THE DEMOGRAPHY
OF FAMINES

An Indian Historical Perspective

ARUP MAHARATNA

DELHI
OXFORD UNIVERSITY PRESS
BOMBAY   CALCUTTA   MADRAS
1996

Oxford University Press, Walton Street, Oxford OX2 6DP

Oxford   New York

Athens   Auckland   Bangkok   Bombay
Calcutta   Cape Town   Dar es Salaam   Delhi
Florence   Hong Kong   Istanbul   Karachi
Kuala Lumpur   Madras   Madrid   Melbourne
Mexico City   Nairobi   Paris   Singapore
Taipei   Tokyo   Toronto

and associates in
Berlin   Ibadan

© *Oxford University Press 1996*

ISBN 0 19 563711 9

Typeset by Rastrixi, New Delhi 110070
Printed in India at Rekha Printers Pvt. Ltd., New Delhi 110020
and published by Manzar Khan, Oxford University Press
YMCA Library Building, Jai Singh Road, New Delhi 110001

Preface

There can be hardly any dispute that India is today relatively free of major large-scale famines, especially when compared with recent famine experiences in some countries of sub-Saharan Africa. However, compared with these African countries India does not appear to have fared particularly well in respect of per capita food consumption and general nutritional level. Indeed, it is worth remembering that India's past (and not too distant past) has witnessed very widespread and severe famines, each taking millions of lives. And the significance of a detailed study of famines in India's past cannot be fully realized if such an investigation does not analyse how India eventually managed to free itself (at least relatively) of large-scale famines. In fact, lessons derived from a careful study of the historical trend of India's famine experience can, understandably enough, be relevant for preventing such crises in vulnerable regions of the contemporary world. The present study has been largely guided by this broad objective.

While famine is a complex socio-economic phenomenon, demographic considerations are central to an understanding of famine. In fact, famine is often viewed as a demographic crisis, especially its adverse mortality effects. However, the demographic impact of famine is not restricted to mortality; famine also affects two other prime demographic variables, namely fertility and migration. The present study analyses, in considerable detail, demographic responses to Indian famines in historical perspective. During the late nineteenth and early twentieth centuries, four major famines occurred in the Indian subcontinent. These famines—precipitated by droughts—involved large-scale excess mortality. After the early twentieth century, India was relatively free of major famine until a severe famine, affecting mainly the eastern province of Bengal, occurred in 1943–4 largely because of the war. Since independence in 1947, India, though it has not experienced any famine of comparable scale, has continued to be vulnerable to occasional droughts and food crises. This book makes use of the wealth of historical material available for India to investigate famine demography from a historical perspective. The prime source of demographic information for this book is the vital registration system which was established in the 1870s. Despite deficiencies, registration data have proved to be quite useful for our present purposes. Besides, detailed official reports on these famines have also been profitably used.

A decline in the frequency and severity of famines since the 1870s can be observed in India. The present study of the trend in patterns of demographic consequences of famines has provided support for the view that this secular amelioration of the fury of famines in India is not a simple story of growth of food production surpassing the growth of population size. Rather, this trend appears to have corresponded with the evolution of relief policy towards greater effectiveness and liberality—a trend which was sometimes backed by improved communications and diversification of the economy. The characteristic features of demographic responses to famine have been much the same throughout, however.

Chapter 1 provides a survey of the major issues of famine demography. It also describes the setting for the present study and includes a discussion of the usefulness of India's registration data. In Chapter 2 demographic responses to major historical famines have been investigated at province level. Chapter 3 examines the demography of some historical famines which involved relatively small numbers of deaths. Chapter 4 presents a detailed study of the demography of the Bengal famine of 1943–4 at province level, while Chapter 5 is devoted to an analysis of regional (district-level) demographic variation during this crisis. The demographic consequences of the Maharashtra scarcity of 1972–3 have been analysed in Chapter 6. Chapter 7 presents a summary and conclusions.

The major part of the research for this book was financially supported by a doctoral scholarship offered by the Association of Commonwealth Universities in the United Kingdom. In the final stages of research the award of the Population Council Fellowship for 1991–2 proved very useful. I would also like to thank the

Population Investigation Committee at the London School of Economics and Political Science for providing me with a travel grant for data collection. The University of Burdwan, West Bengal, has been very generous in granting me leave for carrying out my research at the London School of Economics.

Much of the material used in this study was collected from the British Library of Economics and Political Science (i.e. the London School of Economics Library) and the India Office Library and Records. The enormous wealth of material in these libraries is remarkably matched by an extremely efficient work environment. Indeed, I feel highly privileged to have worked in these libraries.

On the intellectual plane I am indebted to many. I am immeasurably grateful to Tim Dyson who not only introduced me to the hitherto untouched Indian mine of historical demographic information, but who also supervised the core of my doctoral research (of which this is an outcome) with great patience, unfailing interest and sharp insights. I am also grateful to Chris Langford who agreed to supervise my work during the last several months, and offered valuable comments and suggestions. Special thanks are due to Amartya Sen and Jean Drèze not only for offering useful comments and suggestions on the entire draft but also for their invaluable advice and encouragement towards its publication. Thanks are also due to Elizabeth Whitcombe, Mike Murphy, Chris Fernandes and Ken Wilson who have always been very friendly in my discussions with them. I also wish to thank an anonymous referee for useful comments and suggestions.

I am very grateful to Pranab Mukhopadhaya, Pradip Chakrabarty and Alok Bhattacharya for their co-operation and help in collecting material from Calcutta and Delhi.

Finally, I express my heartfelt gratitude to my wife, Paramita, who, despite her own pressing constraints, has provided me with unfailing and indispensable support throughout.

Contents

List of Figures

List of Tables

1

Introduction

1. Famine Demography: The Major Issues

There is no single definition of famine. As one author succinctly remarked, 'famine is . . . hard to define but glaring enough when recognized'.[1] Some scholars have defined famine as a state of extreme hunger, starvation, and malnutrition affecting a substantial proportion of the population of some sizeable area.[2] Another approach toward defining famine emphasizes excess mortality, thus drawing a distinction between hunger, starvation, and malnutrition on the one hand, and famine on the other.[3] In another approach, famine is defined as a community syndrome consisting of early signals, societal manifestations leading to starvation, and/or excess mortality on a wide scale.[4] In fact, the multiplicity of definitions of famine clearly suggests that it is a complex socio-economic phenomenon. On the conceptual plane, famine is of course an 'event' in the sense of being 'an exceptional episode standing apart from the course of everyday life that surrounds it'.[5] Yet the occurrence of famine cannot be understood meaningfully without reference to the economic, social and political structures of a specific society.

However, the existing literature on famine abundantly indicates that demographic considerations are central to an understanding of famine. In fact, famine, especially in its adverse mortality effect, is often viewed as a demographic crisis.[6] Critically

---

[1] A.E. Taylor quoted in Currey (1978), p. 87.

[2] See, e.g. Masefield (1963), p. 2, Bhatia (1967), p. 1, and Keys et al. (1950), p. 784.

[3] See, e.g. Masefield (1963), p. 3–4, Mayer (1975), p. 572, Aykroyd (1974), p. 1, and Blix et al. (1971), p. 190, Johnson (1973), p. 58. See also Sen (1981), p. 40.

[4] See Currey (1978).

[5] See Arnold (1988), p. 6.

[6] See Arnold (1988), pp. 19–20 and Alamgir (1980), p. 5.

reviewing different approaches to the definition of famine, Alamgir considers famine as 'a general state of prolonged foodgrain intake deficiency per capita giving rise to a number of accompanying substates (symptoms) involving individuals and the community that ultimately lead, directly or indirectly, to excess deaths in a region or in a country as a whole'.[7] The different substates, according to Alamgir, include increase in interregional migration, increase in crime, increase in incidence of fatal disease, loss of body weight, changes in nutritional status, eating of alternative 'famine foods', mental deterioration, uprooting of families, separation of families, transfer of assets, and breakdown of traditional bonds. Thus, while famine is a complex socio-economic phenomenon, its demographic impact is rarely restricted to mortality. Famine, in Chen and Chowdhury's words, 'is a complex syndrome of multiple interacting causes, diverse manifestations, and involving all three demographic variables—mortality, fertility, and migration'.[8]

While demographic processes are central to the famine phenomenon, our understanding of their inter-relationships is rather limited. In fact, investigations—both analytical and empirical—of demographic responses to famine are rare. Reviewing the literature on demographic responses to famine, Hugo concluded in 1984 that 'demographers have generally neglected the response to famine as a field of study'.[9] This is probably partly related to the fact that food crises still occur in the developing world where adequate systems of demographic data collection are often nonexistent. The related need for an adequate conceptual framework for examining the inter-relationships between demographic processes and famine has also remained largely unfulfilled. Apart from being useful for planning and disaster-intervention programmes and policies, development of such models of demographic responses to famine may also produce insights into the nature of demographic behaviour in general. Indeed, in the recent past a few attempts have been made towards identifying model patterns of demographic processes during famine.[10]

[7] See Alamgir (1980), p. 7.
[8] See Chen and Chowdhury (1977), p. 409.
[9] Hugo (1984), p. 28.
[10] See Hugo (1984), Bongaarts and Cain (1982), and Watkins and Menken (1985).

In considering demographic effects of famine a distinction between short-term and long-term responses is commonly made. The model patterns of demographic responses to famine, advanced by Bongaarts and Cain, include the hypothesis that, during famine, elevated mortality and reduced fertility are two short-term responses involving population loss. However, for reasons discussed below, the post-famine period is hypothesized to experience a lower death rate and higher birth and population growth rates than in the pre-famine period. One can even distinguish here between the immediate and longer term post-famine periods.

Elevation in mortality during a subsistence crisis is expected because of the adverse influence of acute undernutrition on morbidity and mortality.[11] The social disruption (e.g. aimless wandering, congregation in relief camps, breakdown of sanitary arrangements) caused by famine conditions is also thought to contribute to the spread of epidemic diseases, and hence to a mortality crisis. An above-normal level of mortality may be expected to continue a little longer after famine because of its debilitating and disruptive effects.[12] The most commonly used concept for measuring the mortality impact of famine is 'excess deaths' which is 'the number of deaths over and above those that would have occurred if previous nutritional conditions had prevailed'.[13]

Reduction in fertility, on the other hand, is hypothesized to occur during a famine through several mechanisms. First, acute undernutrition and psychological stress associated with the crisis have fecundity-reducing effects. Below a critical minimum nutritional level, women stop ovulating, and male sperm mobility and longevity are reduced.[14] And psychological stresses induced by the crisis may also partly cause amenorrhea and anovulation.[15] Second, a reduction in the frequency of intercourse may result from a combination of factors, namely decline in libido, general physical weakness and also spousal separation consequent upon temporary

---

[11] Reviewing relevant medical literature, Foege concludes that 'multiple nutritional deficiencies enhance the ability of infectious agents to produce disease'; see Foege (1971), p. 71.

[12] See Bongaarts and Cain (1982), p. 45.

[13] Ibid.

[14] See, e.g. Bongaarts (1980).

[15] See Bongaarts and Cain (1982), p. 48.

migration of males. Fear and anxiety in the wake of the famine may also exert negative influence on the coital frequency.[16] Third, there may be a reduction in the number of new marriages during the famine. Postponement of marriages may occur partly due to the elevated mortality and consequent familial bereavement, and partly due to financial strains within individual households (e.g. because of depletion of resources and savings in coping with the crisis). Moreover, there is evidence of increased numbers of divorces and separations during the crisis.[17] Fourth, the crisis may induce an increase in voluntary birth control efforts through contraception, abstention, or induced abortion. However, this effect may be expected to be rather minor especially in countries with a normally low prevalence of birth control practices (e.g. poor countries). Thus a reduction in conceptions in the face of famine conditions seems, in large part, to be the outcome of circumstances, rather than a result of deliberate decisional response.

However, as Bongaarts and Cain suggest, '[t]here is no apparent lasting damage to the population's ability to reproduce'.[18] Indeed, an above-normal level of fertility (or what is called 'excess fertility') is expected to occur in the immediate post-famine period for the following reasons: first, the decline in fertility and raised infant mortality rate during famine reduces the proportion of women that are pregnant or anovulatory due to breastfeeding. This in turn implies a greater than normal proportion of women in the exposed ovulatory state (i.e. fecund and susceptible to pregnancy) during the immediate post-famine period. Thus, this phenomenon of 'excess fertility' is not due to any deliberate change in fertility behaviour, and its explanation rather lies in the biology of the reproductive process. Second, there may well be a larger than normal number of marriages in the immediate post-crisis years because many marriages postponed during the famine are likely to be added to the normal number of marriages occurring just after. On the other hand, a fall in overall mortality in the immediate post-famine years is hypothesized to occur because the

---

[16] See Chen and Chowdhury (1977), p. 422.

[17] See Hugo (1984), p. 21. Mortality crises may well have longer-term effects on fertility especially through increased marital disruption. For an elegant case study of an influenza pandemic in the Indian context and its implications for fertility, see Mills (1986), especially pp. 26–32.

[18] See Bongaarts and Cain (1982), p. 48.

surviving population just after famine is presumably selected in such a way (i.e. on the Darwinian 'survival of the fittest' principle) as to be fitter and hence experience comparatively higher survival chances. Thus both the expected surge in the fertility rate and the depression in the death rate during the immediate post-famine years result mainly from biological processes rather than any behavioural changes.

Compared with the other demographic variables, the migration response to famine depends more on particular circumstances and thus it is much less predictable. One may generally expect a considerable out-migration from the famine-affected areas during famine and a return migration in the months afterwards. The magnitude of out-migration should vary directly with the availability of food or work in nearby areas (e.g. towns, cities, unaffected rural areas, and sometimes neighbouring countries). Large-scale population movement may reduce the mortality impact of famine by reducing local food shortages through reduction of the number of local consumers as well as via inflow of remittances. On the other hand, extensive movement of people facilitates the spread of infectious diseases and epidemics. Thus, migration may influence the regional variation in the demographic consequences of the famine. However, if large areas are affected by famine and few relief centres are within the reach of the famine victims, migration may be relatively small. The extent of post-crisis in-migration depends on the prospects for a return to normal economic conditions. If the famine is due to an unusual crop failure and the future potential for agricultural production is not damaged, then most out-migrants may be expected to return.

There may also be longer-term implications of famines for birth, death, and population growth rates. In the post-famine period population is likely to contain a larger proportion of people in the main reproductive years; this is hypothesized because of fertility reduction during the famine as well as relatively high mortality of young children and elderly people. This can be expected to cause an elevation in the birth rate over the pre-famine level. At the same time, since some of these age groups, those in the prime adult years, are also normally less vulnerable to death, such a change in population structure may tend to lower the death rate below the pre-famine level. Consequently, lower death and higher birth and population growth rates than those in the pre-famine period may continue for some years after the famine. All these longer-term post-famine demographic responses may thus be expected to offset the loss of population which occurs during famine. If the majority of out-migrants return after the crisis, the expected immediate and longer-term post-famine effects on the population growth rate can be summarized as follows: in the year immediately following the famine the growth rate should fall below the pre-famine level, as the birth rate declines markedly, but growth thereafter should rise to a high level when excess births combine with reduced mortality; this above-normal growth rate should then continue for some time. Thus population loss that famine entails for a relatively brief period is likely to be compensated for by a rather quick resumption of a higher than pre-famine growth rate in post-famine years. Reviewing the likely demographic responses to famine Bongaarts and Cain have concluded that 'changes in mortality and fertility have provided little in a way of a check on longer-term trends in overall size of the affected population'.[19]

The time required for recovery to the pre-famine population level would, in fact, depend on several factors: the normal rate of population growth in the pre-famine period, the extent of mortality increase during the famine, the famine duration and the magnitude of the effects of changes in age composition. In an interesting simulation exercise Watkins and Menken have demonstrated that the effects on recovery time of changes in age composition are much smaller than those of famine duration and magnitude and of the initial population growth rate.[20] However, the recovery time is further shortened by allowing for an increase in fertility (other than that due to the changed age structure of the population). In fact, it has been argued that under normal circumstances pre-famine population seems to be recovered fairly rapidly (except, for example, in a situation of a very thinly spaced occurrence of successive famines). To give some idea of the recovery time: if a famine reduces population by 5 per cent in a society with an initial annual population growth rate of one per cent, the recovery time as indicated by this simulation model (with

[19] Bongaarts and Cain (1982), p. 52; see also Watkins and Menken (1985).
[20] See Watkins and Menken (1985).

the assumption of age-neutrality of famine) is found to be five years.[21]

While most of the 'short-term' demographic responses to famine mentioned above (except migration and postponement of marriages) can be viewed as biological, one may expect some long-term behavioural responses in an environment characterized by a high frequency of famine and other natural disasters. Such high-risk environments are likely to induce the long-term response of high fertility, because under these circumstances (where alternative forms of insurance against crisis are either unavailable or inadequate) children are viewed as a form of insurance.[22] During crises, mature sons provide opportunities for spreading risk and preventing property loss and even starvation through diversified earnings and temporary migration for work. Another long-term behavioural response to famine may be an increased level of permanent emigration from famine-prone areas and a larger flow of rural–urban migration.

Also of considerable interest in connection with famine demography is the interaction between famine conditions and epidemics. Although famine entails large-scale undernutrition, famine mortality does not consist only of direct starvation deaths. In fact, the vast majority of people die of various diseases. It is traditionally held that undernutrition lowers human resistance and leaves the affected population relatively defenceless against infectious disease, thus increasing their vulnerability to death (i.e. via increased susceptibility to infection). Thus, although the recorded cause of death may be an infectious disease, nutritional crisis remains the root cause of mortality. But recently the existence of such a simple nutrition–epidemic relationship has been challenged. First, the relationship between undernutrition/malnutrition and infectious disease is well established as synergistic.[23] Since famine causes a considerable decline in food consumption, undernutrition presumably initiates the synergy leading to increased mortality.[24] However, famine represents not only acute

---

[21] Note that the assumption of age-neutrality of famine, if anything, overestimates the recovery time; see Watkins and Menken (1985), p. 663.

[22] See Bongaarts and Cain (1982), p. 54.

[23] See Scrimshaw et al. (1968). See also Taylor (1985).

[24] In fact among scholars, including medical scientists, there is a continuing debate (and controversy) on the inter-relationship between the level of

nutritional crisis, but it also entails severe social dislocation (e.g. population movements, overcrowding in relief camps, breakdown of sanitary standards). Indeed, evidence on the subsistence crises of eighteenth-century Europe suggests that the breakdown of social relations—and the resulting migration, vagrancy, and over-crowding in insanitary conditions, without the benefit of ade-quate welfare provisions—was a major cause of mortality elevation even from diseases (like smallpox) which are not nor-mally identified synergistically with malnutrition.[25] If a higher mortality rate is found for the more undernourished classes, this may, it has been argued, result from poor living conditions and higher risk of exposure to disease rather than undernutrition *per se*.[26] Moreover, the nutritional status of a population depends not only on availability of food but also on other non-food inputs including health care, basic education, quality of drinking water, and sanitary conditions.[27] Thus, increase in mortality during famine can occur either through an increase in susceptibility to potentially fatal diseases or through an increase in exposure to them or a combination of the two. Thus, while undernutrition and associated debility appear to play some role in raising sus-ceptibility to fatal infections, increased exposure during famine—through various social dislocations (e.g. population movements and large congregations of people at relief camps) —seems to contribute to spreading epidemic diseases. Indeed, there is a continuing debate on the nature and significance of the famine–nutrition–disease–epidemics–mortality relationship.

Another important aspect of the famine–mortality relationship is the differential mortality impact of famine upon different sub-groups in the population and in different sub-regions of the area affected. Differences by age and sex will be considered first. The age–sex composition of famine mortality is usually the outcome of two factors, namely physiological vulnerability and social pro-tection. Infants (whose mortality rate is normally very high anyway in poor countries) might be expected to be particularly vulnerable

---

malnutrition and risk of infection and death; see, e.g. Chen et al. (1980), Tomkins (1986), and Martorell and Ho (1984).

[25] See Post (1990).

[26] See Walter and Schofield (1989), especially p. 19, and de Waal (1989b), especially p. 116.

[27] See Drèze and Sen (1989), p. 44.

to the protein–calorie malnutrition associated with famine and to be adversely affected by decline in birthweight. In analysing the impact of famine on infant mortality, one may distinguish between the effects of 'prenatal exposure' and 'postnatal exposure'.[28] The former work through maternal nutritional stress and associated maternal infections while the latter include postnatal nutritional deficiency, poor care, etc. However, infants can be relatively protected from extreme mortality during famine as they depend on breast milk, the infant's ideal form of nutrition. Moreover, many neonatal deaths in poor countries are due to chronic maternal malnutrition, tetanus, and inadequate prenatal care—variables which seem unlikely to be influenced by acute events such as famine.[29]

Indeed, it may be young children rather than infants who are physiologically most vulnerable to nutritional deprivation as they, in their period of body growth, have comparatively small reserves of nutrients and energy. As Rivers writes, 'the child seems to become more vulnerable to all manner of diseases as it falls further and further behind its expected size'.[30] However, the extreme physiological vulnerability of young children to food shortage may partly be offset by cultural norms which tilt intra-family food distribution during crisis in their favour.[31] Conversely, children's vulnerability during food shortage may be worsened by 'a cultural pattern in which adult males eat first and women and children eat what is left'.[32] The old people, too, can be expected to be physiologically vulnerable to famine. They generally show the signs of famine osteomalacia (gradual softening and deformation of the bones) and they are particularly vulnerable to hypothermia (below-normal body temperature).[33] Difficulty in meeting the heavy additional nutritional demands makes pregnant and lactating women vulnerable to famine. However, decline in fertility during famine causes a corresponding decline in deaths related to pregnancy and childbirth. Thus, although the death rate of

[28] See Stein et al. (1975), chapter 12.

[29] See, e.g. Chen and Chowdhury (1977), p. 415.

[30] Rivers (1988), p. 91.

[31] On this possibility and relevant empirical evidence for various places, see Drèze and Sen (1989), pp. 79–80 and the references cited there.

[32] See McAlpin (1983), p. 57 and the references cited.

[33] See Rivers (1988), p. 91.

women of prime childbearing age is normally high compared to that of males, the increase in female mortality in this age group during famine may be comparatively small. While adult males are physiologically less vulnerable to nutritional stress, they may be expected to move out of their villages in search of food or work, thereby exposing themselves to the dual risks of coming into contact with more diseases and of exhaustion from wandering.

Since some age (and also sex) groups are highly vulnerable to death even in normal times (e.g. infants, young children, women in the prime reproductive years, and the elderly), during crisis they may be expected to experience relatively large absolute increases in mortality, compared with other age groups. But, because of the very high normal levels of death rates of these age groups, the scope for further increases in death rates in proportionate terms during famine may be comparatively limited. Thus, it seems possible that the age–sex pattern of proportional mortality increases does not always coincide with the corresponding pattern in terms of absolute increases.

Turning to the mortality impact of famine on the two sexes, it should be noted first that females are physiologically less vulnerable to death than males. Abundant evidence shows that male infants have higher mortality than female infants.[34] In addition, females have hormonally determined higher immune resistance to infections.[35] Moreover, because of certain physiological advantages relating to body-fat content, females have greater biological capacity to withstand temporary nutritional stress than males.[36] But sex differentials in mortality are also influenced by socio-cultural factors including sex-discrimination. For example, there is evidence of systematic anti-female discrimination in the distribution of food and medical care even in normal times in parts of South Asia.[37] It might be expected that such discrimination against women would worsen during crisis situations.

As regards socio-economic differentials in famine mortality, it is generally expected that increases in mortality and decreases in fertility would be disproportionately large for the poor and

---

[34] See Waldron (1976), p. 349.

[35] Ibid., p. 355.

[36] See Drèze and Sen (1989), p. 55 and references cited there; see also Rivers (1982), pp. 259–63.

[37] See Drèze and Sen (1989), pp. 51–5 and the references cited there.

landless.[38] Regional variation in the demographic impact of famine is understandably much less predictable because it depends upon specific circumstances. Moreover, regional variation is likely to be the result of the interaction of several factors including intensity of crop failure, food availability, pre-famine economic conditions, migration, ecological factors, transport networks, and relief allocation.

2. Famines in India: The Setting for Our Study

It is true that present-day India appears to be relatively free of major famines (especially when compared with many countries of contemporary Africa). But severe famines abound in India's past.[39] Despite recurrent famines in India throughout recorded history, demographic data are extremely scant and probably unreliable for the period before the 1870s, since censuses and vital registration were established only after the 1860s.[40] However, during the closing decades of the nineteenth and the first decade of the twentieth century, India experienced four large-scale famines, each of which caused several million excess deaths. The first crisis was the famine of 1876–8 which has sometimes been labelled as the 'Great Famine'. This crisis was particularly severe in the southern, central, and western parts of India. Indeed, the severity of this famine (especially in terms of excess deaths) partly prompted the establishment of the first Indian Famine Commission (of 1880), which, in turn, laid the foundation of India's subsequent relief system, namely the Famine Codes (i.e. guidelines to the local administration for anticipation, recognition, and relief of famines).[41] During the period between 1880 and 1896, several local

[38] For limited and also scattered evidence on this, see Currey and Hugo (1984), pp. 18–19, 28.

[39] For detailed chronologies and brief descriptions of south Asian famines (often including estimates of excess mortality), see Census of India 1951, vol. 1, *India, Part 1B—Appendices to the Census Report 1951*, New Delhi, 1955; see also Greenough (1982), Appendix A, Bhatia (1967), and Dando (1980).

[40] For the possible sources of information (and their difficulties) about the famines prior to the 1870s in the context of south India, see Murton (1984). Two useful studies of India's famines and food crises since about 1860 are Bhatia (1967) and Srivastava (1968).

[41] The first 'Draft Famine Code' was submitted along with the Famine Commission Report of 1880. Each province was asked to frame its own code

famines occurred but they did not develop into major large-scale crises. Then, in quick succession, the famines of 1896–7 and 1899–1900 devastated wide areas of the subcontinent. They were followed by the establishment of the Indian Famine Commission of 1898 and 1901, respectively.[42] The next major famine was that of 1907–8. This was probably not as widespread as the preceding two; but its effects were particularly acute in the United Provinces of Agra and Oudh (henceforth called United Provinces).[43]

The reasons behind the emergence of such large-scale famines have understandably been the centre of a long-standing debate. Factors like colonial exploitation, population pressure, etc. are sometimes held as responsible for these disasters.[44] However, it is widely agreed that failure of monsoon rains (i.e. so-called drought) was the single most important 'proximate' or precipitating factor in all of these major historical famines in the Indian subcontinent.

Fairly heavy rains during the three monsoon months of July, August, and September, and some further rains in December and January, are generally considered necessary for good harvests in most parts of India. The former rains, resulting from the southwest monsoon, give what is known as the *kharif* cropping season; the latter rains result from the northeast monsoon, and give the *rabi* season. Given the weather-dependence of south Asia's agriculture, the failure of the monsoon can mean crop losses, decline in food availability, sharp rises in prices of staple foodgrains (exacerbated by hoarding), and the threat of famine conditions and associated distress. Indeed, severe droughts in late nineteenth-century India used to shatter the rural economy. The drastic reduction in the area cultivated or sown and the resultant loss in farm activities left the mass of rural labourers jobless and deprived of their basic entitlements to food. On the other hand, the sharp price rises generally contributed to the overall deterioration in exchange

---

by adapting the model contained in the Draft Code to its own circumstances.

[42] For discussion of the modifications that these subsequent Famine Commission reports included, compared with the first report, see Srivastava (1968), chapters 6–8, Bhatia (1967), Drèze (1990), especially pp. 25–32, and Klein (1984).

[43] Note that until 1901 the name of this province was North-Western Provinces and Oudh.

[44] For the different views on this question, see, for example Bhatia (1967), McAlpin (1983), Klein (1984), Hebert (1987).

entitlements too. Indeed, such a major decline in the economic well-being of the agricultural population also adversely affected the conditions of rural artisans.[45] Consequently, aimless wandering and migration in search of work and food was a common response during famine. The sale of assets was a resort of the relatively less vulnerable groups.

The chief governmental effort to tackle famine consisted of relief provision. There was no governmental control over prices, supplies, and distribution of food, which were basically left to market forces and private traders.[46] Organization of relief measures was the responsibility of the local-level administrations.[47] For example, a district was entitled to government relief provision only after local-level administrators had declared the existence of famine conditions. Official declaration of famine in a locality was usually based on some 'tests'. For example, 'test works' (i.e. provision of paid works on a very small scale) were set up initially to test whether or not the provision of large-scale relief work in that locality was justified. Sometimes provision of relief (either gratuitous or relief work) was opened in far-flung places to test whether people were desperate enough to go to such distant centres for relief. Relief measures were in two basic forms: direct and indirect. The most important measure of relief was the provision of massive public works at subsistence wages (paid in cash) for those who came forward for it. Complementary to public works was gratuitous relief for those who were unable to work. Gratuitous relief usually took the form of either cash doles or

[45] Descriptions of these devastating consequences of drought on the rural economy abound in contemporary official documents; see Drèze (1990), pp. 16–19. On this, see also Ghosh (1982).

[46] While governmental participation in trade and distribution of food during the subsistence crisis is sometimes seen as an effective means of protecting the food entitlement of vulnerable sections of population, the British administration was almost obsessively against the policy of state intervention in free-market operations and private trading; on this, see Drèze (1990), pp. 27–8. For a discussion on the influence on the British famine relief policy of the classical ideas favouring operation of free-market forces and its implications, see Ambirajan (1978), especially pp. 69–100, and also Sen (1981), pp. 160–2.

[47] For a useful discussion of the basic principles and rationale behind the relief policy—and also its evolution—during the closing decades of the nineteenth and early twentieth centuries, see Drèze (1990), pp. 25–32, and also Srivastava (1968).

cooked food in the relief kitchens and also poorhouses. Indirect relief measures usually included remissions from land revenue, and agricultural loans for both subsistence and production.[48]

However, acute undernutrition on a large scale seems to have been very common in the affected regions. The widespread under-nutrition—combined with various disruptions—paved the way for epidemic diseases to take their toll. Sometimes analysts denote the first situation described above as the 'starvation' phase, while the latter is termed the 'epidemic phase' of famine.[49]

An examination of the quantum of overall excess mortality caused by the four major famines referred to above would provide an understanding of the time trends in famine mortality over the period of the late nineteenth and the early twentieth centuries. In this context, Table 1.1 provides some rough estimates of the excess deaths during the four major famines. It should be noted that determination of the mortality attributable to famine is not a very easy task. It involves several issues—both conceptual and statisti-cal. For example, the number of excess deaths during famine has to be measured with reference to some non-famine (or pre-famine) mortality level. This non-famine mortality level may or may not represent the 'normal' situation, because there seem to have been occasional bad mortality years (often due to epidemics). Thus it is possible to derive different estimates of excess deaths during famine, depending on what is taken as the normal level. Another issue is the period for which excess deaths should be attributed to famine, since an elevation in mortality may sometimes continue after the famine as such.

While the estimates provided by Visaria and Visaria and by Seavoy have actually been derived from the official estimates made separately for different regions,[50] the detailed procedure in the production of these estimates has not been made explicit. Conse-quently, new estimates have been attempted here. Any attempt to estimate excess deaths during these famines is fraught with dif-ficulties. The major problem, of course, relates to the determina-tion of the level of under-registration of deaths. Some of the newly

---

[48] The hardship loan to agriculturists was called *taccavi.*

[49] See, for example Sen (1981), especially Appendix D, and also Lardinois (1985).

[50] The official estimates were made by either the relevant government department or the Famine Commission Reports.

TABLE 1.1

Estimates of Excess Mortality in the Major Famines in India During the Late Nineteenth and Early Twentieth Centuries

Famine	Seavoy	Visaria and Visaria	Present author	
			Lower estimate	Upper estimate
1876–8	6,135,000	5,550,000	8,217,692	8,217,692
1896–7	5,150,000	5,150,000	2,624,574	4,055,396
1899–1900	3,250,000	n.a.	2,968,757	4,399,579
1907–8	n.a.	n.a.	2,148,788	3,218,776

Notes: 1. The all-India figures provided by Seavoy, and Visaria and Visaria, have been derived by adding the official estimates for only those areas which were officially declared as famine-affected. According to Seavoy his figures are the 'highest [officially] estimated mortalities'.

2. The approach adopted here consists in calculating the excess death rate for the whole of India for each famine year over a pre-famine baseline average annual figure for five years. Two estimates of excess death rates have been made according to two baseline average figures used—one including all the five years preceding famine, and the other excluding some abnormal years. Applying these excess death rates to the respective populations under registration, total registered excess deaths during the famine period were obtained. To take account of under-registration of deaths, registered excess deaths were inflated by a correction factor. The correction factor for each relevant intercensal decade was derived by taking the ratio of the average of four different estimates of the decadal CDR (those by Indian census actuaries, Davis, Visaria, and Das Gupta) to the average decadal CDR calculated from registration data. The estimated correction factors for the 1870s, 1890s, and the decade beginning in 1901 were respectively 1.74, 1.45, and 1.27.

3. n.a. = not available.

Sources: R.E. Seavoy, *Famine in Peasant Societies*, London: Greenwood Press, 1986, Fig. 10, p. 242; L. Visaria and P. Visaria, 'Population (1757–1947)', in D. Kumar (ed.), *The Cambridge Economic History of India, vol. 2: c. 1757–c. 1970*, Cambridge: Cambridge University Press, 1983, Appendix 5.2, pp. 530–1. For various estimates of CDR for each intercensal decade, starting from 1871, and also the relevant references, see Visaria and Visaria (1983), p. 501.

discovered methods, namely growth balance method and intercensal survivorship method were tried. But none of these methods worked well because of serious deficiencies in the census data on age distribution. However, in order to gain an understanding of the temporal trend in famine mortality, the level of under-registration of death (i.e. the correction factor) was estimated for each decade with major famines, by comparing decadal estimates of the all-India death rate with the corresponding decadal death rates derived from registration data.[51] Using these correction factors, we have provided two estimates of excess mortality: lower estimates have been derived on the basis of baseline averages involving all the five years preceding the famine, and upper estimates from baseline averages excluding some years with abnormal mortality. One possible source of discrepancy between the official figures (provided by Visaria and Visaria and by Seavoy) and our estimates is that the former figures stem from the summation of excess deaths occurring only in those areas which were officially declared as famine-affected. In addition, the reference level of mortality for calculating excess deaths, the famine period employed, the adjustment for under-registration of deaths—none of these was made explicit either by Visaria and Visaria or by Seavoy —may well be different.

Despite considerable discrepancy between official figures and our estimates, Table 1.1 suggests a somewhat declining trend in the magnitude of famine mortality over the period of the late nineteenth and early twentieth centuries. This has sometimes been attributed to a more effective and rational relief policy, perhaps helped by both improved transport networks and diversification of the economy.[52]

Indeed, for about four decades after the famine of 1907–8, India was relatively free of major famines. Although some local crop failures occurred during 1908–1940, they involved few excess deaths. However, interestingly, during the three decades preceding the Second World War per capita food output in India was not increasing. It has sometimes been argued that improved communications and more effective policies of famine relief played a crucial role in the absence of major famines during this period.[53]

However, any complacency that major famines had become a

---

[51] For various estimates of decadal death rate for all India, see Visaria and Visaria (1983), p. 501.

[52] See, e.g. Klein (1984), McAlpin (1983).

[53] See Drèze (1990), McAlpin (1983, 1985).

thing of India's past was suddenly smashed by the occurrence of the 'great' Bengal famine of 1943–4 which again caused a large number of excess deaths. Unlike earlier major famines, this crisis, however, was not precipitated by drought. It occurred under unusual circumstances related to war. The main impact of this famine was restricted to the large eastern province of Bengal, though Orissa and Madras were also somewhat affected. Thus, this crisis, though it certainly caused very many excess deaths, probably did not assume quite the same scale at the all-India level as the late nineteenth century famines. It appears that the number of excess deaths during the famine of 1943–4 was somewhat above two million.[54]

However, the famine of 1943–4 is widely believed to be the last major famine in the Indian subcontinent. Indeed, since independence in 1947, India has never experienced a major famine of a scale and severity comparable with that of the previous major famines. However, India's per capita foodgrain output has changed little from the 'dangerously low' pre-independence level.[55] Per capita food availability has also remained stagnant over the post-independence period. Indeed, India is by no means free of occasional visitations of droughts and food scarcities (often within some specific states). In fact the relative stagnation in agricultural output over the large unirrigated tracts still makes these locations potentially vulnerable to famine. The most important crises that have occurred since independence are the Bihar famine of 1966–7 and the Maharashtra drought in 1971–3. Both these events have caused some excess mortality, but the magnitude is small compared to that caused by major famines in the past.[56] Massive food imports (particularly during the 1960s), comparatively effective measures of relief (sometimes combined with effective state control over food supplies and prices), use of a considerable buffer stock (that had been accumulated by the 1980s) are among the main factors that have contributed to preventing such crises from developing into large-scale famines.

[54] The quantum of excess deaths in the Bengal famine has been a hotly debated issue. However, our own re-estimation of excess deaths in Bengal (with hitherto unutilized registration data for the whole of Bengal) provides a figure of 2.1 million; see Dyson and Maharatna (1991), and also chapter 4 below.

[55] See Drèze (1990), pp. 36–7.

[56] See Dyson and Maharatna (1992), and also chapter 6 below.

The foregoing discussion suggests a broad long-term decline in the frequency and severity of famines in India since the 1870s. The chief purpose of the present study is to examine the characteristics of demographic responses to Indian famines since the late nineteenth century. Hopefully, this should throw light on the question of why famines have disappeared in India.

3. The Demographic Data in Our Study

The study will use detailed demographic information provided by India's vital registration system. Since the inception of the registration system (i.e. since the 1870s), the Sanitary Commissioner of each province was responsible for producing an annual report, containing fairly detailed registration data. On the basis of this provincial information, an annual report for the whole of India was produced by the Sanitary Commissioner with the government of India. The information on vital events was collected by village watchmen (or *chowkidars*), each being responsible for a particular jurisdiction. Vital rates in these official reports were almost always based on constant denominators—being the respective enumerated population under registration according to the preceding census.

There were, of course, several deficiencies of registration data, the most apparent of which was the under-registration of births and deaths. This problem was particularly pronounced during the early days of the registration system. It is possible that there has been a long-term improvement in registration after its inception. If, over time, we find a rising trend in registered vital rates, it is impossible to demarcate the relative influence of increase in actual numbers of births and deaths on the one hand, and of improvements in registration on the other. However, since the level of under-registration is unlikely to have changed drastically within short periods, registration data can be used for the purpose of examining the demographic impact of a famine.[57] It should also be remembered that there has been a significant provincial variation in quality of registration. For example, the registration system was relatively good in Central Provinces, Hyderabad Assigned Districts (henceforth called Berar), Madras Presidency, Punjab,

[57] See also McAlpin (1983), pp. 50–1.

United Provinces, and Bombay Presidency. However, during periods of social disruption such as famine, it is possible that the quality of registration sometimes deteriorated. Difficulties of recording deaths among people on distant roads or in jungles have sometimes been mentioned by administrators.[58] Increased work pressure of *chowkidars* in the wake of famine and the attendant mortality crisis may also be responsible for deterioration in registration coverage,[59] though it seems doubtful that registration coverage invariably deteriorated during famines. In fact, one stated motive behind the establishment of the registration system in India was to monitor mortality trends during periods of crisis.[60] Official documents suggest that famine conditions often led to augmented registration efforts. For example, the Sanitary Commissioner of Bombay Presidency, while attributing a large part of the increased mortality in 1877 to the existence of famine, added that 'there can be no question that the increased attention paid to the registration by the large staff of village inspectors throughout famine districts had led to much greater accuracy in the number of deaths returned in 1877. With the exception of the comparatively few cases of persons dying far away from any village, I believe that the great majority of deaths was reported'.[61] The 1901 census report on Punjab, while discussing the quality of registration data during the 1890s, writes that '[i]t is not necessarily true that the completeness or accuracy of data are adversely affected by the dislocation of the administrative agencies in the famines . . . the presumption is that they were not affected one way or the other . . . any laxity would be counterbalanced by the extra supervision necessitated in times of scarcity'.[62]

However, there is a difficulty in basing the analysis of vital rates based on constant denominators (as was the practice of the

---

[58] See Dyson (1991a), p. 10 and references cited.

[59] For this and other related possibilities, see Census of India 1911, *United Provinces, Volume XV, Part 1—Report*, Allahabad, 1912, pp. 46–55.

[60] To quote from a monograph on India's civil registration system, 'An important landmark in the development of vital statistics was the stress laid by the Indian Famine Commission on the importance of these statistics'; see Government of India (1972). See also Dyson (1991a), p. 10.

[61] See Government of Bombay (1878), p. 139.

[62] See Census of India 1901, *Punjab, Volume XVII, Part 1—Report*, Simla, 1902, pp. 41–2.

Sanitary Commissioners). As famine entails a reduction in population size, use of constant denominators may introduce a downward bias in both death and birth rates for the famine and post-famine years. Again, if there was a positive growth of population between the census and the occurrence of the famine, the 'pre-famine' vital rates will be biased upwards. Thus, while changes in the constant-denominator vital rates reflect essentially the changes in the numerators, i.e. registered vital events, the implications of such 'numerator-based' analysis should be borne in mind. For example, a change in population size (e.g. through excess deaths and/or migration) may be partly responsible for a change in the total number of registered vital events. Thus, one should be careful while interpreting the changes in the total number of registered events.

Registered deaths were usually classified under five major causes: cholera, dysentery/diarrhoea, smallpox, fevers, injuries, and all others. Subsequently, plague and respiratory diseases were also included. Distribution of registered deaths from each specified cause—both by district and by month—is available. There is no doubt that cause of death data are not accurate especially because village officials can hardly be assumed to have had much skill in assigning deaths to appropriate categories. However, statistics for categories such as cholera, smallpox, and plague are generally thought to have been relatively reliable because of their very distinctive symptoms. Fevers—under which most deaths are normally classified—seems to have been a catch-all category in the sense that several diseases which cause temperature are likely to have been included under this heading. As the Sanitary Commissioner of Bombay Presidency in his annual report for 1894 writes, 'in every case where fever occurs as a symptom of the illness which terminates in death, this death is recorded as due to fever'.[63] On that count, a certain degree of misclassification of deaths between fever and dysentery/diarrhoea seems possible. Past investigations of malaria have also shown that malaria becomes particularly fatal for children below five years, and it often predisposes the patient to respiratory diseases and dysentery/diarrhoea.[64] As the official

[63] See Government of Bombay (1895), p. 63.
[64] See Census of India 1911, *United Provinces of Agra and Oudh, Volume XV, Part I, Report*, Allahabad, 1912, p. 45.

report on the United Provinces famine of 1896–7 also noted, '[t]his heading [fever] is very general and probably includes most cases of pneumonic and lung diseases, so fatal to people of reduced stamina (especially the young and very old) employed on relief works and elsewhere'.[65] However, malaria is generally taken to have been the most important component of the fever category. The surge in fever mortality during the monsoon and post-monsoon months has often been attributed to the increased incidence of malaria following the rains. Since the early 1920s, 'fever' began to be divided into different sub-heads, namely malaria, enteric fever, measles, relapsing fever, kala-azar, and other fevers. Although a degree of misclassification of deaths between these fever sub-heads seems also likely, malaria generally constituted the most dominant share in the fever category.[66]

However, these problems of using registration data should not be exaggerated. Putting the issue of under-registration aside for a moment, most of the possible defects of the registration system (e.g. misclassification of age at death and cause of death) were common to the periods before, during, and after a famine. Thus, the probable unchanging nature of some reporting biases leaves registration data useful for examining the basic patterns of demographic changes during famines.

However, there are rather strong indications that the civil registration system in post-independence India has been deteriorating.[67] Estimates of under-registration for the period 1941–50 have been found to be lower than estimates for more recent periods.[68] The reasons for this deterioration include, among others, a large increase in population which has increased the work-load of the village headman.[69] Since the mid-1950s, the reorganization of states and subsequent efforts to unify the divergent provisions

---

[65] See Government of the North-Western Provinces and Oudh (1897), p. 135.

[66] See, e.g. Chand (1939), p. 119.

[67] India became independent from British rule in 1947. Note that since then the connotation of India in territorial terms is not the same as that of the pre-independence period. Pakistan and Bangladesh were parts of pre-independence India.

[68] See Mari Bhat et al. (1984), p. 29.

[69] For the reasons, see Mari Bhat et al. (1984), pp. 28–9 and the references cited.

prevailing in different parts of the country have also apparently contributed to its further deterioration. Again, '[t]he *Panchayats*, village-level civic bodies, that took over the work of registration in most states, had neither the necessary personnel nor the zeal to undertake the arduous task'.[70] In terms of under-registration, the civil registration system is especially poor in Rajasthan, Bihar, and Uttar Pradesh, and only moderate in West Bengal, Karnataka, and Andhra Pradesh. Punjab, Maharashtra, and Tamil Nadu, however, possess a more complete registration system.

In the absence of any sign of quick recovery of civil registration in most parts, the Sample Registration System (SRS) was initiated by the Registrar General of India in 1964–5 (initially in certain states) as an alternative. This is a dual-record system with the primary objective of providing reliable vital rates at national and sub-national levels. The data collection process of the SRS consists of continuous enumeration of births and deaths from sample populations by an enumerator and an independent survey every six months by an investigator-supervisor. In addition to the fact that the SRS provides neither detailed demographic data (only the CBR and CDR) nor disaggregated vital rates (say, by district), the SRS data are not entirely free from deficiencies. However, it is generally agreed that SRS vital rates are fairly reliable—though there is usually a slight underestimation of the true rates.[71]

---

[70] See Mari Bhat et al. (1984), p. 29.
[71] For details, see Mari Bhat et al. (1984), pp. 29–34.

2

The Demography of Some Major Historical Famines in the Indian Subcontinent

1. Introduction

Systematic and detailed demographic study of Indian famines cannot be undertaken for a period before the 1870s (i.e. until the establishment of the censuses and vital registration). However, several large-scale famines that occurred during the last few decades of the nineteenth and early twentieth centuries (i.e. those of 1876–8, 1896–7, 1899–1900, and 1907–8) provide a good opportunity for examining the demographic characteristics of Indian historical famines. First, they were major famines both because of their acute severity (and associated excess mortality) and because of their widespread effects, and it is reasonable to expect that during such major famines, characteristic demographic responses would be comparatively pronounced. Second, these famines are all comparatively well documented.

Although Indian historical demography is a very new field of research, some demographic aspects of the major famines of the late nineteenth century have been examined in a few studies.[1] However, a recent analysis by Dyson appears to be the most comprehensive and systematic demographic study.[2] Consequently we summarize here Dyson's main findings.

Using mostly registration data, Dyson analyses three major

---

[1] For a review of the literature on Indian historical demography and also for some recent researches in this area, see Dyson (1989b), chapter 1.

[2] See Dyson (1991a). A few other studies on some specific demographic aspects of the late nineteenth-century Indian famines, sometimes in the context of particular locations, are those by Lardinois (1985), McAlpin (1983) chapter 3, Guz (1989).

nineteenth-century famines in particular locations: the famine of 1876–8 in the Madras Presidency, and the famines of 1896–7 and 1899–1900 in both the Central Provinces and the Bombay Presidency. Thus, the northern parts of the subcontinent are not represented in this study. One of the issues addressed rather thoroughly is the evolution through time of fertility and mortality responses to famine.[3] Average monthly prices of staple foodgrains are used to trace the development of famine distress.[4] The monthly numbers of conceptions are taken to be equal to the monthly births displaced backwards by nine months. Thus, Dyson assumes that only a small proportion of conceptions result in foetal loss.[5] A decline in conceptions corresponding to the rise in food prices— even at an early stage of famine with little or no elevation in death rate—appears to be a common feature. Dyson describes such fertility effects 'at a far earlier stage in the build-up to famine' than the mortality effects, as 'anticipatory'. In addition to the several well-known famine–fertility links (e.g. fertility-reducing effects of nutritional stress, spousal separation, deferment of marriages), Dyson suggested (albeit 'cautiously') an element of planned decision behind such reductions in conceptions.[6] However, the peak mortality phase seems to have exerted an additional independent short-term fertility-reducing effect.

The monthly movements of death rate during these famines show that the main mortality peak not only occurred late, but it also lasted for a short span. As Dyson writes, 'In each case it happened in or around August and was almost certainly related to the resumption of monsoon rains'.[7] Thus, the peak of famine

---

[3] Note that longer-term demographic responses are beyond the scope of Dyson's study.

[4] The concern for, and the attempt to establish, such relationships between fertility, mortality, and food price was rather elaborately shown long back by W.R. Cornish, the Sanitary Commissioner for the Madras Presidency, in his reports covering the Madras famine of 1876–8; see Government of Madras (1878, 1879).

[5] On the validity of this assumption that the births displaced backwards by nine months represent the conceptions even during a famine situation especially because of the insignificance of the variations in the foetal loss, see Chen and Chowdhury (1977).

[6] On this issue, see also Caldwell et al. (1992), Greenough (1992), and Dyson (1992).

[7] See Dyson (1991a), p. 22.

mortality appears to have matched the normal seasonal mortality pattern—occurring during and just after the rains.

Among the few classified causes of death, the importance of 'cholera' and 'fever' mortality is apparent. 'Dysentery and diarrhoea' also seem significant in some cases. The famine mortality due to cholera (and dysentery and diarrhoea) usually peaked somewhat earlier, broadly corresponding to the phase of maximum starvation and social disruption (e.g. wandering, and crowding). Assuming that malaria constituted the major part of 'fever' mortality, the seasonal pattern of fever deaths in most cases suggests that 'malaria was probably the single most important component of the main death rate peaks which accompanied the return of the rains . . . when field activities were resuming, employment prospects were improving, relief works were being run down, and people were returning home'.[8] However, as Dyson notes, the occurrence of such a peak in famine mortality in a year following drought did not depend entirely upon the resumption of the rains—since mosquito breeding and disease transmission also depended on the 'particular conditions of precipitation, temperature, atmospheric humidity, etc.' For outbreaks of epidemic malaria particularly after the resumption of both rains and normal farm activities (which in turn are supposed to improve the nutritional status of the population) another possible mechanism has been proposed. This is 'malaria refeeding'. According to this hypothesis severe undernutrition may obstruct the multiplication of malarial parasites in the human body and arrest both the development and the transmission of the disease; conversely, improvements in nutritional status induce parasite multiplication, and hence contribute to major outbreaks of malaria.[9]

In the baseline periods, age-specific death rates were found to be highest in infancy, childhood, and old age. The largest absolute increases in death rates during the famines occurred in these age groups. This certainly implies absolute vulnerability of these groups compared with other age categories in both normal times and in times of crisis.[10] However, proportional increases in deaths

---

[8] Dyson (1991a), p. 22.

[9] See Dyson (1991a), p. 24 and also the references cited by him.

[10] McAlpin has reported a similar finding in the context of the Bombay famine of 1876–8; see McAlpin (1983), p. 59.

in the peak mortality year were relatively small for infants and old people. This was usually the case for young children (aged 1–4 years) too. But the proportional increases in mortality in most of these famine locations tended to peak in later childhood (i.e. the 5–9 or 10–14 age groups). Thus, these findings suggest, in Dyson's words, 'comparatively small proportional increases in famine mortality in age groups where death rates were already high, and, conversely, comparatively large proportional increases at ages where death rates were relatively low'.[11]

In all famine locations in Dyson's study, the male population from the teens through to about fifty years experienced greater proportional increases in mortality. Most other ages showed insignificant sex differentials. But in each of these famines the female infant mortality rate increased by a larger proportion than that for males. However, the net result was a higher proportional rise in male deaths (all ages combined). In accounting for this, Dyson stresses the importance of greater male mobility and the reduced number of maternal deaths (consequent upon the considerable fall in the number of conceptions).

While Dyson's study provides some interesting findings on the short-term demographic responses to Indian historical famines, there still remains much scope to extend this study. We will make our demographic study of major historical famines more detailed on at least three counts: first, by covering a larger geographical area; second, by examining some issues in greater detail (e.g. interaction between famine and epidemics), and also investigating several additional issues (e.g. longer-term demographic responses, interaction between relief provision, and demographic responses); and third, by using alternative methods of analysis, when appropriate. Moreover, in addition to the three pre-eminent famines of the late nineteenth century (i.e. those of 1876–8, 1896–7, 1899–1900), we will include in our study the famine of 1907–8.

Since the vital registration system was at its nascent stage during the 1870s, demographic analysis of the famine of 1876–8 should be made with particular caution. In fact, for the famine of 1876–8 the Bombay and Madras Presidencies have been selected for two major reasons: one, the south-west of the Indian subcontinent was most severely affected by this famine; and

---

[11] See Dyson (1991a), p. 21.

second, the quality of demographic data was relatively superior for these provinces as early as the 1870s.[12] For the famine of 1896–7, the Bombay Presidency, the Central Provinces, and Berar have been chosen partly because they were severely afflicted, and partly because the registration system was working relatively well in these parts during the 1890s. For broadly similar reasons, the Central Provinces, Berar, Bombay, and the Punjab have been studied for the famine of 1899–1900.[13] While the famine of 1907–8 was probably not as widespread as the others, its effects were particularly acute in the United Provinces.[14] The selection of Punjab and the United Provinces has partly been influenced by our desire to include northern areas within the study. Consequently, our study covers much of the north, central, west, and southern regions of the Indian subcontinent (see Fig. 2.1).[15] Analysis of these major famines at the province level has the advantage that migration should not appear to be important in influencing the demographic impact.

Table 2.1 provides the broad census-based information for each of these provinces. As can be seen, most of these famine locations involved large populations (except Berar). Near-zero or negative rates of population growth occurred in these provinces during the decades of the famines (probably except in Punjab), while the growth rate was considerably higher in both preceding and subsequent decades.[16] Although it is not easy to demonstrate

[12] On the issue of the severity of this famine, see, e.g. Bhatia (1967), pp. 89–98; on the vital registration system in Madras Presidency, see Government of Madras (1878, 1879); on the registration system in Bombay Presidency, see McAlpin (1983), p. 50.

[13] On the question of the geographical spread of the severity of the famines of 1896–7 and 1899–1900, see Bhatia (1967), pp. 239, 250–3; on the vital registration system in the Central Provinces and Berar, see Dyson (1989a), and also Dyson (1989b), chapter 6. The registration system in Punjab improved significantly after 1892 because of the introduction of a more effective supervision; see Census of India 1901, *Punjab, Volume XVII, Part I—Report*, Simla, 1902, pp. 41–2.

[14] On the severity of this famine, see Bhatia (1967), pp. 265–6.

[15] Although the eastern region is not represented in this chapter, we will have occasion to make a detailed study of the eastern province of Bengal later on (see chapters 4 and 5 below).

[16] Negative growth rate during 1911–21 in the United Provinces occurred due to the severe influenza epidemic of 1918.

FIG. 2.1 Famine Locations

Note: N.W.F.P. – North-West Frontier Province (which was included in Punjab till 1901).

the exact contribution of famine to the reduction in population size during the intercensal decade, the considerable scale of excess mortality in these famines cannot be doubted (see below). It may also be noted that the sex-ratio (male–female) declined in all locations during the decade of famine except in the north Indian provinces, namely Punjab and the United Provinces; in Bombay, Madras, the Central Provinces, and Berar, the decline seems to have been significant. Note, too, a considerable decline in the dependency-ratio in the census following famine conditions in Bombay, the Central Provinces, Madras, and Berar; however, this seems to have remained unchanged in Punjab and the United Provinces.

TABLE 2.1
Census-based Information on the Major Historical Famine Locations in the Indian Subcontinent

Province & census year	Population enumerated	Annual growth rate (%)	Sex ratio (M–F)	Dependency ratio
Bombay				
1872	16,228,774	–	1.095	0.78
1881	16,454,414	0.15	1.068	0.62
1891	18,820,346	1.34	1.072	0.66
1901	18,481,362	–0.18	1.065	0.59
1911	19,587,383	0.58	1.084	0.60
Madras				
1867	27,004,452	–	1.005	
1871	30,749,401	3.30	1.006	0.70
1881	30,835,771	0.03	0.980	0.54
1891	33,733,121	0.90	0.980	0.69
Central Provinces				
1881	8,817,185	–	1.019	0.72
1891	9,501,401	0.75	1.000	0.67
1901	8,926,934	–0.62	0.966	0.41
1911	10,518,330	1.64	0.982	0.50
United Provinces				
1881	44,107,869	–	1.081	0.65
1891	46,904,791	0.61	1.075	0.64
1901	47,691,782	0.17	1.067	0.60
1911	46,835,108	–0.18	1.094	0.60
1921	45,375,787	–0.31	1.073	0.62
Punjab				
1881	18,850,437	–	1.181	0.64
1891	20,553,982	0.87	1.160	0.65
1901	22,159,414	0.75	1.160	0.64
1911	23,550,749	0.61	1.215	0.66

(cont.)

Table 2.1 (*cont.*)

Province & census year	Population enumerated	Annual growth rate (%)	Sex ratio (M–F)	Dependency ratio
Berar				
1881	2,672,673	–	1.070	0.67
1891	2,852,825	0.65	1.060	0.67
1901	2,721,342	–0.47	1.026	0.53
1911	3,057,162	1.16	1.029	0.54

Notes: 1. All data refer to the enumerated population under vital registration system.
   2. Dependency ratio is defined as the ratio of population aged 0–9 and 50+ to those aged 10–49 years. But for Bombay Presidency in 1872 dependency ratio is calculated as a ratio of population aged 0–11 and 50+ to population aged 12–49; this was necessary because of different age categories adopted in the 1872 census. For Berar in 1911, it is taken as the ratio of population aged 0–9 and 60+ to those aged 10–60 years.
   3. The population of North-West Frontier Province which was a part of Punjab before the 1901 census, has been included in the Punjab populations for both 1901 and 1911 censuses; this is done simply for the purpose of calculating growth rates during 1891–1901 and 1901–11.

Sources: *Annual Report of the Sanitary Commissioner for Madras,* Madras, various years; *Annual Report of the Sanitary Commissioner for the Government of Bombay,* Bombay, various years; *Report of the Sanitary Commissioner of the Central Provinces,* Nagpur, various years; *Annual Report of the Sanitary Commissioner for the Government of Punjab,* Lahore, various years; *Report on the Sanitary Administration of the Hyderabad Assigned Districts,* Hyderabad, various years; *Annual Report of the Sanitary Commissioner of the North-Western Provinces and Oudh (from 1901 United Provinces of Agra and Oudh),* Allahabad, various years.

2. Aggregative Short-term and Long-term Effects on Fertility and Mortality: An Analysis with Annual Vital Rates

Table 2.2 presents estimated crude birth, death, and natural increase rates (CBR, CDR, and CRNI respectively) during the pre-famine, famine, and post-famine periods for the different major famine locations examined here. The registered vital rates for the 1870s seem to be distinctively low compared with those

Table 2.2
CBR, CDR, and CRNI in Major Historical Famine Locations in the Indian Subcontinent

	Madras			Bombay		
	CBR	CDR	CRNI	CBR	CDR	CRNI
Pre-famine						
1872–5	19.12	18.22	0.90	18.83	21.37	-2.54
Famine						
1876	20.91	22.51	-0.60	21.29	22.69	-1.40
1877	16.38	53.39	-37.01	19.56	39.40	-19.84
Post-famine						
1878	12.15	28.27	-16.12	15.54	34.04	-15.54
1879	16.70	19.19	-2.49	18.50	24.91	-6.41
1880	22.90	15.76	7.14	23.77	21.06	2.71
1881	25.52	16.24	9.24	27.94	23.18	4.76
1882	25.92	16.24	9.68	29.58	20.67	8.91
1883	27.07	18.53	8.54	30.05	25.17	4.88
1884	28.10	22.09	6.01	31.78	24.27	7.51
1885	27.78	20.75	7.03	33.81	22.51	11.58

(cont.)

Table 2.2 (*cont.*)

	Madras			Bombay		
	CBR	CDR	CRNI	CBR	CDR	CRNI
1886	28.51	18.47	10.04	33.93	22.23	11.70
1887	28.07	19.99	8.08	36.26	26.27	9.99
1888	27.31	19.57	7.74	36.27	26.75	9.52
1889	28.23	21.51	6.72	34.15	29.49	4.68
1890	28.83	24.12	4.71	36.08	26.09	9.99
1891	27.44	22.19	5.25	36.27	27.26	9.01

	Bombay			Punjab			Central Provinces		
	CBR	CDR	CRNI	CBR	CDR	CRNI	CBR	CDR	CRNI
Pre-famine									
1891–5	35.09	29.30	5.79	39.88	32.37	6.51	37.41	33.43	3.98
Famine									
1896	35.85	30.91	4.94	41.83	30.64	11.19	31.87	49.53	-17.66
1897	32.84	39.11	-6.27	40.90	29.84	11.06	28.16	72.76	-44.60
Post-famine									
1898	30.32	28.57	2.05	38.99	29.56	9.43	25.35	31.90	-6.55

Famine

	CBR	CDR	NRM	CBR	CDR	NRM	CBR	CDR	NRM
	Bengal						United Provinces		
1899	35.66	34.97	0.69	45.23	27.65	17.58	50.84	40.23	10.61
1900	27.27	71.64	−44.37	38.64	44.88	−6.24	33.24	87.86	−54.62

Post-famine

1901	25.20	37.13	−11.93	35.40	36.10	−0.70	28.83	23.46	5.37
1902	34.32	39.22	−4.90	43.95	44.28	−0.33	47.51	25.40	22.11
1903	31.75	44.66	−12.91	43.34	49.49	−6.15	43.10	30.39	12.71
1904	35.91	42.35	−6.44	42.22	49.93	−7.71	50.19	29.19	21.00
1905	33.79	32.53	1.26	45.36	48.55	−3.19	47.42	31.32	16.10
1906	34.62	35.87	−1.25	44.28	37.47	6.81	44.52	34.80	9.72
1907	33.79	33.57	0.22	42.46	64.37	−21.91	45.07	33.12	11.95
1908	36.20	27.52	8.68	43.71	53.08	−9.37	45.25	33.12	−12.13
1909	35.75	27.50	8.25	36.57	32.17	4.40	42.85	27.30	15.55
1910	37.22	30.22	7.00	44.09	34.33	9.76	46.97	35.99	10.98
1911	36.00	28.35	7.65	43.90	34.10	9.80	49.43	34.20	15.23
1912	34.96	34.88	0.08	43.60	25.63	17.97			

Table 2.2 (cont.)

(cont.)

Table 2.2 (cont.)

	Berar				United Provinces		
	CBR	CDR	CRNI		CBR	CDR	CRNI
Pre-famine							
1891–5	38.29	38.62	−0.33	1901–5	43.46	35.67	7.79
Famine							
1896	38.70	44.30	−5.60	1907	40.09	42.30	−2.21
1897	40.77	54.03	−13.26	1908	37.02	52.11	−15.08
Post-famine							
1898	31.90	23.83	8.07				
Famine							
1899	50.84	40.23	10.61				
1900	33.24	87.86	−54.62				
Post-famine							
1901	30.82	27.63	3.19	1909	33.06	37.05	−3.99
1902	55.56	31.96	23.60	1910	40.58	38.27	2.31
1903	46.69	40.47	6.22	1911	43.84	44.95	−1.11
1904	52.54	35.48	17.06	1912	44.69	29.45	15.24
1905	51.30	40.19	11.11	1913	46.37	33.88	12.49

Year	CBR	CDR	CRNI
1906	50.69	52.18	-1.49
1907	49.77	48.19	1.58
1908	49.75	34.14	15.61
1909	49.85	32.53	17.32
1910	47.97	46.41	1.56
1911	49.61	36.32	13.29
1914	43.22	32.18	11.04
1915	41.28	28.52	12.76
1916	40.38	27.65	12.73
1917	42.86	35.25	7.61
1918	38.63	79.75	-41.12
1919	31.64	40.72	-9.08
1920	34.78	36.43	-1.65
1921	34.39	39.57	-5.18

Notes: 1. CRNI = CBR–CDR.

2. The annual CBR and CDR have been calculated on the annual populations estimated by bringing forward the preceding census population, depending upon the natural increase (or decrease) determined by the difference between the registered numbers of births and deaths. However, the adjustment, when necessary, has been made for the differential in the level of registration coverage between births and deaths. The adjustment factor for annual natural increases or decreases during an intercensal decade has been determined by the ratio of census (or actual) population size to the derived population brought forward from the preceding census. When the ratio is higher than one, which means lower level of registration coverage for births than the deaths, it is used as the multiplier for each of the positive annual natural increase during the decade.

3. The year 1892 has been excluded from the average CDR and CBR during 1891–5 for Punjab as it was a year of malaria epidemics.

Sources: See Table 2.1.

during the following decades, reflecting the difficulties of the newly introduced registration system. However, in almost all cases (except Punjab during 1896–7), the CDR in the prime famine year is substantially higher than in the pre-famine normal period; and all these famine years involved substantial population losses as indicated by negative CRNIs.

TABLE 2.3

Indices of Birth and Death Rates and Rates of Natural Increase During Famine and Immediate Post-famine Years and Subsequent Period: Ten Major Famine Locations

Famine locations	Year of maximum deaths	Indices				
	t	t	t + 1	t + 2	t + 3 to t + 7	t + 8 to t + 12
Birth Rates						
Madras	1877	86	64	87	135	146
Bombay	1877	104	83	98	152	185
Central Pro.	1900	88	77	127	123	123
Berar	1900	87	80	145	131	129
Bombay	1900	78	72	98	97	102
Punjab	1900	97	87	110	109	106
United Pro.	1908	85	76	93	101	87
Central Pro.	1897	75	68	136	n.a.	n.a.
Berar	1897	106	83	132	n.a.	n.a.
Bombay	1897	94	86	103	n.a.	n.a.
Death Rates						
Madras	1877	293	155	105	97	110
Bombay	1877	184	159	117	107	119
Central Pro.	1900	262	70	76	95	98
Berar	1900	227	72	82	112	97
Bombay	1900	244	127	139	129	101
Punjab	1900	139	111	137	154	100

(*cont.*)

Table 2.3 (*cont.*)

Famine locations	Year of maximum deaths	Indices				
	t	t	t + 1	t + 2	t + 3 to t + 7	t + 8 to t + 12
United Pro.	1908	146	104	107	95	234
Central Pro.	1897	217	95	120	n.a.	n.a.
Berar	1897	140	62	104	n.a.	n.a.
Bombay	1897	133	98	119	n.a.	n.a.
Rates of Natural Increase						
Madras	1877	−38	−17	−3	7	7
Bombay	1877	−17	−13	−4	8	12
Central Pro.	1900	−58	1	18	10	9
Berar	1900	−54	3	24	7	48
Bombay	1900	−50	−17	−10	−9	0.5
Punjab	1900	−13	−7	−7	−13	0
United Pro.	1908	−23	−12	−5	2	−15
Central Pro.	1897	−48	−10	6	n.a.	n.a.
Berar	1897	−12	8	10	n.a.	n.a.
Bombay	1897	−12	−4	−5	n.a.	n.a.

Note: 1. The proportional indices of birth and death rates are constructed with reference to the respective baseline average figures being set equal to 100; and indices of rates of natural increase show absolute changes from the respective baseline figures being set equal to zero.

2. n.a. = Not applicable because of the occurrence of the second famine.

Sources: Based on Table 2.2.

Table 2.3 summarizes the broad demographic effects in both famine and immediate and longer-term post-famine periods. In most cases, there seems to have been a reduction in CBR (sometimes considerable) during the prime famine year (i.e. peak mortality year). Given the lag between conceptions and births, this partly implies the existence of the fertility-reducing effects of nutritional stress and other disruptions during the early phase of famines.[17] In all cases, the CBR seems to be significantly reduced

[17] Here we, of course, assume that famine conditions had insignificant influence on the registration of births.

in the year immediately following the year of peak famine mortality, implying a reduction in conceptions during the prime famine period. It then usually shows a sudden upward jump (in the second year following famine, t+2), reaching a much higher level than the baseline average (see Table 2.3). This implies that in the year immediately following famine, the registered conception rate very often shot up above the baseline level, confirming the hypothesis of the existence of 'excess fertility' in the immediate post-famine period. The absence of a sudden rise in births in the second year immediately after the mortality peak in 1877 (in both Bombay and Madras) seems largely due to the persistence of the mortality crisis during 1878, which resulted from a successive drought in 1877 itself. Thus, a large part of the negative effects on conceptions during 1878 were reflected in the births of 1879. But looking at the CBR for 1880, the phenomenon of a sharp rise in fertility in the immediate post-famine period seems to be supported also by the famine of 1876–8 (see Table 2.2). In most cases the CBR also remains higher than normal for roughly a decade following the famine itself. The main exception to this seems to be Bombay Presidency during the first decade of the present century when the CDR remained high due to outbreaks of plague and famine which probably helped to depress the CBR. Low average CBR in the long-term post-famine period in the United Provinces seems largely due to the influenza epidemic of 1918 which is known to have had significant negative fertility effects.[18] On the whole, however, all this largely supports the hypotheses relating to the immediate and longer-term post-famine fertility effects.

While direct data for examining the hypothesized mechanisms behind immediate post-famine effects on the CBR are lacking (namely TFR, proportion of fecund women, number of marriages, etc.), we may enquire whether there were longer-term indirect effects produced by any change in the age structure of the population. An increase in the proportion of people in the main reproductive years is expected in the post-famine period because of fertility reduction and relatively high mortality of young children and elderly people during the famine. And this can be expected

---

[18] For a case study of an influenza pandemic in the Indian context and its implications for fertility, see Mills (1986), especially pp. 26–32.

TABLE 2.4
Proportion of Population aged 20–49 years to
Total Population in Censuses both Preceding
and Following the Famine

	Proportion of population aged 20–49 years to total population			
	Total	(Change)	Female	(Change)
Bombay				
1872	0.414		0.412	
1881	0.425	(+0.011)	0.425	(+0.013)
1891	0.426		0.424	
1901	0.431	(+0.005)	0.431	(+0.007)
Madras				
1871	0.391		0.389	
1881	0.439	(+0.048)	0.446	(+0.057)
Central Provinces				
1891	0.404		0.406	
1901	0.432	(+0.028)	0.436	(+0.030)
Berar				
1891	0.436		0.419	
1901	0.458	(+0.022)	0.447	(+0.028)
Punjab				
1891	0.398		0.404	
1901	0.408	(+0.010)	0.408	(+0.004)
United Provinces				
1901	0.425		0.411	
1911	0.433	(+0.008)	0.439	(+0.028)

Notes: Most of these ratios refer to the census-enumerated population under registration system; in a few cases, they refer to total census population.

Source: See Table 2.1.

to cause an elevation in the birth rate over the pre-famine level. In this context Table 2.4 presents census-based results on the proportion of population aged 20–49 years both before and after famines. It is clear that in all locations there seems to have been some rise in the proportion of population in the reproductive period in the post-famine census. For Madras, Central Provinces, and Berar, this rise was quite sharp. Note, too, that in four out of six cases this rise appears to have been larger for the female population. This may at least partly explain our finding of a post-famine long-term elevated CBR in most cases. While this explanation for the longer-term CBR elevation is biological, there are also some indications of conscious societal responses. For example, a reduction in age at marriage in the post-famine period has been noticed in many of the most affected districts during the Madras famine of 1876–8. The possibilities of a rise in marital fertility as well as an increased incidence of widow remarriage have also been suggested.[19]

As Table 2.3 shows, in 5 out of 10 cases, the CDR in the year just following the famine seems to show a sudden drop from its pre-famine level. Given the high proportion of infant deaths to total overall mortality, this seems to be a likely outcome of a reduction in the CBR in that year.[20] This explanation is also consistent with an observed rise in the CDR in the majority of cases in the second post-famine year (t+2)—a year which usually contains a jump in the CBR. However, raised mortality in 1878 which is year (t+1), in both Bombay and Madras Presidencies, was primarily due to the effects of the successive droughts occurring in 1877. However, in the Bombay and Punjab famines of 1899–1900, the elevated mortality (largely due to epidemics of plague and malaria) continued for a few post-famine years. Thus, the persistence of elevated mortality in the immediate post-famine years does not appear to be a rule. On the other hand, recovery to pre-famine normal mortality in the longer-term post-famine period is also not always apparent. At least two reasons may be

[19] See Guilmoto (1991), pp. 10–11.

[20] A simple calculation may illustrate this point: an 8 point reduction in birth rate in the year following the Berar famine of 1899–1900 seems to have caused a reduction in total deaths by about 4900 (given the normal IMR = 233.33, being the average for 1891–5), which is equivalent to 5 per cent of total average annual deaths during 1891–5.

suggested for this: first, a possible secular rise in the registration coverage over time, especially during the early days of the registration system, may have influenced the long-term vital rates. This possibility may be particularly strong for the 1876–8 famine when the whole registration system was in a nascent stage. Second, and probably more importantly, the hypothesized longer-term post-famine demographic responses may have been obscured by occasional independent outbreaks of epidemics (e.g. the outbreak of plague epidemics during 1901 and the influenza pandemic of 1918). Thus it may be suggested that the data for the major historical famines in India do not generally support a lower CDR in the longer-term period after famine.

In the year just following a famine, the CRNI appears, as hypothesized, to be lower than the pre-famine normal level in most cases (7 out of 10 cases). But in some cases (e.g. Berar and the Central Provinces in 1901) a quick recovery to the pre-famine natural growth rate is also clear. In the second year (t+2) after famine, however, the CRNI was still low in 6 cases out of 10, reflecting the persistence of elevated mortality. But in the longer-term periods, the CRNI in most cases (except for the United Provinces during the period 1915–20, which includes the influenza pandemic of 1918) exceeds the pre-famine rate. This confirms the hypothesis of a fairly quick recovery of the pre-famine rate of population growth. However, in the context of late nineteenth and early twentieth-century India, this recovery of population growth seems to have resulted mainly from a higher (than pre-famine) level of birth rate rather than from a lower death rate, during the longer-term post-famine period.

3. The Time Path of Famine Distress, Fertility and Mortality Responses: An Analysis Using Monthly Data

In this section, we trace the evolution through time of demographic responses. In so doing, basically, the time path of fertility and mortality effects in the course of the development of famine is examined. The following famine locations have been selected for such detailed analysis: the Bombay Presidency for the famine of 1876–8; Berar for the famines of 1896–7 and 1899–1900; Punjab for the famine of 1899–1900; and the United Provinces for the famine of 1907–8. We have selected these locations partly

TABLE 2.5

Annual Rainfall in the Pre-famine Normal Period and Famine Years: Five Major Historical Famine Locations

Province & period	Rainfall (inches)	Province & period	Rainfall (inches)
Bombay		Punjab	
Pre-famine		Pre-famine	
1872–5	58.49	1891–5	31.72
1875	60.12	1898	23.27
Famine years		Famine years	
1876	36.06	1899	14.30
1877	38.57	1900	25.45
1878	71.76		
Berar		United Provinces	
Pre-famine		Pre-famine	
1885–95	40.57	Normal Average	41.84
1895	27.31	1906	42.09
Famine years		Famine years	
1896	26.62	1907	27.03
1897	31.34	1908	33.23
Pre-famine			
1898	28.09		
Famine years			
1899	12.92		
1900	33.07		

Notes: The number of years involved in calculating the normal average is not always clearly specified in the official sources. However, sometimes the averages are based on the 25 normal years. We have used the normal pre-famine average as given in the government gazettes for the United Provinces.

Sources: Punjab: Census of India 1901, vol. XVIII, *Punjab, Part 1*, p. 42 (original data were collected from the metereological department); United Provinces: *The United Provinces Government Gazettes, Part II*, Allahabad, various years; Bombay: *The Bombay Government Gazettes Part II*, Bombay, various years, Berar: *Report on the Sanitary Administration of the Hyderabad Assigned Districts*, Hyderabad, various years.

because they have not been adequately studied so far and partly because of the availability of reasonably good data.[21] As has been mentioned earlier, an additional reason for selecting the Punjab and the United Provinces is to include in our analysis the northern regions.

Table 2.5 summarizes the rainfall data for both the pre-famine and famine years. As can be seen, considerable shortfalls in monsoon rains were the proximate triggers for each of these famines. While the development of famine distress is perhaps better described in terms of food intake, distress sale of assets etc., the time-series data on such variables are unavailable. The sole economic index used here to reflect the build-up of famine is the monthly movement of the average price of a staple foodgrain, namely *jowar* (large millet) in the province. Although rise in foodgrain prices is not a necessary condition for the existence of famine,[22] dramatic price rises (causing deterioration in exchange entitlement and associated distress) appear to have been a common feature of these historical famines.[23] And, rises in the prices of staple food have widely been used as proxies for the timing and severity of famines. Weekly prices of different foodgrains for the districts of these provinces are available in the respective provincial gazettes (except for Berar).[24] Accordingly, averages of these district-level prices for the weeks ending in the middle of each month have been calculated, and they are taken here as the monthly provincial foodgrain prices.

[21] Each of these provincial governments published quite detailed official reports on these famines.

[22] In fact there is substantial literature on the extent to which rises in food prices reflect famine distress; see, e.g. Sen (1981), especially chapters 1–5. The exclusive use of jowar price in our analysis can be justified partly in terms of its relative importance among the poorer people and partly due to its relative price stability compared to prices of other grains, say wheat, which were subject to international influences.

[23] See Drèze (1990), pp. 16–17, and also Bhatia (1967).

[24] The sources of price data are as follows: Bombay Presidency: *The Bombay Presidency Gazette*, Part III, Supplement: Bombay (various years); Punjab: *The Punjab Gazette*, Supplement, Statistical, Part I: Lahore (various years); United Provinces: *The United Provinces Gazette*, Part II: Allahabad (various years). For Berar (for which we could not find any provincial gazettes), see *Report on the Sanitary Administration of the Hyderabad Assigned Districts*: Hyderabad (relevant years). It may be noted that prices were expressed in terms of *seers* (about two lbs weight) per rupee.

When analysing short-term demographic responses to famine it is important to recognize seasonality in the 'normal' annual distribution of births and deaths. The monthly data show a distinct seasonal variation in the registered numbers of both births and deaths during the pre-famine baseline period (see Appendix A). To account for such seasonal influences on the monthly fertility and mortality effects during the famine we have constructed monthly conception and mortality indices (CI and MI).[25] These are respectively the monthly ratios of numbers of conceptions and deaths to the respective pre-famine baseline average figures (the base being taken as 100). Consequently, our indices reflect proportional (rather than absolute) changes in conceptions and deaths from the respective baseline numbers. Monthly average numbers of persons on relief have also been plotted in order to better describe the course of each famine.[26] The number of persons on relief includes those who were on relief works.[27]

The Bombay Famine of 1876–8

The Bombay famine of 1876–8 began with the failure of both the summer and autumn monsoon rains during 1876. The summer

[25] While constructing the CI, we also assume, like Dyson, that the number of registered births for a month is approximately the number of conceptions nine months previously. A part of a reduction in births may indeed be a consequence of higher foetal wastage (rather than a reduction in conceptions) associated with nutritional stress during famines. But this possibility should not seriously distort our present analysis dealing with *trends* of CI. In fact the foetal wastage rates remained 'unaffected' during the crises of 1971 and 1974 in Bangladesh; see Chen and Chowdhury (1977) and also Dyson (1992). For sources of demographic data, see Table 2.1.

[26] Sources of monthly data on the numbers of persons on relief are as follows: Bombay Presidency: *The Bombay Presidency Gazette for 1878*, Part III, Supplements: Bombay, 1879; Berar: J.A. Crawford, *Report on the Famine in the Hyderabad Assigned Districts during 1899 and 1900*, vols I and II: Nagpur, Chambers Press, 1901; Punjab: *The Punjab Famine of 1899–1900*, vol. I, Lahore, 1901; United Provinces: *Resolution on the Administration of Famine Relief in the United Provinces of Agra and Oudh during 1907–1908*: Allahabad, 1909.

[27] To facilitate comparison, monthly movements of price and relief (of course, with different scales) have been plotted alongside demographic measures. Although these scales are not shown on the diagrams, the range of variation for each measure is provided in the note.

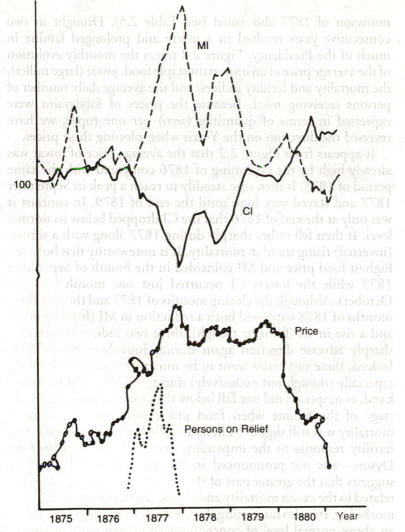

FIG. 2.2 Price of Jowar, Mortality Index (MI), Conception
Index (CI), and Average Daily Number of Persons on
Relief, by Month, Bombay 1875–80

Notes: Ranges of variation: MI, 94 (Oct. 1880) to 261 (Sept. 1877); CI,
65 (Oct. 1877) to 165 (May, 1880); jowar price, 26.12 (Jan. 1875)
to 8.3 seers per rupee (Sept. 1877); average daily number of persons
on relief, 98,422 (Nov. 1876) to 528,951 (June, 1877)

Sources: See Table 2.1 and footnotes 24 and 26.

monsoon of 1877 also failed (see Table 2.5). Drought in two consecutive years resulted in a severe and prolonged famine in much of the Presidency. Figure 2.2 traces the monthly evolution of the average price of an important staple food, jowar (large millet), the mortality and fertility indices, and the average daily number of persons receiving relief. Because the prices of foodgrains were expressed in terms of quantities (*seers*) per one rupee, we have reversed the direction on the Y-axis when plotting these prices.

It appears from Figure 2.2 that the average price of jowar was already high by the beginning of 1876 compared with the same period of 1875. It then rose steadily to reach a peak in September 1877 and stayed very high until the end of 1879. In contrast it was only at the end of 1876 that the CI dropped below its normal level. It then fell rather sharply during 1877 along with a similar (inverted) rising trend in mortality. It is noteworthy that both the highest food price and MI coincided in the month of September 1877 while the lowest CI occurred just one month later (in October). Although the closing months of 1877 and the first three months of 1878 witnessed both a reduction in MI (from its peak) and a rise in CI (from its trough), these two indices moved in a sharply adverse direction again during June–September 1878. Indeed, these two series seem to be mirror images of each other, especially (though not exclusively) during 1877–8. On the other hand, conceptions did not fall below their normal level at an early stage of the famine when food prices were rising and excess mortality was still slight.[28] Therefore, the 'anticipatory' nature of fertility response to the impending crisis—as was suggested by Dyson—was not pronounced in this case. Instead Figure 2.2 suggests that the greater part of the reduction in conceptions was related to the excess mortality and its associated presumed elevated morbidity. It is also interesting that in the pre-famine year of 1875, an above-normal level of conceptions co-existed with an above-normal level of deaths. Even if better registration in 1875 is partly

---

[28] In a similar study of movement of births through time along with the progress of famine distress (measured in terms of calories) during the Dutch famine of 1944–5, a lag between the onset of famine and the fertility reduction was also found, and this was explained in terms of the time required for exhausting the 'nutritional resources of couples'; see Stein and Susser (1978), p. 128.

TABLE 2.6
Cause-specific Death Rates in the Pre-famine (Baseline) and Famine Years: Five Major Historical Famine Locations

Cause of death	Bombay		Berar			Punjab		United Provinces	
	1871–5	1877*	1891–5	1897*	1900*	1891–5	1900*	1901–4	1908*
Cholera	0.35 (1.79)	3.53 (16.51)	1.83 (4.81)	3.49 (12.08)	6.34 (10.40)	0.14 (0.45)	1.37 (7.31)	0.91 (2.66)	1.75 (4.56)
Smallpox	0.80 (4.12)	1.69 (4.62)	0.13 (0.34)	0.21 (0.58)	0.29 (0.37)	0.27 (0.87)	0.51 (1.42)	0.15 (0.44)	1.26 (6.02)
Fever	11.92 (61.40)	20.76 (45.90)	18.66 (48.96)	22.64 (28.97)	29.00 (23.84)	21.24 (68.75)	33.37 (72.20)	24.55 (71.57)	41.31 (90.94)
Dysentery/ Diarrhoea	1.85 (9.52)	3.71 (9.66)	6.02 (15.81)	10.20 (30.42)	22.04 (36.94)	0.76 (2.45)	1.26 (3.00)	0.63 (1.84)	0.41 (-1.19)
Plague	—	—	—	—	—	—	—	2.16 (6.30)	0.48 (-9.12)
Injuries/ Accidents	0.38 (1.97)	0.46 (0.42)	0.38 (1.00)	0.46 (0.58)	0.54 (0.36)	0.33 (1.06)	0.37 (0.29)	0.50 (1.40)	0.57 (0.37)
All other	4.12 (21.21)	8.53 (22.90)	11.07 (29.06)	14.84 (27.44)	23.25 (28.08)	8.16 (26.42)	10.80 (15.78)	5.40 (15.74)	6.95 (8.41)

(cont.)

Table 2.6 (cont.)

Cause of death	Bombay		Berar			Punjab		United Provinces	
	1871–5	1877*	1891–5	1897*	1900*	1891–5	1900*	1901–4	1908*
All causes	19.42	38.68	38.11	51.85	81.46	30.89	47.69	34.30	52.73
	(100)	(100)	(100)	(100)	(100)	(100)	(100)	(100)	(100)

Notes: 1. The years marked (*) are the prime famine years.
2. All these rates are based on constant denominators being the respective enumerated population under vital registration according to the last census prior to famine.
3. For all baseline periods, the figures in parentheses are the respective percentage shares to total average deaths while for all the famine years they are the respective shares to the total excess deaths. Total excess deaths for each cause of death in a famine year have been calculated over the respective average number of deaths during baseline period.
4. As 1902 was an epidemic year in Punjab it has been excluded from the baseline average figures for 1891–5.
5. In the United Provinces, plague began to be included as a separate cause of death only from 1902; so, baseline period average for plague is based on three years, 1902–4.
   Respiratory diseases were included as a separate cause of death only from 1905. Its percentage share to total excess deaths in 1908 was below 1 per cent.

Sources: See Sources in Table 2.1.

responsible for this, it seems clear that the considerable excess mortality peak in 1875 did not bring forth a corresponding decline in conceptions. A plausible inference may be that excess mortality (and morbidity) does not always exert a perceptible negative influence on conceptions. Instead it may be that conditions of acute food shortage and nutritional stress are an important ingredient in explaining conception (and fertility) decline. We return to this below.

Relief operations in this famine started only around November 1876. Given the employment losses and high prices from the beginning of the *kharif* season (June), the very scant start of relief in November may well be considered as late (see Fig. 2.2). As can be seen, relief provision reached a peak in July 1877. It then began to fall, although mortality and food prices were both still rising. Relief operations were closed by the end of 1877.

Table 2.6 presents the changes in the cause-specific death rates and their relative importance. It shows that deaths from cholera were proportionately more important in the excess mortality of both 1877 and 1878 than in the baseline period. But fever deaths constituted the largest share of mortality in both normal and famine years—especially 1878. Figure 2.3 plots the monthly numbers of deaths from cholera, fever and bowel complaints. It shows that deaths from these causes were all rising from the beginning of 1877. Cholera deaths peaked around April and began to decline from about August; deaths from bowel complaints peaked in September; and the fever deaths two months later in December 1877. Thus, while cholera mortality occurred mostly during the pre-monsoon and early monsoon months, mortality from bowel complaints and fever (presumably in part malarial) tended to peak during and after the monsoon. However, it also seems significant that all major causes of death show a similar rising pattern from the beginning 1877. Although the fever mortality peak in November of 1877 may be related to the unusually heavy rains of October (see Fig. 2.4), its sharp rising trend throughout the year is noteworthy. Misclassification of deaths is likely, especially at this time when the registration system was still in its infancy. It seems probable that some deaths from cholera and dysentery/diarrhoea were recorded in the fever category. However, as the Sanitary Commissioner of Bombay Presidency in his annual report for 1877 writes, '[it] is impossible

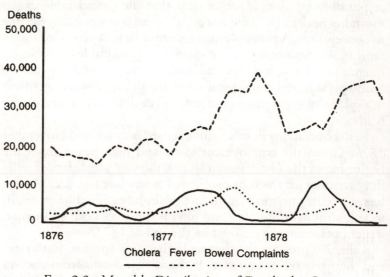

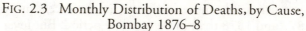

Cholera Fever Bowel Complaints

FIG. 2.3 Monthly Distribution of Deaths, by Cause,
Bombay 1876–8

Sources: See Table 2.1.

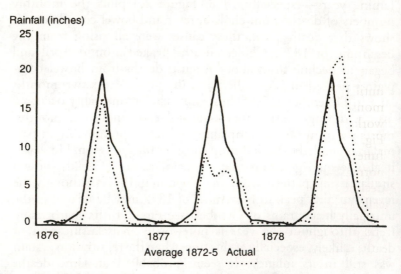

Average 1872-5 Actual

FIG. 2.4 Monthly Distribution of Rainfall in Normal and
Famine Years, Bombay 1876–8

Sources: See Table 2.5.

therefore to say how many of these [fever] deaths were due to malarial fevers, though I think there is but little doubt that the mortality recorded under this heading in the famine districts, was at all events during the latter half of the year, principally due to remittent fever'.[29] By 'remittent fever' he seems to have had malaria in mind.

Thus, excess mortality from fevers (which has sometimes been expected to occur after the resumption of rains following a drought year) can happen even in the second successive year of drought. As Figure 2.4 shows, in terms of rainfall 1877 was little better than 1876. Assuming that fever mortality represented much of the malarial deaths, this implies that the malaria epidemic in 1877 was largely related to famine and undernutrition. In 1878, the MI initially peaked in May, though it rose slightly higher still during the period up to September (see Fig. 2.2). In 1878, the cholera deaths peak in June was followed by bowel-complaint deaths peak in August, which was followed by fever deaths peak in November (see Fig. 2.3). The delayed fever mortality peak in 1878 was probably related to the above-normal rainfall, especially in August and September (see Fig. 2.4). Figure 2.3, thus, suggests that in *both* 1877 and 1878 cholera deaths tended to peak around the beginning of monsoon; bowel-complaint deaths peaked in the mid-monsoon period; and fever deaths peaked after the end of the monsoon.

The number of persons on relief was rising along with the MI until the middle of 1877 (see Fig. 2.2). The beginning of the monsoon period in June probably reduced the demand for relief works; but the monsoon of 1877 was also largely a failure (see Fig. 2.4). Therefore, a steady decline in the relief provisions from June 1877 presumably did not correspond to a recovery of the normal farm activities. Thus, overall relief provision was on the decline during the months when the MI was still rising dramatically (see Fig. 2.2). About the class composition of recipients of relief, the Governor of Bombay reported that '[t]hose who received relief mainly belonged to the humbler castes of the Hindu Community and to the classes of field labourers, of rude artisans, and of village menials'.[30]

---

[29] Government of Bombay (1878a), p. 176.
[30] Quoted in Government of Bombay (1879), p. 114.

The Berar Famines of 1896–7 and 1899–1900

The Famine Commission of 1880 described Berar as 'one of the parts of India particularly free from apprehension of calamity of drought'.[31] However, in 1896–7, the province fell under the grip of a serious famine. Berar experienced a considerable shortfall of rain in 1895; and the successive drought and consequent crop failure in 1896 brought famine conditions (see Table 2.5). Unfortunately, Berar experienced another and more severe drought in 1899 when annual rainfall amounted to less than one-third of its normal level (see Table 2.5). The crop output during 1899–1900 was estimated to be only 2.5 per cent of the average output during the preceding ten years (excluding 1896–7).[32] The famine of 1896–7 was described as a 'famine of high prices rather than of scarcity of food'.[33] However, the 1899–1900 famine was both much more severe and much more widespread.

Figure 2.5 presents the monthly series of the MI and the average price of jowar during 1895–1901. Unfortunately, monthly data on births are not available for the famine years; also price information before September 1896 and after December 1900 could not be found. The MIs in 1895 show some excess over the baseline level. However, such pre-famine excess mortality does not seem to have affected fertility, since the CBR in 1896 was not below either that of 1895 or the baseline average for the period 1891–5 (see Table 2.2). Again, the beginning of 1896 witnessed a sharp rise in mortality which peaked around May and then fell fairly fast. However, mortality during the closing months of 1896 and the first three months of 1897 was below its pre-famine baseline level—although food prices were rising dramatically (see Fig. 2.5). The MI peaked rather sharply during the monsoon period of 1897, and reached a maximum in September when food prices also peaked. Peak famine mortality, thus, seems to have lasted for only a short duration, mainly the latter half of 1897. Relief works which began at the end of 1896, peaked in April 1987. In fact, as Figure 2.5 indicates, relief

---

[31] Quoted in Census of India 1901, *Report on Berar, Volume VIII, Part 1,* Allahabad, 1902, p. 30.

[32] See Census of India 1901, *Report on Berar, Volume VIII, Part I,* p. 31.

[33] See Crawford (1901), vol. I, p. 2.

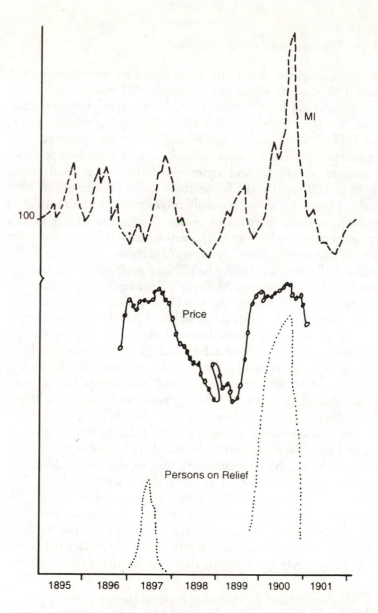

FIG. 2.5 Price of Jowar, Mortality Index (MI), and Average Daily Number of Persons on Relief, by Month, Berar 1895–1901

Notes: Ranges of variation: MI, 43.9 (Aug., 1898) to 423.5 (July, 1900); jowar price, 33 (April, 1899) to 7 seers per rupee (July, 1897); average daily number of persons on relief, 788 (Dec., 1896) to 601,424 (July, 1900).

Sources: See Table 2.1 and footnotes 24 and 26.

provision declined drastically from the first monsoon month (June 1987), while at the same time the MI was rising.

Among the specified causes of death, cholera, dysentery/diarrhoea, and fever were the major killers during the baseline period (see Table 2.6). However, comparing the relative proportion of deaths from different causes indicates an increased importance of cholera, smallpox, and dysentery/diarrhoea in total excess deaths in 1897 and also a fall in the relative importance of fever deaths. Figure 2.6 shows monthly movements in the number of deaths from these three major causes. It suggests a fairly similar time pattern of deaths from all these diseases in the main mortality year. While deaths from dysentery/diarrhoea, and from fever, peaked in September 1897, the cholera peak occurred just one month before in August. As Berar's Sanitary Commissioner in his report for 1897 writes, '[i]t was the experience at all our relief centres that after the rains set in sickness greatly increased, especially fevers and bowel-complaints. Indeed, the most common termination of life in those debilitated by famine was diarrhoea or dysentery, aggravated by damp and exposure after the setting in of the south-west monsoon. Cold and damp had a most detrimental effect upon the starving poor, and those in a physically reduced condition from chronic insufficiency of food'.[34] The report also noted that 'the number of deaths from starvation returned by village registrars numbered 377. These take no account of the deaths at poorhouses due to diarrhoea, dysentery etc., primarily the cause of chronic deprivation of food'.[35] It is also notable that in 1897—a year of huge fever mortality—there was a marked *decline* in admissions from fever in several medical institutions of the province. According to the Sanitary Commissioner for Berar, this largely reflected the fact that most of the excess fever mortality in that year occurred 'amongst the

---

[34] See Government of the Hyderabad Assigned Districts (1898), p. 7.

[35] Ibid., p. 32. It also states that 'the official definition of death from starvation signifies that so long as a person has food before him, or the means of procuring it, he cannot die from starvation. This is a mistake, for physiologically the human body may be starved of every[thing] essential to its vitality in spite of the most nutritious food if digestion has been so impaired by the effects of chronic starvation that nutrients cannot be assimilated and this form of starvation caused directly or indirectly many deaths throughout the province and explains the excess mortality under "other causes"'; pp. 32–3.

famine-stricken poor, with whom the question of medical relief was secondary to that of food . . . '[36] All these considerations suggest that the general course of mortality rise during the famine was largely determined by the general course of famine distress and its lagged effects on human survival, being, of course, partly mediated by both environmental factors and social disruptions.

The mortality was below its baseline level throughout the post-famine year of 1898. While mortality was somewhat higher than its normal level during the early months of 1899, interestingly, it was below its baseline level in late 1899—when the food price had risen dramatically (see Fig. 2.5). As in 1896, this mortality improvement during the initial phase of famine may, as suggested by the Sanitary Commissioner in his report for 1900, have been due to the dryness of the weather and the consequent lower incidence of fever.[37] Moreover, there may well be a time lag between the onset of famine and its excess mortality outcome. Note that the price of food remained extremely high throughout 1900.

From the beginning of 1900 the MI rose drastically to reach a huge climax within a few months—peaking in July (see Fig. 2.5). It then declined with similar rapidity and by the end of 1900 mortality came down to its baseline level—remaining below this level throughout 1901. The relief provision reached a maximum in June of 1900, after which it fell sharply—probably due to the resumption of rains and normal farm activities. In contrast to the famine of 1896–7, in this second famine the rise in the number of persons on relief better corresponds to the rise in the MI (see Fig. 2.5).

As Table 2.6 suggests, there has been, as with the former famine, an increase in the importance of cholera and dysentery/diarrhoea, and a reduced role of fever mortality in accounting for overall excess deaths in 1900. Indeed, as Figure 2.6 shows, deaths from cholera, dysentery/diarrhoea, and fevers all tended to rise steadily from the closing months of 1899. According to the Sanitary Commissioner for Berar, many cholera deaths (about 10,000 by his estimate) were registered under other heads.[38] While cholera

---

[36] Ibid., p. 16.
[37] See Government of the Hyderabad Assigned Districts (1901), p. 10.
[38] See Government of the Hyderabad Assigned Districts (1901), p. 8.

Deaths

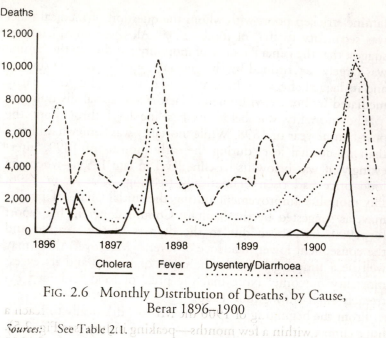

FIG. 2.6   Monthly Distribution of Deaths, by Cause,
Berar 1896–1900

Sources: See Table 2.1.

Rainfall (inches)

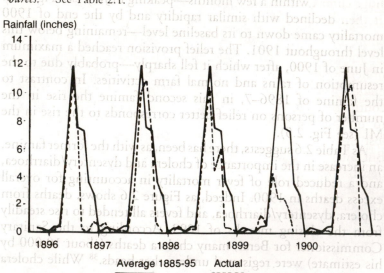

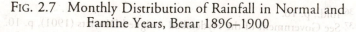

FIG. 2.7   Monthly Distribution of Rainfall in Normal and
Famine Years, Berar 1896–1900

Sources: See Table 2.5.

deaths peaked in July 1900—coinciding exactly with the highest MI—the other two causes reached a maximum just one month later in August, when deaths from dysentery/diarrhoea actually exceeded the number of fever deaths. Therefore, the indications are that the huge elevation in mortality which lasted throughout 1900 did *not* result mainly from an outbreak of malaria following the resumption of rains. In an extract from the Proceedings of the Resident at Hyderabad No. 2936 dated 12 August 1901, much of the famine mortality was attributed to the prevalence of cholera and bowel complaints due to 'excessive consumption of rank vegetables and foul water after the first heavy rain of the monsoon'.[39] In fact, Mr J.A. Crawford, the Commissioner of Berar, in his foreword to the Sanitary Commissioner's report for 1900 specifically stated that '[t]he death rate in Berar in 1900 was increased largely by the famine'.[40]

The scanty rainfall and the related dryness of weather may have suppressed the expected post-monsoon peak in fever mortality in both 1896 and 1899. However, the occurrence of peak fever mortality during the pre-monsoon months in 1900 is of interest. This, as reported by the Sanitary Commissioner of Berar, was due in large part to influenza and other simple fevers. As he wrote in his report for 1900, '[a]s the year 1900 advanced, "influenza" became prevalent, and deaths from it were registered under the head "fevers", and the number of cases of fevers also gradually commenced to increase—mostly of the type of simple continued [fever] . . .' This, according to him, was largely due to 'unwholesome water and food' consumed by people who had lost their stamina and were exposed to the heat and the rains. But after the resumption of the rains, the malarial fever with hepatic complications and jaundice symptoms increased till the end of the year.[41] Thus, as with the former famine, the monthly data on cause-specific deaths during the famine of 1899–1900

---

[39] Quoted in Crawford (1901), vol. I, p. 2.
[40] Quoted in Government of the Hyderabad Assigned Districts (1901), (no page number).
[41] See Government of the Hyderabad Assigned Districts (1901), pp. 10–11. Indeed there is more evidence in the context of other locations that famine may cause deaths from 'some fatal types of fever other than malarial fevers, aggravated by the debilitating effects of want of food'; see Guz (1989), p. 204.

also indicate the effects (presumably lagged) of the general course of nutritional deprivation on the general course of mortality increase, although environmental and other factors seem to have influenced the exact timing of the peaks from specific causes. In this connection, note the excess rainfall in August of both 1897 and 1900—a fact which may have contributed to the mortality peak in the following months.

Although in these famines we are unable to examine monthly variations in conceptions, it is clear that both famines affected aggregate births in the short run. The CBR fell from an average of 38.29 during the baseline period (1891–5) to 31.90 in 1898 and 30.82 in 1901 (see Table 2.2). However, this does not give a precise estimate of the fertility-impact of the famines. Comparing these major famines in Berar, that of 1899–1900 appears to have been far more severe in respect of monsoon failure, crop losses, and excess mortality, (e.g. see Figs 2.5 and 2.7).[42] The percentage of stillbirths to total livebirths in 1897 (4.7) was little different from the average figure of 4.5 during the baseline period 1891–5. But it rose to 5.2 in 1900.[43] However, interestingly, the extent of the food-price rise was similar in these famines. This probably suggests that the extent of food-price rises during a famine does not necessarily reflect the degree of nutritional stress and associated subsequent excess mortality. Indeed, the extent of failure of food entitlements for the majority of the rural population depends crucially on employment opportunities, which, in turn, are determined largely by rainfall in such weather-dependent agriculture. The birth rate in 1897, was slightly *higher* than the baseline level, whereas in 1900 it was significantly lower than the baseline level. This suggests a little overall 'anticipatory' fertility reduction in the former famine (see Table 2.2). However, it partly reflects both the greater severity and the very closely spaced occurrence of the latter famine.

[42] The relatively greater severity of the famine of 1899–1900 than that of the one in 1896–7 is also affirmed by the data on sales and mortgages of land: the number of land sales rose from 12,683 in 1895–6 to 12,981 in 1896–7, and to 13,850 in 1899–1900; the respective numbers of land mortgages are 11,931, 13,342 and 21,661; see Crawford (1901), vol. II, Appendix Table XXI, p. 51.

[43] See Census of India 1901, *Report on Berar, Volume VIII, Part I*, p. 44.

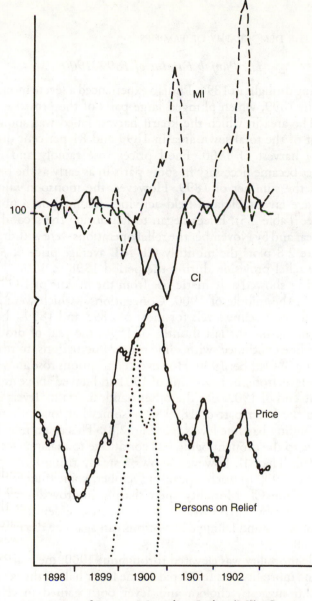

FIG. 2.8 Price of Jowar, Mortality Index (MI), Conception
Index (CI), and Average Daily Number of Persons on
Relief, by Month, Punjab 1898–1902

Notes: Ranges of variation: MI, 77 (Oct., 1899) to 309 (April, 1902); CI:
61 (Oct., 1900) to 132 (June, 1902); jowar price, 26 (Dec., 1898)
to 11 seers per rupee (July, 1900); average daily number of persons
on relief, 29,763 (Sept., 1899) to 242,755 (March, 1900).

Sources: See Table 2.1 and footnotes 24 and 26.

The Punjab Famine of 1899–1900

Following drought in 1896, Punjab experienced a severe monsoon failure in 1899, which plunged large parts of the province into crisis. The area in which the kharif harvest failed was about 51 per cent of the total sown area in 1899 and 81 per cent during the rabi harvest of 1900. Food prices rose rapidly and relief measures became necessary in some parts in as early as the beginning of the summer of 1899. However, the monsoon rains of 1900 were favourable and field activities resumed on a normal scale (see Table 2.5). Prices began to fall during the second half of the year and by November the relief operations were withdrawn.

Figure 2.8 plots the monthly CI, MI, average price of jowar and the relief provision during the period 1898 to 1902.[44] The food prices showed a dramatic rise from the middle of 1899 and peaked in the middle of 1900. Conceptions—which were marginally above baseline levels for most of 1898 and 1899—began to decline during the last months of 1899, the year of drought. This decline continued, with some minor fluctuations, to reach a minimum in October 1900. However, conceptions rose above the baseline level from the beginning of 1901 and stayed above normal until the end of 1902. On the other hand, mortality levels especially in the latter part of 1899 were somewhat lower than the corresponding baseline levels (see Fig. 2.8). This again may have been due to the drought being less conducive to malaria (see also Fig. 2.10). The MI, however, shows a steady rising trend from the start of 1900 to reach a peak in October, coinciding with the trough in the CI. Mortality then sharply improved—reaching normal levels by early 1901. A strong correspondence between rising mortality and falling conceptions can again be discerned in Figure 2.8.

While mortality was elevated throughout 1900, the main peak in famine mortality was restricted to the latter half of the year. As Table 2.6 suggests, cholera and fever both gained in relative importance during 1900. But fever alone, in fact, seems to have

[44] On 25 October 1901 some areas were taken out of Punjab to constitute a separate province called North-Western Frontier Province. So, for the sake of comparability, the registered numbers of births and deaths in Punjab from that date onwards have been inflated by a factor which is the inverse of the proportion of total population remaining in truncated Punjab according to the 1901 census.

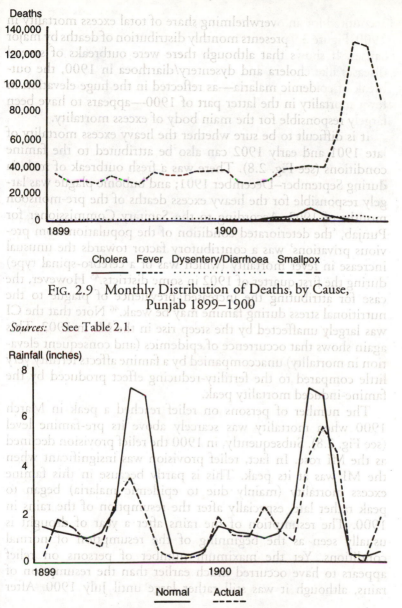

FIG. 2.9 Monthly Distribution of Deaths, by Cause,
Punjab 1899–1900

Sources: See Table 2.1.

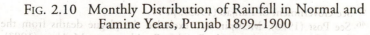

FIG. 2.10 Monthly Distribution of Rainfall in Normal and
Famine Years, Punjab 1899–1900

Sources: See Table 2.5.

accounted for an overwhelming share of total excess mortality in 1900. Figure 2.9 presents monthly distribution of deaths by major causes. It shows that although there were outbreaks of several diseases like cholera and dysentery/diarrhoea in 1900, the outbreak of epidemic malaria—as reflected in the huge elevation in fever mortality in the latter part of 1900—appears to have been largely responsible for the main body of excess mortality.

It is difficult to be sure whether the heavy excess mortality of late 1901 and early 1902 can also be attributed to the famine conditions (see Fig. 2.8). There was a fresh outbreak of malaria during September–December 1901; and bubonic plague was largely responsible for the heavy excess deaths of the pre-monsoon months of 1902. According to the Sanitary Commissioner for Punjab, 'the deteriorated condition of the population from previous privations' was a contributory factor towards the unusual increase in fever mortality (which was of a cerebro-spinal type) during the first quarter of 1902 in some districts.[45] However, the case for attributing the increased prevalence of plague to the nutritional stress during famine may be weak.[46] Note that the CI was largely unaffected by the steep rise in the MI in 1902. This again shows that occurrence of epidemics (and consequent elevation in mortality) unaccompanied by a famine affects fertility very little compared to the fertility-reducing effect produced by the famine-induced mortality peak.

The number of persons on relief reached a peak in March 1900 when mortality was scarcely above its pre-famine level (see Fig. 2.8). Subsequently, in 1900 the relief provision declined as the MI rose. In fact, relief provision was insignificant when the MI was at its peak. This is partly because in this famine excess mortality (mainly due to epidemic malaria) began to peak rather late, especially after the resumption of the rains in 1900. The resumption of the rains after a year of drought is usually seen as the beginning of the resumption of normal conditions. Yet the maximum number of persons on relief appears to have occurred much earlier than the resumption of rains, although it was still rather large until July 1900. After

[45] See Government of Punjab (1903), p. 11.
[46] See Post (1976). McAlpin also excluded the plague deaths from the estimates of famine mortality in the Bombay Presidency; see McAlpin (1983).

that, relief works were virtually closed while gratuitous relief, though diminished, continued in response to rising mortality until September. Mortality was much higher among those on gratuitous relief. The Deputy Commissioner of Hissar district stated that 'the increase in mortality was mainly among those in receipt of relief' especially those in poorhouses and those receiving gratuitous relief.[47] This implied that, as he himself argued, 'privation and consequently decreased vitality played a considerable part' in the excess mortality. There may be several reasons for the decline in relief provision in as early as March 1900. Outbreaks of cholera at relief camps were a common source of epidemics 'when people fled the works and took cholera with them to their home villages and other locations'.[48] Moreover, owing to deepening nutritional stress, people also lose their capacity to work. For example, as one district engineer in his official letter dated 20 April 1900 wrote, 'people . . . are in a starving condition and half of them [are] unfit to work . . . they are living skeletons and crying from hunger'.[49]

The United Provinces Famine of 1907–8

The famine of 1907–8 in the United Provinces was brought about by the premature cessation of monsoon rainfall in August 1907, following a generally poor start to the monsoon (see Table 2.5). In large parts of the province the rains lasted for only 5 to 8 weeks, instead of their usual 12 weeks. The failure of the kharif season in 1907 against the backdrop of some partial weather failures in the preceding two years ultimately produced famine conditions.[50] Drought continued until January 1908, and there was a very small rabi crop in early 1908 as well. According to the official report on the famine the kharif harvest was only 31 per cent of normal output and only about 60 per cent in the case of rabi production.[51]

---

[47] Government of Punjab (1901), vol. II, Appendix XVIII, pp. 163–4.
[48] See McAlpin (1985), p. 167.
[49] See Government of Punjab (1901), vol. II, Appendix XVIII, p. 145.
[50] For details of the antecedents and partial weather failures before this famine, see Government of the United Provinces of Agra and Oudh (1909a), chapter 1.
[51] Ibid., p. 18.

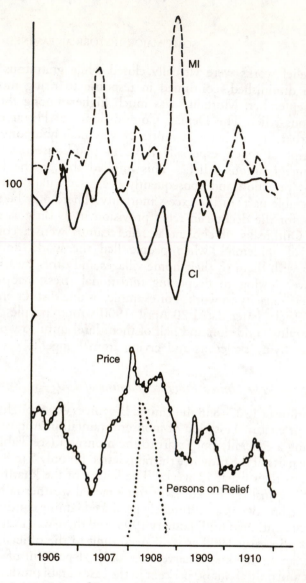

FIG. 2.11 Price of Jowar, Mortality Index (MI), Conception
Index (CI), and Average Daily Number of Persons on Relief,
by Month, United Provinces 1906–10

Notes: Ranges of variation: MI, 84.5 (June, 1909) to 244.5 (Nov., 1908);
             CI, 46.2 (Nov., 1908) to 104.3 (July, 1910); jowar price, 19.6
             (March, 1907) to 7 seers per rupee (Dec., 1907); average daily
             number of persons on relief, 5883 (Nov., 1907) to 1,411,576
             (March, 1908).

Sources: See Table 2.1 and footnotes 24 and 26.

The net loss in food crops in the province in 1907–8 was estimated to be 7 million tons.

The prices of foodgrains, which were already high during the early part of 1906 (owing to the partial drought and famine during 1905–6) declined until early 1907, but then rose sharply to reach a peak around December (see Fig. 2.11). Due to the persistence of high prices during the pre-famine period, people who were net purchasers of foodgrains, were probably already distressed and thus less able to cope with this fresh round of price rises in 1907. There was some delay in the commencement of relief operations. As Figure 2.11 shows, these did not start until the end of 1907. This was because of the official assumption that large advances given early in the autumn (for the sowing and irrigation of the spring crops) and the 'prompt and liberal' suspensions and remissions of land revenue encouraged people to continue the sowing of spring crops until a much later period than was usual.[52]

As Figure 2.11 shows, mortality was somewhat above the baseline normal level during most of 1906 and the CI was slightly below baseline level. There was a considerable MI peak during the first half of 1907—largely due to the prevalence of plague. Interestingly, this peak occurring during the pre-famine months of 1907 seems to have had no significant effect upon the level of conceptions. This lends support to the view (indicated earlier in the contexts of the Bombay famine of 1876–8 and the Punjab famine of 1899–1900) that the negative effect of epidemic diseases on conceptions and subsequent fertility was minor if unaccompanied by famine conditions. There seems to have been a considerable reduction in conceptions during late 1907 when food prices were rising and (proportional) excess mortality was not yet great. However, as Figure 2.11 shows, in the main famine period there was a clear correspondence between the extent of excess mortality and the amount of conception shortfall. Indeed, the minimum CI occurred in November 1908 when the MI reached its peak. By the middle of 1909 both conceptions and deaths recovered to baseline levels. It is also notable that conceptions declined below the baseline level late in 1909.

[52] Ibid., p. 28.

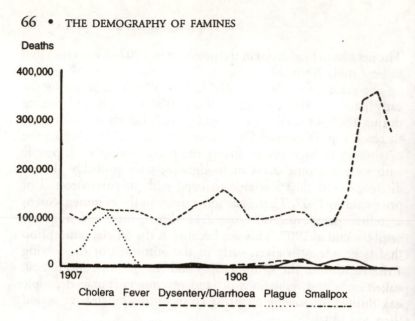

FIG. 2.12 Monthly Distribution of Deaths, by Cause,
United Provinces 1907–8

Sources: See Table 2.1.

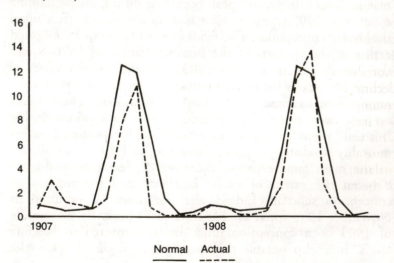

FIG. 2.13 Monthly Distribution of Rainfall in the Normal and
Famine Years, United Provinces 1907–8

Sources: See Table 2.5.

It is clear both that the MI peak of this famine was of rather short duration and that it was largely accounted for by a sharp rise in fever mortality during the last months of 1908, i.e. after the resumption of monsoon rains (e.g. see Figs 2.11, 2.12 and 2.13). As Table 2.6 also shows, although there was an increase in the relative importance of cholera in 1908, about 91 per cent of the total excess deaths were recorded under the fever category. Note, too, that there was no rise in the mortality from dysentery/ diarrhoea, and according to the Sanitary Commissioner for the United Provinces 'this no doubt to some extent is due to the measures adopted and to the judicious feeding of the people on the relief works especially young children and suckling mothers'.[53] Cholera deaths peaked in September, which usually marks the end of the monsoon; fever mortality rose steeply in September and peaked in November (see Fig. 2.12). Although the cholera deaths peak thus preceded the fever mortality peak, both seem to have followed the same broad time pattern and occurred rather late, and note also that it occurred at a time when relief was nearly over. The sharp and huge fever deaths peak, according to the official reports,[54] corresponds to a malaria epidemic. There was, indeed, an enormous rise in the attendance of malaria patients at hospitals and dispensaries: it rose from an average annual figure of 625,885 during 1904–7 to 1,369,583 in 1908.[55] It is also notable that the number of persons on relief peaked in February 1908 and subsequently declined during the main period of excess mortality. Here again we find evidence that the beginning of the decline in relief operations did not always coincide with the resumption of the rains. Indeed, the number of persons on relief was insignificant by the time of the huge peak in excess mortality. This was (as in the Punjab famine of 1899–1900) probably because the main mortality peak (largely as a result of epidemic malaria) started in the later months, especially after the resumption of the rains.

[53] See Government of the United Provinces of Agra and Oudh (1909b), p. 14.

[54] Ibid., p. 11; see also Government of the United Provinces of Agra and Oudh (1910a).

[55] See the Sanitary Department Resolution dated 7 July 1910 in Government of the United Provinces of Agra and Oudh (1910b), p. 1.

4. Monthly Movements of Prices, Mortality and Conceptions: A Statistical Analysis using Time-series Data for Ten Major Famine Locations

The previous diagrams generally suggest that the monthly CI and MI respectively have had a somewhat negative and positive relationship with monthly movements of food prices. Also very clear was an inverse relationship between the monthly MI and CI movements. However, coming to a precise view about the appropriate lags involved in these relationships is difficult on the basis of diagrams alone.[56] Cross-correlation coefficients may help us to explore the precise nature of lags in the various time-series data on food prices, the MI and the CI.

A cross-correlation function describes the extent of correlation between two time-series X_t and Y_t, allowing for different lags in the series. For each integer k (positive or negative), the cross-correlation measures the correlation between Y_t and the shifted series X_{t-k} (or equivalently, between Y_{t+k} and X_t).[57] The calculation of the cross-correlation function is as follows:

r_{xy} (k) = sample cross-correlation coefficient of lag k

$$\frac{\sum_{t=1}^{T-k} (X_t - \bar{X}) (Y_{t+k} - \bar{Y})}{\sqrt{\sum_{t=1}^{T} (X_t - \bar{X})^2} \sqrt{\sum_{t=1}^{T} (Y_t - \bar{Y})^2}}$$

$$k = \ldots -3, -2, -1, 0, 1, 2, 3 \ldots$$
$$T = \text{series length}$$
$$\bar{X} = \text{mean for } X_t$$
$$\bar{Y} = \text{mean for } Y_t$$

However, it is important to note that the cross-correlation function can only be easily interpreted if both time-series are made stationary.[58] Working with first differences is one way of making the series stationary for this purpose. Moreover, the cross-correlation coefficient only describes the linear association between the

---

[56] See Figs. 2, 3 and 4 in Dyson (1991a) for diagrammatic presentations for the Madras famine of 1876–8 and for the famines of 1896–7 and 1899–1900 in the Central Provinces and Bombay Presidency.

[57] See Fornum and Stanton (1989).

[58] 'Broadly speaking a time series is said to be stationary if there is no systematic change in mean (no trend), if there is no systematic change in variance, and if strictly periodic variations have been removed'; see Chatfield (1984), p. 14.

two series. However, the estimated cross-correlations obtained with different lags help one to make inferences about the direction of causality and, of course, the approximate length of the appropriate lags.

It has become clear from all the famines examined so far that the lag in the time-series of food prices is only expected to produce correlations with both the CI and the MI series, and not the other way round. In other words, the direction of causation is fairly clear. Since excess mortality in the wake of famines appears to have exerted additional negative effects on fertility, the lag in the MI is expected to produce cross-correlation with the CI, and not the reverse. However, these relations do not seem to hold in the context of non-famine periods. For example, we have noted some occasions of considerable excess mortality in non-famine years which were unaccompanied by price rises or reductions in fertility (e.g. the United Provinces in 1907, Bombay in 1875, and Punjab in 1902). Consequently, we have restricted ourselves here to time-series data mostly for the officially declared famine years when calculating cross-correlations. We present estimates based on differenced time-series data for ten major famine locations (i.e. those that have been considered in section 2).[59] The main results are summarized in Table 2.7.

Table 2.7 shows that the magnitude of the cross-correlation coefficients is somewhat considerable (in many cases), and all are in the expected directions. However, the correlations between food prices and the MI (r_1) are relatively weak; also, the results suggest that fairly long lags (of at least several months) are sometimes involved. Indeed, in some famines this relationship appears to be very weak (e.g. the United Provinces famine of 1907–8 and the Central Provinces famine of 1899–1900). As we have seen, peak famine mortality often occurred within a relatively short time span when prices, though high, were not rising any further. In contrast, movements in prices and CI (r_2) and the MI and CI (r_3)

---

[59] The demographic data and also the data on food prices for the Madras famine of 1876–8, and the famines of 1896–7 and 1899–1900 both in Bombay Presidency and Central Provinces were collected from Tim Dyson; for relevant information, see Dyson (1991a), especially Table 1, and also footnotes 25, 26, 28, 29. For the monthly data on relief provision in the latter two locations, see Government of Bombay (1903), vol. II, Table 10, p. 21; Government of the Central Provinces (1901), vol. II, Statement VI, p. 47.

TABLE 2.7

Estimates of Cross-correlations with Monthly Time-series (differenced) Data on Food Prices, Conception Indices and Mortality Indices: Ten Major Historical Famine Locations

Famine locations	Highest cross-correlation coefficients with the corresponding lags (in months)					
	r_1	lag	r_2	lag	r_3	lag
1. Madras famine, 1876–8, n = 36	0.39*	2	–0.52*	1, 2	–0.47*	1
2. Bombay famine, 1876–8, n = 36	0.28	0	–0.56*	1	–0.51*	1
3. Berar famine, 1896–7, n = 16	0.28	6	n.a.		n.a.	
4. Bombay famine, 1896–7, n = 24	0.32	2	–0.63*	0	–0.41	0
5. Central Prov., 1896–7, n = 24	0.42	0	–0.66*	0	–0.60*	0
6. Berar famine, 1899–1900, n = 24	0.28	4	n.a.		n.a.	
7. Bombay famine, 1899–1900, n = 24	0.38	6	–0.63*	0	–0.58*	1
8. Central Prov., 1899–1900, n = 24	0.20	0	–0.53*	3	–0.62*	0
9. Punjab famine, 1899–1900, n = 29	0.33	3	–0.46*	2, 3	–0.68*	0
10. United Prov., 1907–8, n = 30	0.26	3	–0.41*	2, 3	–0.61*	0

r_1 = cross-correlation coefficient between monthly variations in food prices and mortality indices (MI)

r_2 = cross-correlation coefficient between monthly variations in food prices and conception indices (CI)

r_3 = cross-correlation coefficient between monthly variations in mortality indices (MI) and conception indices (CI)

Notes: 1. * significant at less than five per cent level.
   2. Only the cross-correlation coefficients with the expected directions in lags are considered here.
   3. n = number of observations.

Sources: For demographic data, see Table 2.1; for data on food prices, see footnotes 24 and 59.

appear to be much more tightly related and operate with relatively minimal lags. The relatively weak cross-correlation found between food prices and the CIs (r_2) in the Punjab and United Provinces famines may partly be due to the fact that in both cases the first famine year witnessed a fertility-recovery (or 'excess fertility'), as a demographic response to a considerable fertility reduction in the preceding year of famine.

In Figure 2.14 we present diagrams (for eight famine locations) plotting the cross-correlation coefficients (i.e. 'cross-correllograms') involving lags of up to 6 months. As can be seen, the cross-correllogram for r_1 (based on food prices and mortality) over different lags for the famines of 1876–8 and 1896–7 generally has a consistent pattern, attaining its highest positive values around lags of roughly 0 to 2 months. However, the famines of 1899–1900 and 1907–8 show relatively weak and longer lag effects of food price movements on the mortality time path. This weakening in the immediate response of mortality to price rises after the 1870s may be thought of as consistent with an increasing growth and benevolence of relief policy. Indeed, it has been argued by several authors that a temporal moderation of excess famine deaths can at least partly be attributed to increasing liberalization and enhancement of relief policy through time in India.[60]

The correllograms for r_2 and r_3 not only show patterns which are more systematic, coherent and close to our expected relationships, but they also show much stronger associations on the whole than those for r_1. For example, the cross-correlation coefficient between food prices and the CIs shows a pattern reaching the highest negative value around a positive lag (in price) of 0 to 1 month, and then declining rather steadily over the higher positive lags. Indeed, this pattern is found rather consistently for all the famines considered here. This provides considerable support for the view that food price rises in the course of drought-related famines reflect the increasing distress, and thus affect fertility adversely rather immediately. On the other hand, the similar consistent and coherent pattern of cross-correlation coefficient

---

[60] On the role of relief policy in the trend in the famine mortality over time, see Klein (1984); see also McAlpin (1983), especially chapter 6, and Dreze (1990). The clear weakening of the association between price and mortality over several centuries has also been observed in the historical context of England; see Lee (1981).

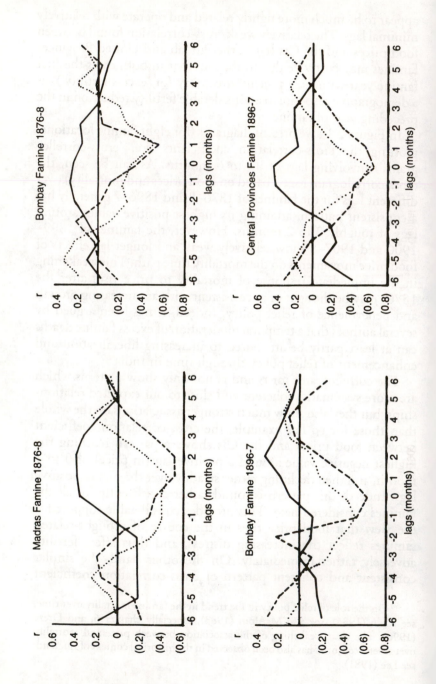

Madras Famine 1876-8

r

0.6
0.4
0.2
0
(0.2)
(0.4)
(0.6)
(0.8)

-6 -5 -4 -3 -2 -1 0 1 2 3 4 5 6
lags (months)

Bombay Famine 1876-8

r

0.4
0.2
0
(0.2)
(0.4)
(0.6)

-6 -5 -4 -3 -2 -1 0 1 2 3 4 5 6
lags (months)

Bombay Famine 1896-7

r

0.4
0.2
0
(0.2)
(0.4)
(0.6)
(0.8)

-6 -5 -4 -3 -2 -1 0 1 2 3 4 5 6
lags (months)

Central Provinces Famine 1896-7

r

0.6
0.4
0.2
0
(0.2)
(0.4)
(0.6)
(0.8)

-6 -5 -4 -3 -2 -1 0 1 2 3 4 5 6
lags (months)

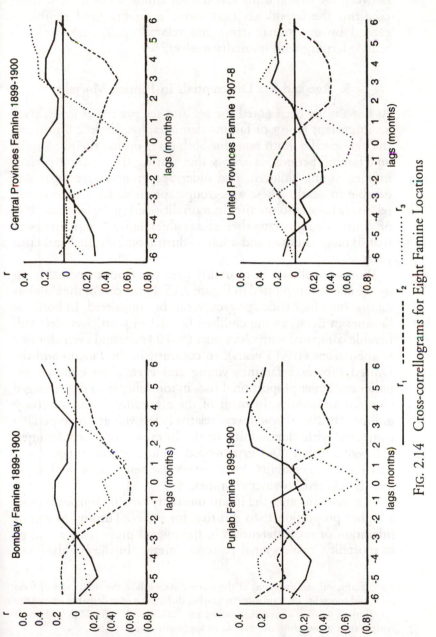

FIG. 2.14 Cross-correllograms for Eight Famine Locations

between the MIs and the CIs (r_3) for almost all of these famines confirms the hypothesis that excess mortality (and morbidity caused by nutritional stress and related epidemics) works to reduce fertility with immediate effect.[61]

5. Age and Sex Differentials in Famine Mortality

As has already been noted the age and sex pattern of mortality is an important aspect of famine demography. Table 2.8 provides the age-specific death rates for both sexes during the pre-famine and famine periods. It shows that during the baseline periods infants, young children, and older age groups were most vulnerable to death. These age groups appear to have experienced relatively large absolute rises in mortality during the famines. This of, course, demonstrates their great vulnerability—compared with that of older children and adults—during both normal and crisis years.

Proportional rises in mortality over pre-famine normal levels by age and sex are plotted in Figure 2.15. In the case of the Bombay famine only four wide age groups can be considered. In both the famines in Berar, young children (aged 1–4 years) were less vulnerable compared with older ones (5–10 years) and even children in their teens (10–15 years). In contrast, in the Punjab and the United Provinces famines young and even older children experienced larger proportional rises in mortality than did teenaged children and adults. In most of these famines young adult age groups (say 20–30 years) were relatively less vulnerable, especially compared with older adults. In the Bombay and Berar famines, old people (aged 60+) experienced a mortality advantage compared to younger adults, while the reverse held true in the Punjab and the United Provinces famines.

In almost all cases, the infant mortality rate for females rose by a higher proportion than did that for males. Turning to a consideration of sex differentials in the overall proportional change in mortality, two regional patterns emerge. In the Bombay and

---

[61] Statistical measurement of the relative strength of the influences of food price and mortality on fertility seems rather difficult, particularly because of the very limited number of observations we are dealing with here. With such small sample sizes it was also not possible to apply any causality tests.

TABLE 2.8

Crude Death Rates by Age and Sex in the Pre-famine Baseline and the Prime Famine Years: Five Major Historical Famine Locations in India

Province & year		IMR	1–4	5–9	(1–11)	10–14	(12–49)	15–19	20–29	30–39	40–49	(50+)	50–59	60+	CDR
Bombay															
1872–4	M	172.6			10.92		14.08					161.55			19.22
	F	161.55			11.05		13.03					97.47			18.07
1877	M	281.23			20.19		34.31					399.30			41.21 (2.14)
	F	275.38			19.44		27.18					209.86			35.47 (1.96)
Punjab															
1891–5	M	215.71	48.30	10.24		7.22		8.18	11.53	15.08	23.52		36.97	105.01	30.35
	F	242.18	49.72	10.94		8.25		9.30	12.53	16.29	21.28		31.95	104.03	31.26
1900	M	280.39	94.97	20.29		13.10		13.31	14.64	20.21	31.03		49.76	146.37	45.53 (1.50)
	F	311.26	106.24	21.96		16.20		17.63	17.84	23.23	29.71		45.24	154.37	50.20 (1.59)
United Provinces															
1901–4	M	246.99	64.57	14.11		9.44		11.79	14.09	16.91	22.97		37.58	67.12	34.20
	F	239.82	65.01	13.63		10.09		16.58	17.02	17.00	21.13		33.84	55.59	34.73
1908	M	336.52	115.96	25.98		13.60		16.12	20.58	25.14	38.32		66.66	130.22	51.79 (1.50)
	F	354.56	117.78	24.30		13.56		19.92	22.97	25.03	35.40		62.90	117.13	53.73 (1.55)

(cont.)

Table 2.8 (*cont.*)

Province & year		IMR	1–4	5–9	(1–11)	10–14	(12–49)	15–19	20–29	30–39	40–49	(50+)	50–59	60+	CDR
Berar															
1891–5	M	233.33	97.16	16.94		8.84		9.78	12.72	16.96	26.70		48.62	105.12	39.80
	F	216.39	84.76	14.90		9.32		12.54	15.78	17.94	18.10		38.06	95.68	37.79
1897	M	307.98	101.10	24.80		14.30		15.30	19.80	27.80	46.80		79.60	150.30	55.30 (1.39)
	F	302.26	91.00	21.60		15.30		16.80	20.60	24.80	28.20		55.70	127.20	49.90 (1.32)
1900	M	492.52	190.00	48.50		27.90		29.10	33.50	47.20	72.20		116.30	194.50	86.10 (2.16)
	F	487.35	166.20	41.70		27.40		30.70	33.40	41.10	44.80		92.20	186.50	79.30 (2.10)

Notes: 1. IMR = Infant mortality rate (per 1000 livebirths). The IMRs have been calculated by dividing the number of infant deaths by the number of livebirths registered in the same year. Strictly speaking, this ratio (which is aptly called the 'infant death rate') is neither an age-specific death rate nor the infant mortality rate in the life table sense. But data constraints do not allow any adjustments for rectifying this defect; see Barclay (1958), p. 141.

2. The year 1871 has been excluded from the baseline period owing to incomplete data on deaths by age and sex for Bombay Presidency.

3. As 1892 was an epidemic year in Punjab, it has been excluded from the baseline period.

4. For calculating death rates (expressed per 1000 population) denominators have been taken from the censuses preceding the famines.

5. Figures in parentheses are the respective ratios of the CDR in prime famine year to that during the baseline period.

Sources: See Table 2.1.

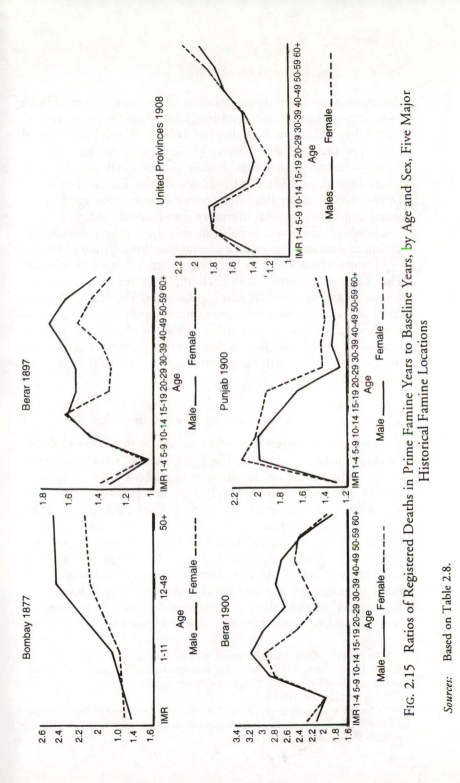

FIG. 2.15 Ratios of Registered Deaths in Prime Famine Years to Baseline Years, by Age and Sex, Five Major Historical Famine Locations

Sources: Based on Table 2.8.

Berar famines—interestingly those in the western region of India —male mortality (all ages combined) rose more (in proportionate terms) than did female mortality (see Table 2.8). But in the United Provinces and Punjab famines—those located in the northern region—females experienced higher proportional rises in mortality. Indeed, as Figure 2.15 shows, in the Punjab famine of 1899–1900 even females in the prime reproductive ages experienced larger proportional mortality rises than did males.[62]

Elsewhere, however, females in this age range generally experienced smaller proportional mortality increases than did males —a feature which seems to be found in other famine locations.[63] This suggests a north–south dichotomy in sex differentials in famine mortality which is also supported by the census data on the changes in sex ratios from pre-famine to post-famine censuses. We have already seen that most of the southern and western locations exhibit a decline in sex ratio in the census following famine while the northern provinces show a distinct rise (see Table 2.1).

6. Concluding Discussion

We now can summarize the main findings on the demography of the major historical famines. The precipitating factor was almost always monsoon failure, resulting in significant losses of agricultural output and employment. But the marginal existence of a large section of the population, who usually had almost nothing in store to withstand threats of subsistence crisis, can hardly be discounted. According to the 1880 Famine Commission's estimate, 'one-third of the land-holding classes were deeply and inextricably in debt'.[64] All these famines involved both substantial excess mortality on the one hand and significant reduction in conceptions on the other; so considerable losses of population seem to have resulted. However, there appears to have been a

[62] In a study of the late nineteenth-century famines in the most severely affected Hissar district of Punjab, Guz also reported a distinct female disadvantage in mortality; see Guz (1989), especially p. 208.

[63] See also Dyson (1991a).

[64] Quoted in Srivastava (1968), p. 330. For more evidence of rural poverty and indebtedness during the late nineteenth century, see Srivastava (1968), pp. 328–35; see also Bhatia (1967).

compensating above-normal rise in conceptions in the immediate post-famine period in most cases, while mortality in some cases declined even below its pre-famine baseline level.

Over the longer term in the post-famine period a continued elevation of the birth rate has generally been found, although the reduction in mortality did not occur in some famine locations. In the post-famine period death rates seem to have been rather less stable than birth rates; this was probably due to a greater responsiveness of mortality to weather and other environmental fluctuations, especially in the past (when India was vulnerable to occasional outbreaks of epidemic diseases such as plague, malaria, smallpox, and cholera). However, in the longer-term post-famine period of 5–10 years the crude rate of natural increase in most cases appears to have exceeded the pre-famine levels. An elevated birth rate over the longer-term post-famine period seems to have played a more important role in this, and this excess birth rate appears to have partly been due to the change in age composition of population, especially for females. The implication is that despite considerable population losses during famines, the longer-term post-famine demographic responses tended to promote the recovery of the pre-famine population sizes.

The major findings from our analysis of the monthly time-series data—both diagrammatic and statistical—can now be reviewed.[65] First, an early indication of the development of famine has almost always been reflected in soaring food prices. This period of rising prices represents the onset of the 'starvation phase' when people presumably pass through acute economic distress, and various social disruptions ensue. In this connection we may note the relatively weak positive link between the movements of food prices and the MI during famine. The reason seems to lie in the fact that the main famine mortality peak usually occurred relatively late in the process (with some lag after the beginning of distress), and it also occurred within a relatively short span of time (i.e. epidemic phase) when food prices were either stabilized at a high level or were only starting to decline. Moreover, food prices often continued to remain quite high when mortality went back to normal levels.

[65] Despite several issues involved in the interpretation of the estimated cross-correlations, the findings in Table 2.7 generally confirm the conclusions drawn on the basis of the diagrams.

Second, fertility (or more strictly conceptions) responds rather quickly to the rise in both food prices and mortality movements. A significant fertility reduction occurring sometimes (but not always) somewhat earlier than the elevation of mortality can hardly be described as 'anticipatory' in the sense of a conscious decisional response. This is because nutritional stress and social disruption during the period of rising prices (i.e. in the peak starvation phase) can considerably reduce conceptions through the well-known mechanisms (e.g. the nutrition–fecundity link or through increased spousal separation). Moreover, a fairly strong negative association has been found between movements of the MI and CI, especially during the prime period of famine. Thus, in addition to the MI and CI movements being partly associated with the development of distress, they also demonstrate the negative effects of increased morbidity and mortality on conceptions.

However, interestingly, we have discovered occasions when outbreaks of epidemics resulted in an apparent mortality crisis, independent of any immediate subsistence crisis and with relatively little negative effect on conceptions. The suggestion is that epidemics and related excess morbidity and mortality exert much stronger fertility-reducing effects when they follow a subsistence crisis than when they do not. This, in turn, probably implies that a reduction in fertility, rather than a rise in mortality, is a more robust index of the existence of famine distress, perhaps especially during the starvation phase.

This is not to suggest that the outbreaks of epidemics that accompanied famine can be treated as independent of famine and the associated mass nutritional stress. The occurrence of epidemics appears to have been caused partly by widespread acute nutritional deficiency and weakened resistance, and partly by the contamination of food and drinking water, increased exposure (to various diseases) associated with 'wandering' and migration, crowding in relief camps and deterioration of sanitation.[66] Epidemics of some diseases are rather easily recognized as famine-caused: for example,

---

[66] The question of how undernutrition enhances the risk of mortality seems to be a complex one. For a summary of the several issues involved, see Walter and Schofield (1989), pp. 17–21. For possible mechanisms linking social disruptions and outbreaks of diseases in the Indian historical context, see Arnold (1991).

cholera and dysentery/diarrhoea. On the question of epidemic malaria, which seems to have accounted for the bulk of excess mortality in most of the famines considered here, three hypotheses (which are not mutually exclusive) have been suggested:

(a)   A relatively low incidence of malaria owing to dryness during the drought year reduces the population's immunity level; and this enhances the chances of a malaria epidemic when the rains resume in the following year.[67]

(b)   Since a fever mortality peak appears to have often occurred after the resumption of rains when (along with the beginning of normal farm activities) people presumably begin to experience an improvement in their nutritional level, it may be an outcome of the 'refeeding of malaria'.[68]

(c)   In view of a strong correlation found (historically) between food scarcity and fever (or malaria) mortality in parts of the Indian subcontinent, the occurrence of malaria epidemics in the wake of famines may be related to acute nutritional stress and its debilitating effects.[69]

Several issues arise in assessing the relevance of the above hypotheses. First, the absence of malaria as a separate category of death in the reports of the Sanitary Commissioners always leaves some doubt as to whether the fever mortality peak does indeed represent epidemic malaria. As already indicated, several other diseases may have been misreported and included in the fever category. For example, on the basis of very careful diagnostic investigation of famine victims admitted to hospitals during the Madras famine of 1876–8, Dr A. Porter found that a considerable number of registered fever deaths were actually due to pneumonia—which was not a recognized cause of death in the registration system. Indeed, in the post-mortem room he found pneumonia ('in a more or less advanced stage') in more than 25 per cent of all cases.[70] In the case of the Berar famines, we have also seen that

[67] See Dyson (1991a), and also de Waal (1989b), especially p. 92.
[68] For evidence in support of this hypothesis, especially in the African context, see Murray et al. (1975, 1976, 1990), and also de Waal (1989b), especially pp. 104–6.
[69] See Christophers (1910), Zurbrigg (1988).
[70] See Porter (1889), p. 131.

the highest number of deaths recorded during the month of peak MI was under the dysentery/diarrhoea category rather than that of fever. However, all this is not to ignore the fact that a large number of the registered fever deaths very often represented malaria mortality, especially during the post-monsoon months. Also, some malaria deaths may have been entered under other headings.

Hypothesis (a) is debatable in the light of our evidence on two counts. First, the Bombay famine of 1876–8 shows that a fever mortality peak can certainly occur even in a year of drought (e.g.1877) (see Figs 2.3 and 2.4). Second, the experience of the Berar famines of 1896–7 and 1899–1900 shows that the time path of mortality movements was similar for all major causes of death (see Fig. 2.6). This implies the existence of a more general time pattern of famine mortality rather than the seasonality of malaria mortality *per se*. In fact, a broad general time pattern of rising mortality in the course of the prime famine year seems to have often been shared by the major causes of deaths, although the exact timing of peak mortality from specific diseases such as cholera, dysentery/diarrhoea, and fever does not necessarily coincide.

There are also some difficulties regarding hypothesis (b). First, since food prices almost always appear to have stayed very high during and even beyond the monsoon months in the year following drought, and since normal harvesting does not take place until late in that year, it seems uncertain whether a perceptible improvement in the nutritional status of the affected population occurred during the period of peak fever mortality. Besides, the available evidence on the malaria refeeding hypothesis suggests that even though the attack rate rises with refeeding (and the consequent recovery in nutritional level) the actual mortality rate probably depends considerably on the previous level of under-nutrition. Reviewing the relevant literature, Tomkins and Watson have recently concluded that while a low plasma nutrient level seems to inhibit the rate of (malaria) pathogen multiplication, 'in every situation this has to be balanced against the effect of malnutrition on the immune host response'.[71] In fact, there is no evidence that malnutrition is advantageous during the recovery from infection.

[71] See Tomkins and Watson (1989), p. 24.

Indeed, there are indications that poor people were more vulnerable to malaria mortality. For example, much greater malaria death rates were reported by Christophers for the poorer classes in the late nineteenth- and early twentieth-century Punjab.[72] The report of an investigation of the epidemic of malarial fever in Assam during 1896 concluded that 'the poor suffer in a disproportionate degree, and have less chance of recovery, owing to their living in more crowded dwellings, and to a deficiency of nourishing diet especially of a nitrogenous nature'.[73] In a recent study of young children admitted to hospitals in the context of an African food crisis, undernutrition, though seemingly protective against clinical malaria, appeared to be associated with a higher overall risk of death.[74] Although information about the class composition of mortality during India's past famines is particularly scant, relief records and contemporary accounts indicate that the main rural victims were often the poor classes—small cultivators, agricultural labourers and petty artisans.[75]

All this, however, does not mean that the malaria epidemics that accompanied several of these major Indian famines occurred solely due to famine-caused food shortage and undernutrition—unrelated to rainfall, temperature, and other environmental and epidemiological conditions. The huge post-monsoon elevation of fever mortality in several Indian famines—appearing often as a magnification of the normal seasonal pattern—suggests a mediating role played by environmental factors. In many cases, low mortality in the drought year itself has been attributed to a relative absence of mosquitoes and malaria. In turn, lowered malaria immunity in the population during a drought year may help aggravate malaria epidemics after the resumption of rains.[76]

[72] Christophers (1910), pp. 38–9.
[73] See Rogers (1897), p. 37.
[74] See de Waal (1989b), especially p. 103. In this connection attention may be drawn to the findings of an early celebrated study with 100,000 English prisoners over 4 years—a study which is probably considered to be an important event in the history of the 'refeeding hypothesis'. This study reported that those receiving least food had four times higher mortality than those consuming most food, although the sickness rate was far higher for the better-fed group; see Murray and Murray (1977), pp. 472–3.
[75] See Currie (1991) and also Ambirajan (1989).
[76] See, e.g. Dyson (1991a), p. 24.

Furthermore, the fact that some famines appear to have involved very small malaria epidemics is sometimes used to cast doubt about the inevitability of a link as is proposed in hypothesis (c).[77]

However, resolving this question fully is probably impossible. And it may indeed involve several factors such as the severity of failures in both rains and crops, the nature of relief, and so on. For example, in the Punjab famine of 1899–1900, although rainfall recovered in the year of peak mortality (i.e. 1900), the crop output turned out to be even lower than in the preceding year of drought.[78] Christophers, while discussing the major factors determining the recurrence of epidemic malaria in Punjab, states that '[t]he facts certainly support the view that scarcity is a factor determining to a large degree the situation, extent and intensity of epidemics'.[79] He also recognized the role of rainfall in creating favourable conditions for mosquito-breeding. The basic argument is succinctly summarized by the following statement: 'Rainfall made the mosquitoes more abundant; famine made the people more susceptible.'[80] This seems to be quite consistent with our finding of peak fever mortality occurring often after the resumption of rains following drought and famine.

To sum up: while a general course of rising mortality seems to have often been shared by most diseases especially during the year following drought, reflecting broadly the lagged effects of nutritional stress on human health and survival, the exact timing of peak mortality from specific epidemics was probably partly shaped by environmental factors (monsoon in the case of malaria, heat and lack of drinking water in the case of cholera) and partly by other influences (e.g. period of maximum congregations at relief camps causing maximum spread of cholera and dysentery/diarrhoea).

We now turn to the time path of relief operations. Relief

---

[77] See Whitcombe (1990).

[78] While in the drought year, 1899, the cropped area in the whole of Punjab was 22.75 million acres, it declined even further to only 15 million acres in the following year (i.e. 1900), the year of peak famine mortality; see *Census of India 1901, Volume 18, Part I*, p. 42.

[79] See Christophers (1910), p. 39. S.R. Christophers was one of the leading malariologists in the colonial public health service. He made a celebrated study of malaria epidemics in Punjab.

[80] See Harrison (1978), p. 202.

operations were usually adopted after some administrative tests and were often rather late (e.g. Figs 2.2, 2.5, 2.8, and 2.11).[81] This late start of relief presumably had especially adverse implications, especially for those who had few reserve stocks of food or assets. In turn, there is a strong implication that a large number of people were already debilitated by considerable nutritional stress when they joined relief works.

As we have also noted, while relief works were to provide employment and income for those who suffered job losses in the wake of drought, the timing of the decline in relief provisions did not always correspond closely to the resumption of the monsoon rains. Official documents sometimes attribute the early decline of relief provision to villagers' unwillingness to join relief works. For example, the reduction in the number of persons on relief work during the pre-monsoon months (i.e. March–April, 1900) in Hissar—one of the most affected districts in the Punjab famine of 1899–1900—was reported to be 'due in the first instance to the employment afforded to large numbers by the harvesting of canal crops and to many earning sufficient in this way to save them from having to return to the works, and later to jungle fruits being available for food and to the great heat coupled with the conditions of our relief works driving off such as were not in absolute want'.[82] But it is also likely that people, being already debilitated, found the relief works extremely harsh; often they may have acquired diseases in relief camps and thus lost their chances of continuing with their job.[83] Moreover, the fall in the number of relief workers was often the result of deliberate government policy to discourage relief, rather than the workers' willingness to return home.[84] There is evidence that the government often made the relief system oppressive by enforcing

[81] For a detailed account of different kinds of relief that were in operation during these famines, see Bhatia (1967), Srivastava (1968), Drèze (1990), and also the official reports on the famines in different provinces.

[82] See Government of Punjab (1901), vol. I, pp. 9–11.

[83] For example, as Reverend C. Harding in his replies to the Famine Inquiry Commission (1878–80) wrote about the Bombay famine of 1876–8, 'People were constantly dying, some labour gangs near Kaladgi were so weak that they could hardly walk. I thought many people on the works should have been in hospital'; quoted in Currie (1991), p. 48.

[84] See Srivastava (1968), especially pp. 210, 255–7.

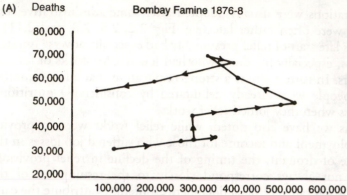

(A) Deaths — Bombay Famine 1876-8

Persons on Relief

Central Provinces Famine 1896-7

Deaths

Persons on Relief

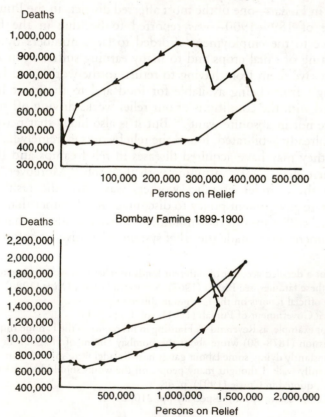

Bombay Famine 1899-1900

Deaths

Persons on Relief

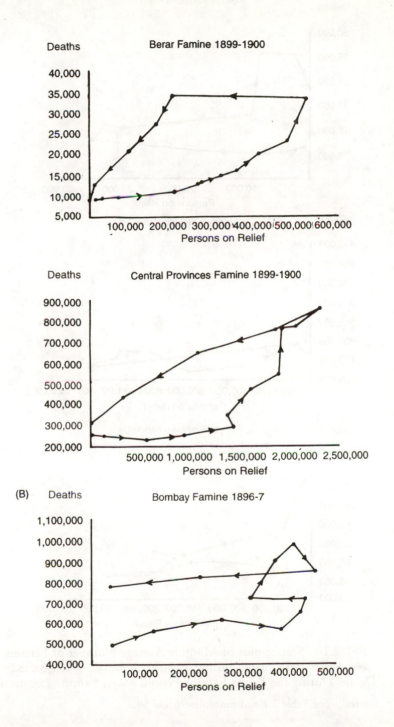

Deaths — Berar Famine 1899-1900

Persons on Relief

Deaths — Central Provinces Famine 1899-1900

Persons on Relief

(B) Deaths — Bombay Famine 1896-7

Persons on Relief

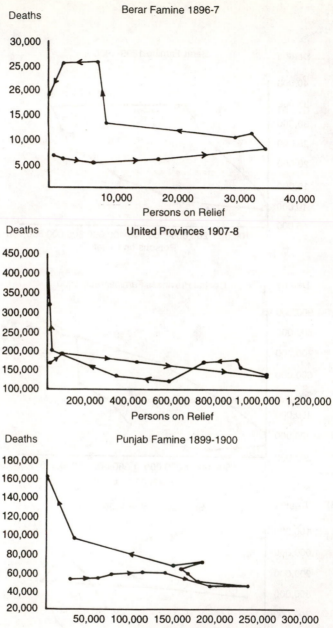

FIG. 2.16 Scatter-plot of Monthly Average Number of Persons on Relief and Corresponding Monthly Number of Registered Deaths During the Prime Famine Period, Major Famine Locations

Sources: See Table 2.1 and footnotes 26 and 59.

distance tests, high standard of tasks, and deductions from wages due to shortfalls from tasks.[85] As a result, the relief policy often made a worker unfit 'for work [and] at the same time it lays him open to the attack of famine diseases'.[86]

However, on the other hand, in some cases the provision of relief works seems to have continued to rise until the early monsoon months or even a bit later (e.g. Berar and Central Provinces in 1900). Such a relatively prolonged maintenance of relief works may have partly reflected a comparatively liberal policy.[87] Figure 2.16 presents scatter plots of monthly data on the numbers of deaths and persons on relief. The overwhelming dominance of relief works in total relief operations should be borne in mind. Two broad patterns seem to emerge. In the first pattern (as depicted in Figure 2.16 (A)), mortality level and provision of works increased together up to a certain point, and then came down roughly hand in hand. The first pattern corresponds to a relatively gradual process of mortality increase (rather than an abrupt rise in mortality due to one or two epidemic diseases) over the year following drought. When deaths from almost all major causes simultaneously showed a considerable upward trend, relief seems to have risen, especially until the arrival of the monsoon.

The second pattern, as shown in Figure 2.16 (B), is when relief works were increasing while there was hardly any significant rising trend of mortality, but mortality rose rather sharply at a time (usually late in the year following major drought) when relief works were almost closed down. This pattern was experienced most clearly in the Punjab crisis of 1899–1900 and the United Provinces famine of 1907–8. In both these cases famine mortality was in large part accounted for by a malaria epidemic which occurred late in the year (i.e. during the post-monsoon months). The suggestion probably is that the time span of relief measures

[85] See Bhatia (1975), pp. 589–90, and also Guz (1989).

[86] This comment was made by a special representative of the *Manchester Guardian*, Vaughan Nash, while covering the famine of 1899–1900; it is quoted in Bhatia (1975), p. 590.

[87] Bhatia cites the experience of the Madras famine of 1896–7 where relief policy was comparatively liberal, and relief works continued to employ an increasing number of workers until late July 1897. According to Bhatia, the relatively liberal relief policy was partly the reason why there was only a small rise in mortality (4 per cent) during this famine; see Bhatia (1975), p. 590.

was partly influenced by the mortality situation; when mortality does not seem to have been rising (particularly before the arrival of the monsoon in the year following drought), relief measures were probably wound up early (e.g. the Punjab and the United Provinces). Conversely, when mortality showed a steady increase over time, relief works were continued even until the early part of the monsoon (e.g. the Central Provinces and Bombay).

In this connection the role played by gratuitous relief is worth noting. Gratuitous relief (e.g. cash or food doles, poorhouses, etc.) usually tended to become important in relative terms rather late in the famine process, when outbreaks of major epidemics had already caused a considerable elevation of mortality. Poorhouses, for example, very often continued to exist well beyond the arrival of the monsoon (when provision of relief works was rapidly declining).[88] Thus, in the Bombay famine of 1876–8, the ratio of persons on public works to those on gratuitous relief declined from 94.92 in December 1876 to 6.17 in June 1877, and further to 1.32 in November 1877.[89] A similar time pattern of gratuitous relief *vis-à-vis* relief works is found in most of the famine locations. This was partly because during the prime epidemic phase people in large numbers qualified for gratuitous relief as they appeared to be unfit for work. This is consistent with the evidence of a very high mortality rate among recipients of gratuitous relief and those in poorhouses. The suggestion therefore is that the timing of gratuitous relief assumes relative prominence as it often coincides with the phase of famine-induced mortality crisis (i.e. the epidemic phase).

Differentials in famine mortality by age and sex can be viewed in both absolute and proportionate terms. Infants, young children and older age groups are usually subject to greater absolute vulnerability compared to older children and adults, even during normal times (see Table 2.8). This pattern is typical of a society where widespread undernourishment coexists with very poor public health facilities. But in terms of proportional rise in deaths during famine, infants (i.e. those under one year) appear to have experienced a relative advantage compared to other ages. However,

---

[88] See, e.g. official reports on famine administration in several locations.

[89] See Minute by the Governor of Bombay, dated 24 December 1877; quoted in Government of Bombay (1878b), Part III, Supplements, p. 118.

our findings on the other age differentials in proportionate terms do not fully conform to Dyson's view that young children are relatively less affected by famine mortality compared to older children and adults. Instead, our results suggest two patterns broadly corresponding to two major Indian regions. First, in the Berar famines we find a pattern similar to the famines in the western, southern and central regions considered in Dyson's study, i.e. young children and old people appear to be proportionately less vulnerable compared to older children and adults. Second, young and even older children turn out to be more vulnerable compared to teenagers and adults in the Punjab and United Provinces famines, both of which are located in north India. In these two northern famines the prime adult age groups experienced relatively small proportional mortality increases (see Fig. 2.15). Moreover, in the southern, western, and central Indian famine locations, adults seem to have had a relative mortality disadvantage compared to older ages,[90] while the famines in the northern region showed the reverse. Since all these famines were very widespread, and also the registration areas were very large (except for Berar), the above age patterns of proportional mortality rises do not seem to have been due to biases introduced by migration.

The relative advantage of infants in terms of proportional rise in famine mortality seems to result partly from their extremely high death rate even in normal times, and partly from the relative insensitivity of infant mortality to acute food shortage and environmental factors.[91] At other ages, patterns of age differentials in famine mortality are the net result of several complex forces. For example, age differentials in biological vulnerability to nutritional stress may work against children; but social disruptions and associated changes (e.g. migration) during famines may act to favour them rather than adults, as adults are more likely to move in search of food or work during a subsistence crisis. There may also be changes in the distribution of food within families in such a manner as to protect children.[92] However, the normal

[90] See also Dyson (1991a), p. 21.

[91] See Behar et al. (1958) on this issue.

[92] During the Greek famine of 1941–2 young children and women seem to have been relatively protected by cultural traditions favouring those household

functioning of a family in the face of a severe famine is likely to be threatened as different members may be scattered in search of either relief or work. In fact the extent to which intra-household distribution of food and other inputs varies during an acute food crisis is not clear. Moreover, some epidemic diseases have sometimes been found to be age-selective.[93]

On the question of sex differentials in famine mortality, we again observe two regional patterns. In the south, west, and central Indian famine locations the proportional rise in overall mortality was higher for males than for females (see Table 2.8).[94] But the reverse was found in the north Indian famine locations, especially Punjab. As noted earlier, the relative female advantage, or disadvantage, in famine mortality is the result of two divergent forces: because of certain physiological advantages, women may be able to withstand famine situations better than men. On the other hand, the anti-female pattern of intra-household distribution of food, health care, etc. may change further against women during a food crisis.[95] Moreover, the relative female mortality disadvantage in the wake of malaria—due to their staying at home for longer periods, which increases their risk of attack—was recognized long ago.[96] Apart from this, reduction in the number of maternal deaths due to a reduction in fertility and also male-dominated distress migration can be some examples of how female populations derive some relative protection in famine mortality.[97] However, it is extremely difficult to separate the relative influences of all the factors involved in the determination of sex differentials in crisis mortality.

However, the existence of a considerable amount of recent research on India's demography has tended to establish a north–

---

members; see Valaoras (1946). There is also evidence in the context of other famine locations to show greater protection given towards children; see Drèze and Sen (1989), pp. 79–80 and references cited.

[93] For example, the 1918 influenza pandemic in India appears to have killed the adult population much more than children and the elderly. For the relevant evidence and some possible explanations, see Mills (1986).

[94] See also Dyson (1991a), Table 4, p. 20.

[95] See Drèze and Sen (1989), pp. 55 and also the references cited; on this, see also Rivers (1982).

[96] See, e.g. Census of India 1911, *Volume 1, India, Part 1, Report*, p. 212.

[97] See, e.g. Mohanty (1989).

south regional dichotomy.[98] There appears to be a distinct female mortality disadvantage in the northern states as compared to the states of south India.[99] A strong preference for males and related female neglect—reflected in mortality differentials by sex—seems to be an old phenomenon in the northern parts of India.[100] The contemporary literature clearly indicates an anti-female bias in the distribution of food and health care, especially in the Punjab.[101] Thus the available evidence suggests that the anti-female changes in the pattern of distribution of food and health care during major famines in northern parts, unlike southern, western, and central regions, probably outweighed the potential biological and other female advantages in coping with such crises. Also, a relative mortality advantage for adults (compared with young children) in north Indian famines may be consistent with the extremely patriarchal nature of the region.

[98] On the 'north–south' divide in India, see Sopher (1980).

[99] See Miller (1981) and the literature cited, and also Kynch and Sen (1983) and Harriss (1989, 1990). There is substantial amount of literature on the possible explanations for such north–south patterns of sex differences in the mortality; see Bardhan (1974), Miller (1981), Dyson and Moore (1983), Basu (1989a), and also Kumar (1989). In fact, recent researches have shown an intrinsic north–south cultural difference in the matter of women's status; see Basu (1989b) and Dyson and Moore (1983). See also Langford and Storey (1991) and Langford (1984).

[100] See the early census reports and other official publications on this possibility.

[101] See Dasgupta (1987), and also Dhillon et al. (1979). See also Harriss (1989, 1990). It is, however, interesting to note that the anti-female bias especially in the matter of food and medical care has probably been becoming more widespread throughout India over the recent past; see, for example, Miller (1989); see also Dyson (1988).

3

The Demography of Lesser-mortality Historical Famines in the Indian Subcontinent

1. Introduction

In the last chapter we analysed, at the provincial level, the demography of several major historical famines which involved large-scale excess mortality. But there is evidence of famines in different Indian locations, which did not kill at all, or killed very much less. In other words, the excess number of deaths over the average 'normal' number was small. While excess mortality is often defined as an essential element of famine, a study of famines with a comparatively small number of excess deaths may provide us with an understanding regarding the essence of famines in general, and also insights about issues such as the interaction of famine conditions with epidemics and the provision of relief. As we saw in the last chapter, it is famine-induced outbreaks of epidemics that generally account for most famine mortality. If in some famines, relatively small excess mortality is accompanied by all the other features of a typical famine (namely high food prices, scarcity, fertility reduction, etc.), then the absence of heavy mortality should largely be due to the absence of major epidemics. Obviously, it is of interest to know why there were no major epidemics in the wake of some famines: for example, was it due to a less severe drought or crop failure in the first place? Or was it due to better relief provision? Indeed, in circumstances where excess mortality was minimal, are we justified in using the word 'famine' at all? Consequently, this chapter focuses on the detailed demographic responses during some famines which involved relatively little excess mortality.

We have included the following four famines which caused

TABLE 3.1

Annual Rainfall in the Pre-famine Period and Famine Years:
Four Lesser-mortality Famine Locations

Province & period	Rainfall (inches)	Province & period	Rainfall (inches)
Punjab		*Bombay*	
Pre-famine		Pre-famine	
1890–5	31.72	1893–1903	48.36
1895	23.72	1904	36.19
Famine years		*Famine years*	
1896	19.46	1905	33.06
1897	24.80	1906–7	36.10
United Provinces		*Bombay*	
Pre-famine		Pre-famine	
Normal average	41.84	1893–1903	48.36
1895	39.43	1910–11	39.56
Famine years		*Famine years*	
1896	26.99	1911–12	24.68
1897	43.92	1912–13	61.61

Notes:
1. The number of years included for calculating 'average normal' rainfall for the United Provinces is not made explicit in the official report.
2. For Bombay Presidency, the years from 1906–7 onwards begin on 1 June and end on 31 May. Since most of the rains of a calendar year fall during June–September, the use of these two accounting definitions of a year does not cause much difficulty in our understanding here.

Sources: Punjab: Census of India 1901, *Punjab, Volume XVIII, Part 1*, p. 42; United Provinces: Based on monthly averages given in *United Provinces Government Gazettes*, Part II, Allahabad: Government Press, various years; Bombay: *Annual Report on the Administration of the Bombay Presidency*, Bombay: Government Press, various years.

relatively little excess mortality: the Punjab famine of 1896–7; the United Provinces famine of 1896–7; and the famines of 1905–6 and 1911–12 which both occurred in the Bombay Presidency. These were all officially declared to be famines, and for each location a fairly lengthy report was produced by the respective provincial governments. In fact, as mentioned earlier, the famine of 1896–7 was a major famine with widespread effects in the subcontinent. But it did not produce major loss of life everywhere. As we have already noted in the preceding chapter, the vital registration system was comparatively good in each of the above locations. The census-based demographic information on these locations has also been given in the last chapter (see Table 2.1).

Table 3.1 shows that each of these famines was related to a monsoon failure. Indeed, the extent of monsoon failure appears to have been considerable, and even comparable with that for the famines of the preceding chapter (see also Table 2.5). However, Table 3.2 shows that the elevation of mortality in these famines was marginal and certainly much smaller than those considered in the last chapter (see also Table 2.2). Interestingly, during the Bombay famine of 1905–6 overall mortality seems to have improved from its pre-famine level. Perhaps the 'best candidate' for famine excess mortality in Table 3.2 is United Provinces in 1897; however, even in that year the CDR was only elevated by about 7 points over its baseline level.

2. Short-term Fertility and Mortality Responses During Lesser-mortality Famines: An Analysis Using Monthly Data

It is of interest to analyse the time path of short-term fertility and mortality responses in relation to the development of these famines. Monthly movements of food prices are again used as indices of the development of famine distress. In fact, we have calculated monthly averages of district-level prices of a single staple food-grain, namely jowar.[1] The short-term demographic effects are captured, as before, in terms of the monthly conception and mortality indices (CI and MI). These have been constructed with reference to the respective averages for pre-famine baseline periods

---

[1] The sources of price data are as follows: Punjab: *The Punjab Government Gazette*, Supplement, Statistical, Part I: Lahore (various years); United Provinces: *The United Provinces Gazettes*, Part II: Allahabad (various years); Bombay Presidency: *The Bombay Presidency Gazette*, Part III, Supplement: Bombay (various years). It may be noted that prices were expressed in terms of *seers* (about two lbs weight) per rupee.

TABLE 3.2

Registered Provincial Vital Rates in the Baseline, Famine and Post-famine Periods: Four Lesser-mortality Famine Locations

Province	Period				
	Baseline	Famine			Post-famine
Punjab	1891–5	1896	1897	1898	1899
CBR	39.2	43.0	42.6	41.0	48.4
CDR	30.9	31.5	31.1	31.1	29.6
United Provinces	1890–4	1896	1897	1898	1899
CBR	38.0	35.4	31.1	37.1	48.1
CDR	33.8	33.3	40.5	27.4	33.2
Bombay	1901–4	1905	1906	1907	1908
CBR	31.4	33.1	33.8	33.3	35.7
CDR	40.4	31.8	35.1	32.8	27.2
Bombay	1907–10	1911	1912	1913	1914
CBR	35.4	36.0	34.9	34.9	37.4
CDR	29.4	30.4	36.9	26.6	28.6

Notes: 1. Because 1892 was a year of epidemic with heavy excess mortality in Punjab, it has been excluded from the baseline period, 1891–5.

2. The vital rates shown are based on constant denominators, being the respective enumerated populations according to the last census prior to the famine. An exception to this is the Bombay famine of 1911–12 for which we have used the 1901 census population as denominator when calculating rates during 1911–14; this was done for reasons of comparability.

Sources: *Annual Report of the Sanitary Commissioner for the Government of Bombay,* Bombay, various years; *Annual Report of the Sanitary Commissioner for the Government of Punjab,* Lahore, various years; *Annual Report of the Sanitary Commissioner of United Provinces of Agra and Oudh,* Allahabad, various years.

of about five years (for details see Table 3.2). The monthly average numbers of persons on relief (all kinds) have also been plotted alongside these demographic measures.[2] As before, scales of all

---

[2] The sources of monthly data on relief provision are as follows: Punjab:

these measures are not shown on the Y-axis, but the range of variation for each variable is indicated in the note.

The Punjab Famine of 1896–7

The early cessation of both the summer and autumn rains of 1896, and the much delayed winter rains of 1896–7—as reflected in lower annual rainfall averages—were responsible for a considerable failure of at least two harvests in substantial parts of Punjab (see Table 3.1). These harvest failures in Punjab, though not uniform across all districts, coincided with widespread crop failures in many other Indian provinces. All this caused a very sharp rise in food prices, bringing famine conditions to much of the province. According to the estimates of the Punjab's Director of Land Records and Agriculture, the province's autumn harvest of 1896 fell short of the normal level by about one-third. In Hissar district the failure was nearly complete. Apart from two districts (Jhang and Muzaffargarh) in which there was almost no harvest failure, output declines ranged between 5 and 50 per cent below normal.[3] Relief measures, especially test works, were opened in the affected districts around November 1896.[4] In the second week of March 1897, the average daily number on relief reached its maximum (which amounted to about 4 per cent of the population in the affected areas).[5] With the reaping of the rabi harvest (Feb.–Mar.) of 1897, which was thought to have reduced both the famine severity and the demand for relief in most districts, relief works began to be curtailed and were virtually closed by May 1897. With the arrival of the monsoon rains in July, food prices tended to decline and the famine started to draw to a close.

Figure 3.1 plots monthly movements of the price of jowar, and the CI and MI during 1895–8. The daily average numbers of persons on relief at the end of each month in the course of the

---

Government of Punjab (1898); United Provinces: Government of North-Western Provinces and Oudh (1898); Bombay: Government of Bombay (1907, 1913).

[3] See Government of Punjab (1898), pp. 5–6.

[4] However, owing to a localized failure of fodder supplies and a partial failure of the rabi harvest of 1896, relief works were opened in as early as August 1896 in Phalia Tahsil of Gujarat district; ibid.

[5] Ibid., p. 14.

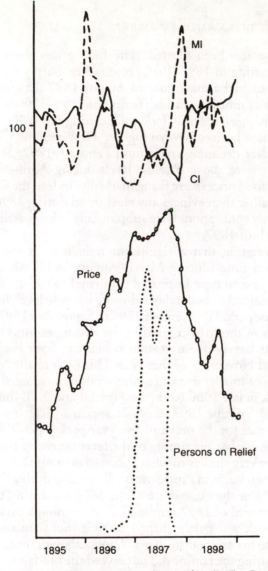

FIG. 3.1 Price of Jowar, Mortality Index (MI), Conception
Index (CI), and Average Daily Number of Persons on Relief,
by Month, Punjab 1895–8

Notes: Ranges of variation: MI, 81.1 (Oct., 1895) to 145.7 (Nov., 1895);
CI, 77.3 (Nov., 1898) to 123.9 (Dec., 1898); jowar price, 27.8
(March, 1895) to 8.27 seers per rupee (July, 1897); average daily
number of persons on relief, 5638 (Sept., 1897) to 128,940 (Feb.,
1897).

Sources: See Table 3.2 and footnotes 1 and 2.

famine have also been plotted. The food prices show a rising tendency starting in 1895. Prices rose rather sharply throughout 1896 and reached a maximum in August 1897. In comparison with the major mortality Punjab famine of 1899–1900 (examined in the last chapter), the peak food price during the 1896–7 famine appears to have been somewhat higher.[6] However, the CI did not show any clear declining trend until February 1897. Strikingly, conceptions were above baseline levels during April–August of 1896 when food prices were rising markedly; indeed the CI simply fluctuates rather than evinces any clear trend during 1896. However, monthly conceptions were substantially below baseline levels during much of 1897.

It is interesting that a significant reduction in conceptions occurred at a time (during March–August 1897) when overall mortality seems to have improved compared to its baseline level. The MI remained considerably below its baseline level during the prime famine period (November 1896 to September 1897). However, a peak in the MI occurred in the closing months of 1897, and this was largely due to a sudden jump in fever mortality in October and November of that year. This peak in the MI, however, is both of smaller size and of shorter duration compared with the MI peak in late 1900 (compare Figs 2.8 and 3.1). Indeed, the annual death rate for 1897 does not appear to have risen above the average rate for the previous five-year period (see Table 3.2). Note, however, that the timing of the fever mortality peak seems to have been very similar to what occurred on a much larger scale in 1900. Fever deaths in Punjab normally peaked during October–December.[7] But the occurrence of the MI peak during the post-monsoon months of 1897 implies that, even though on a smaller scale, the peak was partly shaped by post-monsoon conditions favourable to malaria transmission. Thus, although overall annual mortality during the famine did not exceed the pre-famine normal level, an excess mortality peak in the post-monsoon months—similar to that seen in 1900—does seem to have occurred.

It is also worth remarking that conceptions appear to have

---

[6] In a study of the situation in Hissar—the most severely affected district—price rises in 1896–7 are also reported to have been larger than in the famine of 1899–1900; see Guz (1989), p. 216.

[7] See also Zurbrigg (1988), p. 7.

declined in response to the famine distress and associated disruptions (as detailed earlier). And the lowest CI, as in most of the major famines examined in the last chapter, coincided with the maximum MI, signifying independent and additional negative effects of excess mortality on fertility. Figure 3.1 also shows that during the *early* months of 1896 a significant peak in the MI occurred—actually slightly larger than that in late 1897; but its effect on conceptions was slight compared to the reduction in conceptions in the course of the famine. This seems to confirm our view that a significant elevation in mortality exerts a stronger negative effect on fertility in the wake of a famine than it does in isolation from famine conditions. Moreover, a smaller fertility reduction in this 1896–7 famine (compared to that of 1899–1900 which involved many excess deaths) probably reflects both less intense distress and less excess mortality. Also, note that conceptions rose rather sharply above the baseline level from the beginning of 1898 and continued high thereafter. This conforms with our hypothesis regarding excess fertility in the immediate post-famine period.

Interestingly, the average daily number of persons on relief reached a maximum in a month (February 1897) when conceptions were near the normal level, and mortality was actually below its baseline level by about 25 per cent. However, the number of persons on relief stayed rather high until the beginning of the monsoon in June; at that time the resumption of both the rains and normal farm activity marked a drastic reduction in relief operations (especially relief works). The MI peak occurred at a time when virtually all the relief operations had been closed.. This (as also in the famine of 1899–1900) was largely due to the fact that peak mortality occurred very late in 1897, being essentially a magnification of usual peak fever mortality. Nevertheless, the overall mortality cost of this famine still seems to have been negligible. Table 3.3 shows that the cause composition of deaths did not undergo any perceptible change during the main famine year. Thus, presumably, any famine-induced epidemics were also much less severe.

Part of the explanation for all this may indeed lie in a comparatively low level of distress. In terms of drought intensity, crop losses and their spread, the famine of 1896–7 appears to have been less severe, especially compared with the famine of 1899–1900.

TABLE 3.3

Cause-specific Death Rates in the Pre-famine (Baseline) and Famine Years:
Four Lesser-mortality Historical Famines

Cause of death	Punjab		United Provinces		Bombay			
	1891–5	1897*	1890–4	1897*	1901–4	1906*	1907–10	1912*
Cholera	0.14 (0.46)	0.03 (0.09)	2.70 (7.98)	0.94 (2.32)	0.43 (1.07)	2.50 (7.13)	0.56 (1.90)	3.49 (9.44)
Smallpox	0.27 (0.88)	0.78 (2.25)	0.42 (1.24)	1.86 (4.60)	0.20 (0.50)	0.22 (0.63)	0.19 (0.65)	0.34 (0.91)
Fever	21.15 (68.76)	20.57 (66.25)	24.83 (67.50)	31.20 (77.11)	14.53 (35.99)	14.86 (42.38)	13.41 (45.60)	15.49 (41.91)
Dysentery/Diarrhoea	0.75 (2.43)	0.77 (2.48)	1.05 (3.10)	1.25 (3.09)	3.19 (7.90)	3.34 (9.53)	2.39 (8.13)	3.08 (8.33)
Plague	n.a.	n.a.	n.a.	n.a.	11.07 (27.42)	2.79 (7.96)	2.30 (7.82)	1.57 (4.24)
Respiratory diseases	n.a.	n.a.	n.a.	n.a.	3.21 (7.95)	3.28 (9.36)	3.05 (10.37)	3.83 (10.36)

Injuries/Accidents	0.33 (1.07)	0.35 (1.12)	0.56 (1.66)	0.71 (1.75)	0.37 (0.92)	0.37 (1.06)	0.38 (1.29)	0.39 (1.06)
All other	8.12 (26.40)	8.54 (27.50)	3.48 (10.29)	4.48 (11.07)	8.17 (20.23)	7.71 (21.99)	7.13 (24.24)	8.78 (23.76)
All causes	30.76 (100.00)	31.05 (100.00)	33.82 (100.00)	40.46 (100.00)	40.37 (100.00)	35.06 (100.00)	29.41 (100.00)	36.96 (100.00)

Notes:
1. The years marked (*) are the prime famine years.
2. The above cause-specific death rates (expressed per 1000 population) are based on constant denominators—being the respective populations under registration system according to the census prior to the famine. The rates for Bombay Presidency for 1912 are based on the population according to the 1901 census (instead of the 1911 census) for considerations of comparability.
3. The figures in parentheses are the respective percentage shares of total deaths.
4. n.a. = not available.

Sources: See Table 3.2.

Reviewing both famines in the context of Hissar—one of the most severely affected districts—Guz attributes lower excess mortality in 1896–7 partly to a lesser degree of production failure.[8]

Even so, the famine of 1896–7 was not exactly light. Indeed, the number of people on relief was relatively high. As the Report on the famine states, 'judged by the number of persons relieved, the expenditure incurred, the extent of crop failures, the duration of the drought and dearth of fodder and the high prices which prevailed, the Punjab famine of 1896–7 was probably as severe as any famine which preceded it since annexation, yet as compared with other parts of India the Province must be regarded as having escaped somewhat lightly'.[9] Compared with other provinces the severity of distress in Punjab was probably somewhat less acute.[10] Part of the explanation may indeed lie in the relatively good provision of relief. In comparison with the famine of 1899–1900 relief was certainly more liberal.[11] For example, relief works in connection with the construction of the Jhelum Canal in Gujarat district, which provided employment to a large number of villagers from surrounding areas, paid the dependents an 'extraordinarily high' proportion of the total amount spent on workers (more than 20 per cent); moreover, there were said to be an 'excessive' number of non-working children, constituting about 46 per cent of workers (in day units), while 'in no province has it exceeded 25 per cent'.[12] Such relatively liberal relief in Punjab may have been responsible, in part, for 'less acute' distress and hence almost no overall excess mortality. This view is also shared by Guz who in her study concludes that '[t]he strict and inclement attitude of the relief administration probably accounted, in part, for the greater mortality of the latter famine [of 1899–1900]'.[13] However, the less severe malaria epidemic of 1897 was probably due in part to some specific climatic factors.[14]

[8] See Guz (1989), p. 216.

[9] See Government of Punjab (1898), p. 3.

[10] As Higham writes, 'Distress in Punjab was less widespread and of shorter duration than in other provinces and even where it existed was probably less acute'; see Higham (1897), p. 11.

[11] See Bhatia (1963), p. 253.

[12] See Higham (1897), p. 7.

[13] See Guz (1989), p. 218.

[14] See Whitcombe (1990).

The United Provinces Famine of 1896–7

The drought of 1896 and consequent crop losses also initiated famine in much of the United Provinces (see Table 3.1). In fact, for about three years preceding 1896, the United Provinces experienced somewhat unfavourable weather conditions, which caused partial failures of some crops.[15] There was deficient rainfall in 1895 (especially during the autumn and winter rains), which partially affected the rice districts. And food exports into the United Provinces from the Punjab declined in the latter half of 1895. All these developments raised food prices in 1895; by early 1896 prices were about 25 per cent higher than normal (see Fig. 3.2).[16]

Against this background the monsoon failure of 1896 seems to have been a final blow which plunged the province into a serious famine. An estimate by the Director of Land Records and Agriculture was that the magnitude of shortfalls over normal levels in the autumn food crop of 1896 and spring crop of 1897 (owing to erratic winter rains in 1896–7) was about 60 and 40 per cent respectively.[17] Thus, in terms of both drought and production losses, the famine of 1896–7 seems to have been as severe as that of 1907–8 (which was examined in the last chapter).

Figure 3.2 shows that the price of jowar rose fairly rapidly throughout 1896, reached a maximum in July 1897, and then declined rather swiftly in the closing months of the year. In fact, the price rises seem to have been comparable with those of the 1907–8 famine (compare Figs 2.10 and 3.2). From the middle of 1896, conceptions were below their baseline levels; and they remained so up to the end of 1897. During the first few months of 1897, mortality rose above its baseline level; but it fell back drastically during May and June. Then the MI rose again and finally peaked in October 1897. Thus there were *two* mortality

[15] For details of the antecedents of famine, see Government of the North-Western Provinces and Oudh (1898), chapter 1.

[16] Ibid., p. 7. Test works were opened during the summer of 1895 in Rai Bareli, Sitapur and Hardoi districts; also large remissions and reductions of revenues were made in 1895 by the government for the famine-prone Bundelkhand region.

[17] Ibid., p. 65. It may be noted that damage to crops was mostly on unirrigated lands; pp. 64–5.

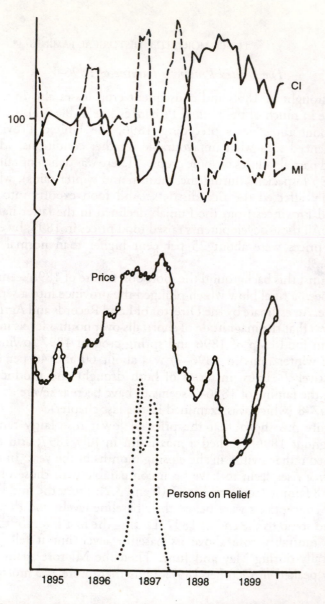

FIG. 3.2 Price of Jowar, Mortality Index (MI), Conception Index (CI), and Average Daily Number of Persons on Relief, by Month, United Provinces 1895–9

Notes: Ranges of variation: MI, 72.7 (May, 1899) to 145.5 (Oct., 1897), CI, 71.6 (Aug., 1897) to 138 (Aug., 1898), jowar price, 28.7 (Dec., 1898) to 8.43 seers per rupee (July, 1897); average number of persons on relief, 6097 (Oct., 1897) to 1,696,722 (Feb., 1897).

Sources: See Table 3.2 and footnotes 1 and 2.

peaks in 1897; and also two corresponding troughs of the CI. The below-normal conception levels during the latter half of 1896 were probably in response to famine distress (as reflected in rising food prices), while the peaks in (proportional) excess mortality reduced conceptions even further to reach minimum levels twice during 1897. However, the peak in the MI during this famine appears to have been much smaller than in the famine of 1907–8. This is also reflected in the smaller trough in the CI (compare Figs 2.11 and 3.2). This confirms the view that the extent of fertility reduction during a famine is largely determined by the severity of distress and the associated excess mortality. However, conceptions returned to normal levels by the end of 1897. But, at the start of 1898, the CI rose rather abruptly much above its baseline level and did not return to near normal until late 1899. This again conforms to the hypothesized above-normal level of fertility ('excess fertility') in the immediate post-famine period. And mortality —in accordance with the hypothesis about post-famine demographic responses—remained significantly below its baseline level, at least for the two years following the year of peak mortality.

The average daily number of persons on relief (of all kinds) reached a maximum in February 1897, and then started to decline. There was virtually no relief being provided at the time of peak MI in October of 1897. Thus in this famine we find another example where relief provisions began to decline much earlier than the resumption of monsoon. However, it is notable that overall relief provision during this famine was both relatively timely and large compared to the disaster of 1907–8 (compare Figs 2.11 and 3.2). Table 3.3 shows that most of the excess mortality in 1897 (the main mortality year) was accounted for by excess fever deaths, although there was also some rise in deaths from dysentery/diarrhoea, smallpox and other causes. Interestingly, there was a significant *decline* in cholera mortality compared to normal. As the Sanitary Commissioner of the United Provinces remarked in his report for 1897: 'Inasmuch as the reduced condition of the people and the accumulation of immense bodies of workers on relief works might have been expected to result in a heavy mortality and extensive diffusion of the disease [i.e. cholera], this result must be regarded as extremely satisfactory.'[18] The official report on the

[18] Ibid., p. 18.

relief administration notes, 'It is impossible to attribute this [i.e. the comparative lack of mortality from cholera] to any other cause than the extraordinary attention paid to sanitation and in particular to securing a pure water-supply on all relief works and in poorhouses'.[19] However, the MI peak in early 1897 was mainly due to mortality from dysentery and diarrhoea. Since this epidemic of dysentery and diarrhoea is likely to have greatly affected people in relief camps, the drastic fall in the number of persons on relief in March may partly have reflected this excess mortality (see Fig. 3.2).

The MI peak in October seems to be a magnification of usual fever (malaria) mortality in the post-monsoon months. But this MI peak appears to have been much smaller than that which occurred in late 1908 (compare Figs 2.11 and 3.2). Thus, while the famine of 1896–7 does not appear to be less severe with respect to food price rises, crop loss, and relief provision than the famine of 1907–8, the scale of overall excess mortality is much smaller. Furthermore, the time patterns of the MI and CI also appear to be broadly similar, except for much smaller respective peaks and troughs in the 1896–7 famine. This, in turn, implies that the famine of 1896–7 involved both less severe distress and smaller associated epidemics. The timing of MI peaks may have partly been shaped by environmental factors and by social disruptions (which assist disease transmission)—factors which were probably common in both the famines. The lesser severity of distress may partly be ascribed to better relief provision.

Compared to the famine of 1907–8, the relief measures provided in 1896–7, especially the large-scale provision of works, seem to have been particularly timely. For example, while in the last week of October 1896—the drought year—the number of persons on relief was about 100,000, in the latter famine there was virtually no provision of relief until the end of November 1907; and a comparable number of persons on relief was not

---

[19] Ibid., p. 137. The report goes on to stress that 'where . . . cholera made its appearance, as it repeatedly did in certain districts, it was on each occasion successfully met by prompt transfer of the workers or poorhouse inmates to another locality, by isolation of the infected gangs, and by the protection and disinfection of the new water-supply. Over and over again were outbreaks of cholera suppressed by these measures on the appearance of the first few cases', p. 137.

reached until January 1908. The total number of persons (including dependents) on public works during 1896–7 was nearly twice the number recorded during 1907–8.[20] According to the official report on relief administration in 1896–7, the relatively small number of excess deaths, 'especially of an epidemic character in the relief centres' should be ascribed to 'the measures taken to secure sanitation and a good supply of pure water and to check epidemic disease on its first appearance'.[21] Moreover, expenditure on gratuitous relief (i.e. on dependents and doles) constituted a higher proportion of total relief expenditure (12 per cent) in the 1896–7 famine than in the 1907–8 one (8 per cent). Such differences in the timing, magnitude, and nature of relief policy thus probably accounted for a large part of the differential severity of famine-induced epidemics. The Famine Commission of 1898 praised the Government of the North-Western Provinces for showing 'incessant activity and watchfulness' during the famine of 1896–7; and it also described its organization of relief as 'a conspicuous success and a great administrative feat'.[22]

The Bombay Famines of 1905–6 and 1911–12

After a year of rainfall which was somewhat below normal, in 1904, the premature cessation of the monsoon, and the almost complete failure of winter rains in 1905 initiated famine conditions in much of Bombay Presidency (especially the famine-prone Deccan region) (see Table 3.1). Crops in 1905–6 failed in more than 50 per cent of the area sown; and the agricultural output was only one quarter of the normal level.[23] However, according to the official Report on the famine, crop failures and famine distress were confined to the following eight districts: Nasik, Ahmednagar, Poona, Sholapur, Satara, Bijapur, Belgaum, and Dharwar. There were fair harvests in other parts of the Presidency and in adjacent native states, to which a large number of agricultural labourers

---

[20] The ratio is 1 : 85; see Government of United Provinces of Agra and Oudh (1909a), p. 150.
[21] See Government of Punjab (1898), p. 130.
[22] Quoted in Bhatia (1967), p. 247.
[23] See Government of Bombay (1907), p. 2.

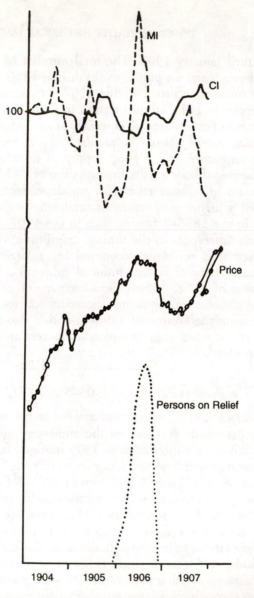

FIG. 3.3 Price of Jowar, Mortality Index (MI), Conception
Index (CI), and Average Daily Number of Persons on Relief,
by Month, Bombay Presidency 1904–7

Notes: Ranges of variation: MI 56.1 (Oct., 1905) to 148.9 (May, 1906);
CI, 90.1 (June, 1906) to 116 (Sept., 1907); jowar price, 25.7 (Jan.,
1904) to 11.5 seers per rupee (Dec., 1907), average daily number of
persons on relief, 4893 (Dec., 1905) to 92,158 (June, 1906).

Sources: See Table 3.2 and footnotes 1 and 2.

probably migrated. Relief measures were opened in the affected areas around December 1905, and they continued in operation until the end of October 1906. On the whole, in terms of both rainfall and crop failure, this famine seems to have been quite severe even when compared to the earlier major famines in Bombay Presidency.[24]

Figure 3.3 presents monthly conception and mortality indices, prices of jowar and average daily number of persons on relief for Bombay Presidency. It shows that food prices were increasing from early 1904, and they rose quite dramatically in 1905; the maximum price prevailed in early 1906. Although food prices declined from this peak in the latter half of that year, they remained very high. Indeed, prices went up again in 1907.

Conceptions did not fall below baseline levels until late in 1905 (when prices were extremely high) and the CI reached its minimum in the middle of 1906 (see Fig. 3.3). This implies that reduction in fertility did not occur until the prime starvation phase. Mortality, however, was far below its baseline level especially during the latter half of 1905 and early 1906. This said, the MI peaked rather abruptly in May 1906 and returned sharply to around normal in August, before becoming relatively low again. Thus, except for the very short-lived elevation of the MI around the middle of 1906, mortality levels for most of the famine period—and 1907—were markedly lower than the respective baseline levels. The sharp MI peak in May was largely related to an outbreak of cholera.

The data on relief show a sharp rise in numbers of people from around February 1906. The numbers then peaked in June and subsequently declined with the resumption of the monsoon. The social disruption associated with relief works probably played a part in the outbreak of the cholera epidemic. It is also notable that there was no elevation in the MI during the post-monsoon period (i.e. the later months of 1906)—the time when an outbreak of malaria might normally be expected. Indeed, to reiterate, mortality during late 1906 was lower than during the baseline period (see Fig. 3.3). Table 3.3 shows an increase in mortality from cholera in 1906, while the number of fever deaths was similar to

[24] See McAlpin (1983).

the baseline level. In fact, there appears to have been a definite improvement in overall registered mortality during the famine (see Table 3.2). This seems to stem solely from the drastic reduction in plague mortality (see Table 3.3). The connection between food shortage and increased plague mortality is probably very weak. In her study of famines in the Bombay Presidency, McAlpin also excluded plague deaths while estimating excess deaths due to famine. Excluding plague from her calculations she arrived at a figure of 2.4 excess deaths per 1000 population in the famine of 1905–6 for the whole of Bombay Presidency.[25] This is indeed a very small quantum of excess mortality compared to earlier major famines. In this connection small rises in deaths from cholera, smallpox, fevers, dysentery/diarrhoea and respiratory diseases are shown in Table 3.3. It may be, then, that a drastic fall in plague mortality in 1906 outweighed modest increases in mortality from some other causes.

However, it is not very clear whether a drastic reduction in deaths from plague was connected with the drought and famine of 1905–6. Outbreaks of plague are related to a variety of environmental conditions. For example, as one authority writes, 'Cold limits the flea's [i.e. the rat flea *X. cheopis*] activity, while heat retards its productivity, and humidity of less than 70 per cent kills it'.[26] It seems plausible, then, that deficient rainfall for the three consecutive years 1904, 1905, and 1906 (see Table 3.1) helped suppress plague mortality. In any case, even putting plague mortality aside, the very moderate mortality effect of this famine is clear.

The failure of monsoon rains in 1911 again precipitated famine in much of the Presidency. As Table 3.1 suggests, this later famine entailed a somewhat larger shortfall of rains. And it was probably more widespread than the previous famine, 11 districts being officially declared as famine-affected.[27] The cropping out-turn during 1911–12 in the most affected tracts (i.e. Gujarat, Deccan and Karnataka) dropped by about 50 per cent compared with

---

[25] See McAlpin (1983), Table 3.13, p. 76.

[26] See Gottfried (1983), p. 9.

[27] The overall percentage of population affected, according to the official estimates, was 29 in the 1905–6 famine, while it was 38 for the famine of 1911–12; see McAlpin (1983), p. 168.

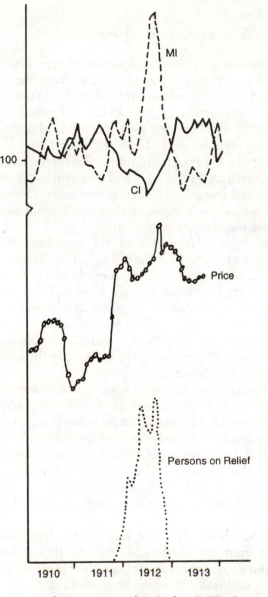

FIG. 3.4 Price of Jowar, Mortality Index (MI), Conception
Index (CI), and Average Daily Number of Persons on Relief,
by Month, Bombay Presidency 1910–13

Notes: Ranges of variation: MI, 84.8 (March, 1913) to 164.7 (July, 1912);
CI, 83.9 (June, 1912) to 113.2 (May, 1913); jowar price, 14.5 (Feb.,
1910) to 9.1 seers per rupee (July, 1911); average daily number of
persons on relief, 115 (Dec., 1912) to 108,888 (April, 1912).

Sources: See Table 3.2 and footnotes 1 and 2.

the out-turn in the preceding agricultural year. Figure 3.4 shows that food prices were on a rising trend from the beginning of 1911, and they rose very sharply after the middle of the year, reaching a maximum in July 1912, and remained very high subsequently. Conceptions were somewhat above normal until the closing months of 1911, when they began to fall below baseline levels; the maximum proportional reduction in conceptions occurred in June 1912; and conceptions then went back above normal levels by the end of the year. Throughout 1913 conceptions were well above baseline levels, again consistent with immediate post-famine excess fertility.

As can be seen from Figure 3.4 mortality was marginally elevated during the second half of 1911. The MI rose dramatically after the first few months of 1912, reaching a peak in June–July; then mortality improved to reach baseline levels by the end of the year. Thus peak famine mortality can be said to have lasted from April to November 1912. Once more there is a clear inverse correspondence between the MI and CI movements. Both the 1911–12 and 1905–6 famines share broadly the same time path of MI and CI movements.

Test works were started in some parts of the Presidency in August 1911; and relief measures of all kinds gradually became more widespread. The average daily number of persons on relief peaked in June 1912, and then declined rather sharply, presumably with the resumption of normal farm activities just after the arrival of the monsoon. The provision of relief had virtually ceased by the end of 1912 (see Fig. 3.4). As in the preceding famine, relief operations can be considered to have been relatively timely.

Table 3.3 shows that, not surprisingly, fever was the single most important specified cause of death during the pre-famine period. But increased mortality from cholera, dysentery/diarrhoea (epidemic outbreaks of which were often associated with social disruptions) and fever together accounted for most of the excess famine mortality. Indeed, the proportional (and absolute) rise in mortality from cholera was much greater than for fever: cholera's share to total excess deaths in 1912 was 41 per cent, while its share of total deaths during the baseline period was less than 2 per cent. The corresponding figures for fever were 29 and 46 per cent, respectively. The fact that in both famines cholera appears to have been the most prominent cause is also consistent with the early occurrence of the MI peaks. This link between the relative predominance of cholera and early occurrence of peak mortality during a famine has also been noted in the last chapter.

Although the famine of 1911–12 led to a somewhat larger number of excess deaths than did the famine of 1905–6, the overall excess mortality associated with both famines can be regarded as modest, especially compared to the major late nineteenth century famines (compare Table 2.2 and Table 3.2). This has also been noted by McAlpin who has clearly demonstrated that the relatively small excess mortality associated with these famines of the first decade of the twentieth century was not related to severity of drought and production failure. Close scrutiny of relevant data suggests that these famines were no less severe in terms of both the degree and extent of crop failure.[28]

Relatively prompt and liberal relief, then, seems to have contributed towards averting large-scale mortality in these famines in Bombay Presidency. As the Report on the famine of 1905–6 notes, 'The relief measures adopted were on the whole timely, adequate and successful'.[29] For example, during the famine of 1905–6, 59 per cent of the average daily number of persons involved were on gratuitous relief (even excluding from the statistics the dependents of relief workers).[30] Relief was also given in the form of suspension or remission of land revenue, and through *taccavi* loans. The emigration of people from the affected districts to relatively unaffected parts (e.g. Khandesh, Berar, and Hyderabad) and to the growing metropolis of industrial Bombay also helped prevent famine distress from developing into major mortality. The official Report on the famine of 1905–6 states that in 1906 'the exodus [from the affected districts] was on an unprecedentedly large scale'. Of course, this large-scale emigration was made possible by demand for labour induced by relatively good harvests elsewhere (e.g. Khandesh, Berar, and Hyderabad)

[28] See McAlpin (1983), especially p. 171. This point has been questioned by Guha, who seeks to argue that these crop failures were less 'extensive and acute' than those of 1896–7 and 1899–1900; see Guha (1985, 1986).

[29] See Government of Bombay (1907), p. 13.

[30] See Bhatia (1963), p. 262.

and industrial development, especially the increase in ginning factories in more favoured parts of the province (i.e. in Bombay and other industrial cities). For example, in spite of a huge immigration of labourers into Khandesh, 'the wages of unskilled labour rose by half'.[31] The Report on the 1905–6 famine remarked that

[t]his exodus proved to be of great service. Although the distress was severe, the numbers on relief were very low and a great saving in expenditure to the State resulted. The emigrants left their dependents behind them and a large proportion of these, who were helpless, had to be brought on the dole lists and relieved gratuitously. On the other hand the returning emigrants brought back with them savings sufficient to enable to carry them on till normal times returned.[32]

And the Report finally concluded by emphasizing these twin beneficial features (i.e. of emigration and relief) for the better tackling of future famines. It stated that:

[e]migration on a large scale of the able-bodied population will, if any conclusions can be drawn from the experience of 1905–6, be one of the most important economic factors in future Deccan famines, and the organization which will require the most careful attention in future will be that of systematic village inspection and the distribution of gratuitous relief to those who are unfit for work and have no means of support, combined of course with measures which pertain to all famines with a view to keeping the cultivator on his legs and enabling him save his useful cattle and sow his land in the year succeeding that of famine.[33]

The relief policy during the famine of 1911–12 was also comparatively liberal; 55 per cent of the total number on relief received gratuitous relief. Another important feature of the policy was its emphasis on the provision of village works alongside large public works. As the Report on the famine states:

The population to be provided for belonged to wild and backward tribes for whom it has been recognized that village works are most suitable. Village works were accordingly from the first made the backbone of the system of relief. A number of such works were opened in each *taluka*,

---

[31] See Government of Bombay (1907), p. 11.
[32] Ibid., p. 11.
[33] Ibid., p. 14.

but, as the famine gradually became more acute and the attendance increased, groups of village works were replaced each by a big central work and other village works were opened in order to close up the gaps. Thus the number of village works remained more or less constant, while the increase in the number of workers was met by an increase in the number of public works. This policy was maintained until the approach of the monsoon, when it became advisable to replace some of the public works by village works.[34]

One implication of this policy was that there was less congregation of people in relief camps and consequently less population movement; both factors presumably acting to limit the outbreak and transmission of epidemic diseases. Moreover, even people engaged on public works apparently preferred to come from their villages every day and return home every evening rather than to reside continuously in camps located at work sites. This was also backed by a programme by which '[t]he dependents of workers on public works were not relieved at the works but by grant of dole in their villages'—a policy which marked a distinct and welcome deviation from 'the ordinary rules of the Famine Relief Code'.[35] Thus, increased gratuitous relief—especially in the form of more care for dependents on the village dole—and large disbursements of taccavi loans not only provided a favourable environment for organized migration in search of employment, but also helped create alternative sources of employment. Thus, relief provisions during the famines appear to have been moderately successful in preventing these major subsistence crises from developing into large-scale mortality crises.[36]

---

[34] See Government of Bombay (1913), p. 4.

[35] See ibid., p. 5.

[36] The success of relief policy in mitigating excess mortality during these famines was partly helped by new employment opportunities created by the expansion of the economy. As McAlpin writes, 'In the first decade of the twentieth century, the interaction of the general expansion of the economy, the increasingly diverse options available to agriculturists, and the famine relief policies of Bombay Presidency combined to prevent crop failures from becoming major demographic and economic catastrophes'; see McAlpin (1983), p. 189.

3. Age and Sex Differentials in Mortality Change During these Lesser-mortality Famines

The age–sex pattern of mortality in the above famines is also of interest. Table 3.4 provides age–sex specific death rates both for the pre-famine baseline periods and prime famine years. As we have seen in the last chapter, infants, young children and elderly people appear to be the most vulnerable to death. It is notable that while these famines entailed minimal overall mortality, infants and children seem to have been the most vulnerable groups, especially compared to most adult age groups. In both Bombay in 1906 and the Punjab in 1897 it is only infants and young children who appear to have experienced adverse mortality, while for most other age groups mortality seems to have improved. Even when mortality of children above 5 years of age recorded a decline the infant mortality rate rose (e.g. Bombay in 1906; and Punjab in 1897). Figure 3.5 presents proportional changes in registered

TABLE 3.4

Death Rates by Age and Sex During the Pre-famine Baseline Periods and the Prime Famine Years: Four Lesser-mortality Famine Locations

| | United Provinces | | | | Punjab | | | |
| | 1891–5 | | 1897 | | 1891–5 | | 1897 | |
Age	M	F	M	F	M	F	M	F
IMR	221.2	217.4	286.9	296.6	215.7	224.7	221.4	242.7
1–4	55.7	53.5	73.6	72.8	48.3	49.7	58.4	66.7
5–9	13.6	11.7	20.2	17.7	10.2	10.9	10.0	10.8
10–14	8.2	7.6	12.2	11.5	7.2	8.3	6.9	8.6
15–19	11.8	16.3	14.7	18.6	8.2	9.3	7.5	9.3
20–9	15.9	17.0	20.0	18.5	11.5	12.5	9.4	11.0
30–9	20.1	17.5	27.7	21.4	15.1	16.3	12.4	14.0
40–9	30.6	25.6	43.7	33.7	23.5	21.3	18.4	16.9
50–9	50.0	39.1	68.0	50.6	37.0	32.0	29.4	26.4
60+	72.3	50.6	85.4	57.5	105.0	104.0	89.7	91.7
CDR	33.1	31.3	42.1	38.7	30.5	31.3	29.6	32.4
			(1.27)	(1.24)			(0.97)	(1.04)

	Bombay Presidency							
	1901–4		1906		1907–10		1912	
Age	M	F	M	F	M	F	M	F
IMR	205.3	193.4	226.0	214.2	199.4	183.9	225.8	211.0
1–4	50.9	49.2	63.5	62.1	54.1	52.3	79.5	78.8
5–9	19.8	22.0	15.4	15.5	10.2	10.9	15.4	15.6
10–14	19.8	24.7	12.0	13.3	8.1	9.6	9.6	11.5
15–19	24.1	27.3	17.7	20.0	13.1	15.4	14.6	18.5
20–9	27.1	27.1	19.7	21.4	15.0	16.7	16.8	19.8
30–9	30.4	30.0	22.5	21.5	17.5	17.1	19.1	19.3
40–9	40.0	34.2	29.2	23.1	24.9	19.3	28.5	22.0
50–9	57.9	50.4	44.6	36.1	38.7	31.1	45.7	37.2
60+	113.4	110.8	94.5	86.0	88.9	79.9	114.7	103.9
CDR	40.2	40.6	35.3	34.9	29.7	29.2	36.9	37.3
			(0.88)	(0.86)			(1.24)	(1.28)

Notes: 1. All death rates have been calculated on the constant denominators being the respective populations according to the last census. Note, however, that death rates for 1912 have been calculated on the respective populations according to the 1901 census for the sake of comparability.

2. Figures in parentheses are the respective ratios of the CDR (all ages combined) in the prime famine year to that of the baseline period.

3. For Punjab the year 1892 has been excluded in the reference period, 1891–5.

Sources: See Table 3.2.

deaths by age and sex. These proportional changes in mortality have been calculated from the respective average levels during baseline periods (see Table 3.4). Figure 3.5 shows that young children were particularly vulnerable in most of these lesser mortality famines. This contrasts with the age pattern found during major famines of heavy excess mortality, in which *older* children and *adults* often appear to have experienced relatively greater mortality increases. The implication may be that even when a major mortality crisis does not result from a famine, the adverse mortality effects of nutritional stress may still show through for infants and young children (and to a lesser extent the old). In

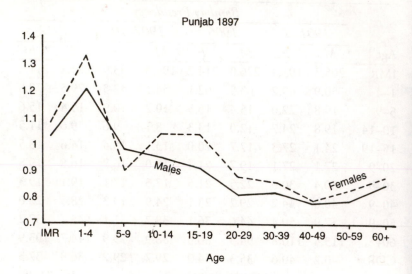

Punjab 1897

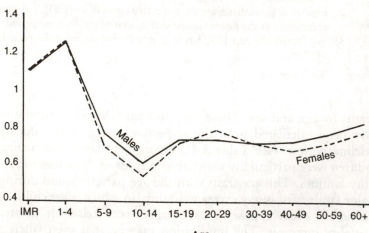

Bombay 1906

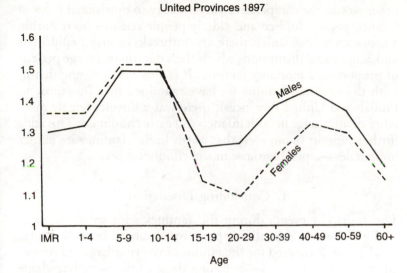

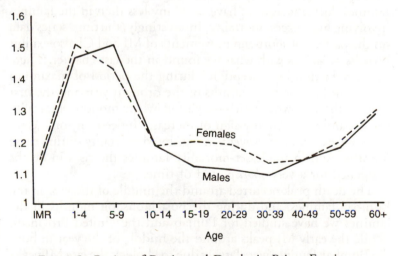

FIG. 3.5 Ratios of Registered Deaths in Prime Famine Years to Baseline Years, by Age and Sex, Four Lesser-mortality Famine Locations

Sources: Based on Table 3.4.

other words, the comparative vulnerability to nutritional stress of infants, young children and elderly people remains overt during a subsistence crisis unless there are outbreaks of major epidemics and acute social disruptions which then dominate the age pattern of proportional mortality increase. It is also worth noting that in both the northern famines we have examined here (i.e. those in Punjab and United Provinces), there was a distinct female mortality disadvantage in both infancy and early childhood. This adds further support to our view that north Indian famines are harder on females—especially those in the childhood years.

4. Concluding Discussion

The course of events during the famines with small (or even negligible) excess mortality appears to have been broadly similar to what we discovered for the famines involving large-scale mortality. All these famines—including those of the preceding chapter—were precipitated by drought (see Table 3.1). And food prices rose sharply, peaking in the year following the drought. Indeed, the extent of price rises during these lesser-mortality famines does not seem to have been any less than in the famines involving huge excess mortality. Interestingly, the time-series data on the pattern of short-run movements of MI and CI also exhibit broad similarities with what we found in the last chapter. There was a reduction in conceptions during the period of maximum starvation (i.e. the later months of the drought year and the first part of the following year)—a period when monthly mortality levels hardly showed any sign of increase. Indeed, in some cases there were even *improvements* in registered mortality during these months. And in the lesser-mortality famines the rises in deaths happened for a very *short* period of time.

The death peak occurred around the middle of the year in the Bombay famines, and during the post-monsoon months in the famines we have studied for Punjab and the United Provinces. While the early MI peaks around the middle of the year in both the Bombay famines were largely due to cholera, the late MI peaks we found in Punjab and the United Provinces were probably mainly due to epidemic malaria. All this is in conformity with our finding (based on the experiences of the major historical famines) that in the process of famine, cholera epidemics tend to precede the occurrence of malaria epidemics. There was also a rough coincidence of the maximum MI and the minimum CI, confirming the additional fertility effects of excess mortality. Thus, while all these features essentially appear to be shared with the famines which caused many excess deaths, the difference lies mainly in the scale of the demographic effects. Both the peaks in the MI and the troughs in the CI are much smaller for the lesser-mortality famines. This almost certainly reflects, in large part, a lesser degree of overall distress and disruption.

Figure 3.6 presents scatter-plots of monthly deaths and relief provision in course of these lesser-mortality famines. As can be seen, the relief provision in most cases (probably except Bombay during 1905–6) was increasing when the number of deaths was somewhat constant (e.g. United Provinces and Punjab) or even declining (e.g. Bombay during 1911–12). And relief provision generally appears to have declined, especially after the resumption of rains when there seems to have been the usual elevation of mortality.

The age–sex pattern of mortality provides an interesting aspect of the lesser severity of distress during these famines; that is, the greater proportional mortality increases for infants and young children (and probably the old) compared to other ages. This finding contrasts with the famines involving large-scale mortality, where older children and adults often experienced larger proportional increases. This may confirm the relatively greater vulnerability of infants and young children to nutritional stress in circumstances in which a famine is prevented from developing into a mortality crisis. And the regional dichotomy of sex differential in mortality increases too—particularly the female disadvantage in the northern parts—has been noticed in the lesser-mortality famines.

Interestingly, the relatively mild overall demographic consequences of these famines do not seem to have been necessarily due to a lesser severity of drought and famine. The Punjab famine of 1896–7 was probably less severe and widespread than the famine of 1899–1900. But judged in terms of the failure in weather and crop output, the extent of food price rises, and the amount of relief expenditure, this famine certainly does not seem to have been a light one. Also, the famine in the United Provinces in 1896–7 cannot be treated as being less severe than that of

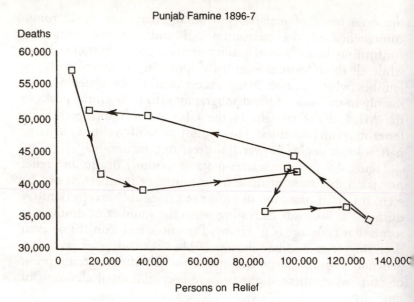

Punjab Famine 1896-7

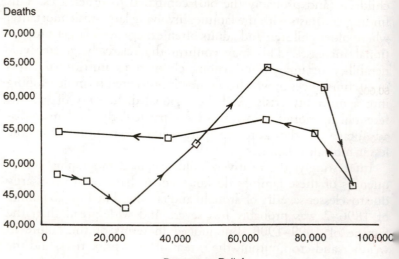

Bombay Famine 1905-6

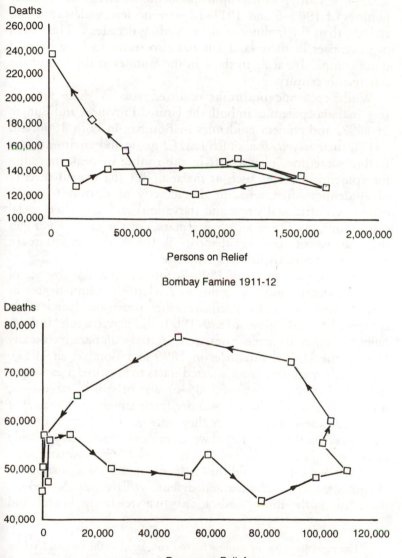

FIG. 3.6 Scatter-plots of Monthly Average Number of
Persons on Relief and Corresponding Monthly Number
of Registered Deaths During the Prime Famine Period,
Four Lesser-mortality Famine Locations

Sources: See Table 3.2 and footnote 2.

1907–8.[37] Lastly, as McAlpin has demonstrated, the Bombay famines of 1905–6 and 1911–12 were no less 'widespread and serious' than the famines of the preceding decades.[38] The extent of price rises in these later famines also seems to have been of quite comparable scale to those in the famines at the end of the nineteenth century.

While epidemic outbreaks occurred also in these famines (e.g. malaria epidemics in both the United Provinces and Punjab in 1897, and cholera epidemics in Bombay in both 1906 and 1912), their *severity* was much less. Climatic and environmental factors sometimes play a part in the timing of peak mortality for epidemic diseases such as malaria. But the overall severity of epidemics often rests on the severity of distress (e.g. the extent of nutritional stress and starvation) and associated social disruptions. As Drèze and Sen remark, 'in the case of famines the collapse of food entitlements is the initiating failure in which epidemics themselves originate'.[39]

In the Punjab famine of 1896–7, for example, the absence of severe epidemics was partly due to a relatively minor degree of crop failure; but more adequate relief provision (particularly compared to the famine of 1899–1900) also played a role. Indeed, relief measures in some cases were started comparatively early (e.g. in the United Provinces in 1896 and Bombay in 1911). Large-scale migration from affected tracts to favoured areas (especially during the famine of 1905–6) was of considerable help, because 'the people did not wander forth aimlessly in search of work, but knew exactly where they were going'.[40] Attention was also placed on the provision of works in the villages; this probably helped to reduce population movements and *large-scale* congregations at relief camps—and thus helped contain the transmission of diseases such as cholera and dysentery/diarrhoea. Moreover, there are fairly strong indications that relatively liberal and

[37] The percentage loss of autumn harvest compared to the normal level for all-United Provinces was 61 and 69 respectively in 1896 and 1907; and corresponding figures for spring harvest was 40 both in 1897 and 1908; see Government of United Provinces of Agra and Oudh (1909a), pp. 18, 32.

[38] See McAlpin (1983), p. 170.

[39] See Drèze and Sen (1989), p. 66.

[40] See Government of Bombay (1907), p. 11.

rational relief policies —sometimes helped by general expansion and diversification in the economy—played a significant role in mitigating the scale of both distress and mortality.[41]

---

[41] Reviewing the evolution of Indian relief policy during the nineteenth century, Klein remarks that '[w]hen more flexible and generous policies were invoked they were dramatically successful in reducing famine mortality'; see Klein (1984), p. 201. It is probably worth noting what Drèze and Sen concluded on the basis of analysis of several famine experiences: 'Many past experiences of famine prevention show the dramatic effectiveness that simple intervention measures can have on famine mortality. These measures have primarily taken the form of early protection of food entitlements, supplemented if possible with provision of drinking water and basic health care (especially vaccination)'; see Drèze and Sen (1989), footnote 5, p. 66.

4

The Demography of the
Bengal Famine of 1943–1944

1. Background

There is little dispute that the famine of 1907–8, marked the end of the period of (drought related) large-scale famines in India.[1] However, more than three decades later a severe famine occurred in 1943–4, particularly in the large eastern province of Bengal, although some other provinces, notably Orissa and Madras, were also affected. The relative absence of major famines during the three decades preceding the Second World War is particularly intriguing because per capita food output in India over this period was not increasing. Indeed, there is rather persuasive evidence of *declining* per capita food output during this time.[2] Nor is there any convincing sign of improved public health and sanitation. Klein, for example, has sought to explain the improved mortality of the 1920s and 1930s as resulting from greater immunity to disease among a population which had passed through a prolonged period characterized by several major crises.[3] Drawing on the experience of Bombay Presidency, McAlpin[4] has attempted to relate these two

---

[1] As Bhatia writes, 'The famine of 1907–8 . . . proved to be a turning point in the long history of food and famine problem in India. Henceforth, drought ceased to be a problem of serious concern'; see Bhatia (1967), p. 270.

[2] For the relevant evidence on this issue, see Bhatia (1967), especially pp. 311–14, Klein (1990) and Drèze (1990).

[3] See Klein (1990); and for a discussion on the difficulties of this hypothesis see Guilmoto (1991), pp. 23–4, and also Guha (1991). In fact Guha has argued that climatic change, enabling greater *stability* (though not the level) of agricultural production (and consumption) during this period (i.e. during the 1920s and 1930s) compared with the preceding decades, was the most important source of improvement of mortality; see Guha (1991).

[4] See McAlpin (1983, 1985).

phenomena of mortality and famine. She argues that the absence of famine-induced mortality was largely responsible for the improved mortality and faster population growth after 1921. On the other hand, while crop failures did occur during this period, they were prevented from developing into major mortality crises. This was achieved by more effective and timely relief provision, greater diversification of the economy, better management of food supplies, and improved transport networks.

One factor which certainly distinguished the Bengal famine was that it was not attributable to drought. At one level, this famine has been viewed as the result of a long-term deterioration in the economic conditions of the poor in Bengal. For example, Alamgir writes that '[f]rom the beginning of the twentieth century, Bengal turned into a region characterized by a large proportion of the population leading a quasi-famine existence'.[5] However, on another level, the events immediately preceding the famine also played an important role. The Bengal famine occurred during World War II. The war caused a cessation of normal imports of rice from Burma which was captured by Japan in early 1942. Government controls brought dislocation of trade. Increased demand for food was created by both the army and the inflow of refugees from Burma. In 1942 there was 'a heavy drain on [food] stocks, with increased exports and decreased imports'.[6] Moreover, a cyclone accompanied by torrential rains and tidal waves in October 1942 caused major crop losses—especially in Midnapore district. All these factors pushed up the price of rice and other essentials, starting from 1941. In turn, rising prices fuelled 'speculation, hoarding and profiteering' and helped to create artificial shortages. Because of this process food prices reached 'astronomical heights' in 1943, which ironically was neither a year of drought nor, probably, of significant food shortage.[7] W.R. Aykroyd, who was a member of the Famine Inquiry Commission, wrote subsequently that 'sheer lack of rice was a less important cause of starvation and death than its enormous price'.[8] It is here that the

---

[5] See Alamgir (1980), p. 79; and see also Chattopadhyay (1991), chapter 1.
[6] See Aykroyd (1974), p. 73.
[7] For detailed treatment of this issue, see Greenough (1982), chapter 3; see also Sen (1981), chapter 6, Famine Inquiry Commission (1945a).
[8] Aykroyd (1974), p. 74.

failure of the Government to control prices and ensure a proper distribution of food really lies.[9]

The majority of the population, who were net purchasers of foodgrains, were near starvation from early 1943.[10] Probably the most appropriate form of relief in these circumstances was direct provision of food to the distressed.[11] But such relief against the failure of food exchange entitlements did not come into operation on a significant scale until September 1943; and by that time, as we shall see, mortality had already risen alarmingly.[12]

With a bumper *aman* harvest during the last months of 1943 the price of rice dropped—but it still remained very high throughout 1944 compared to its normal level. In late 1943 the army at last initiated an efficient distribution of imported foodgrains. However, before any plan for the rehabilitation of famine victims was put into operation, multiple epidemics devastated the province.[13]

2. The Demographic Implications of the Bengal Famine: A Review of the Existing Literature

Demographic considerations have always been an important aspect of writings on the Bengal famine. The quantum of excess mortality understandably constituted a hotly debated issue, not only during the famine, but even today.[14] Several other demographic aspects of the crisis have also received attention. For example, the Famine Inquiry Commission's own *Report on Bengal* gives an account of the nature of mortality, its timing, its causes, including the role of epidemics, and its geographical variation. According to the Report, the period of peak famine mortality was

[9] On this, see Bhatia (1967), chapter 11, Greenough (1982), chapter 3, and also Sen (1981), chapter 6. As Aykroyd wrote, 'The Government of Bengal tried various expedients in a half-hearted way but failed to master the appalling difficulties'; see Aykroyd (1974), p. 78.

[10] For a discussion on the development of distress during 1943, see Mukherji (1965), pp. 41–60.

[11] See Aykroyd (1974), pp. 76–7.

[12] For a discussion of the failure of relief measures, see Greenough (1982), especially pp. 127–38; see also Famine Inquiry Commission (1945a).

[13] This period of famine has sometimes been described as the 'epidemic phase' as against the preceding 'starvation phase'; see, e.g. Sen (1981).

[14] For a brief summary of the debate over the scale of mortality during the famine period, see Sen (1981), especially pp. 195–6.

from the middle of 1943 to the middle of 1944. This conclusion was presumably based on unpublished registration data for the period up to June 1944 which was available only to the Commission. On the basis of registration data for *West* Bengal, Amartya Sen argues that famine mortality lasted at least until 1946.[15] However, using newly found registration data for the whole of undivided Bengal, Dyson has shown that famine excess mortality began in June 1943 and lasted until the middle of 1945. Apart from this, the bulk of mortality occurred during the period previously indicated by the Famine Inquiry Commission.[16] It has also often been suggested that East Bengal suffered a greater severity of famine—though not necessarily in terms of mortality—as compared to the rest of the province.[17]

W.R. Aykroyd wrote that 'in the early days of the famine most deaths were due to sheer starvation, but later hundreds of thousands of deaths were ascribed to smallpox, cholera, and malaria, all rampant in a disorganized and unresistant population'.[18] Greenough notes that epidemic cholera, smallpox and malaria became prevalent between October 1943 and April 1944.[19] He adds that '[t]here is little reason to doubt that the major cause of epidemics was the nutritionally weakened state of the rural populace in combination with unusual concentrations of migrant destitutes'.[20] Indeed, the monthly pattern of registered deaths during the height of the famine was remarkably similar to the pre-famine normal seasonal pattern.[21]

The *Report on Bengal* explicitly deals with the question of the interaction of the famine and epidemics. It recognizes the role of widespread famine-induced starvation in causing these epidemics. While cholera and diarrhoea were thought to be largely related to food shortages and contamination of water and food, the cause of the epidemic of malaria, though more complicated, was largely taken to be the famine. It noted that 'a most formidable epidemic

---

[15] See Sen (1980), and also Sen (1981), Appendix D, especially pp. 196–202.
[16] See Dyson (1991b).
[17] See, e.g. Alamgir (1980), especially pp. 86–7, Aykroyd (1974), p. 72, and also Greenough (1982), p. 163.
[18] See Aykroyd (1974), p. 77.
[19] Greenough (1982), p. 141.
[20] Ibid., p. 141.
[21] See Famine Inquiry Commission (1945a), p. 113.

of malaria was associated with the famine'.[22] Together with other possible explanations such as the interaction of migration and epidemic malaria, Dyson cites[23] Ramakrishnan's suggestion that the occurrence of extremely high malaria mortality during late 1943 and early 1944 followed the establishment of 'feeding arrangements' in September 1943.[24]

Information on the class composition of famine mortality is 'limited and somewhat haphazard'.[25] All available evidence indicates that agricultural labour was the most affected group in terms of both destitution and mortality.[26] Fishermen, artisans, and transport workers were also severely affected. Since distress was primarily due to very high prices, rather than non-availability of food or employment, wage workers were, as expected, among the most vulnerable groups.

The fertility response to the famine has been relatively neglected. However, Dyson has recently used registration data to examine the time path of monthly movements of deaths and conceptions alongside movements in food prices. Given considerable seasonality of conceptions in Bengal during the pre-famine baseline period of 1936–40, he constructs monthly 'conception indices' during 1941–5. These are the absolute (rather than proportionate) deviations of conceptions from those during 1936–40. His analysis shows that in as early as 1941 food prices were higher than usual and the number of conceptions was lower than usual. The fall-off in conceptions continued and reached a minimum absolute level during September–November 1943, which was broadly the period of highest death rates. The fertility of the population was therefore reduced long before the death rate started to rise.

Turning to the age and sex pattern of famine mortality, Sen used data from the Census of India 1951 publication for West

[22] Famine Inquiry Commission (1945a), pp. 119.

[23] See Dyson (1991b) and the references cited therein.

[24] See Ramakrishnan (1954), especially pp. 94–5. More recently, evidence of increased malaria attack following the rehabilitation of famine crisis victims has also been found in the African context; see Murray et al. (1975, 1976, 1990).

[25] Sen (1981), p. 210.

[26] See Sen (1981), especially pp. 209–10. The *Report on Bengal* also noted that 'only one section of the community suffered from starvation—the poorer classes in the rural areas'; see Famine Inquiry Commission (1945a), p. 2.

Bengal.[27] He argued that age and sex differentials were very similar to those of normal times. However, Dyson has shown that Sen's use of the data for West Bengal, which were themselves derived by applying a constant proportional age distribution (i.e. pro-ration), makes this conclusion doubtful.[28]

With this as background, we now consider some of these issues in much greater depth using data contained in the *Bengal Public Health Reports* published for the years 1942, 1943, 1944, and 1945.[29] So far as we are aware, these Reports have *never* been used in any of the previous published work on the Bengal famine. Dyson's recent reanalysis used another publication and in any event pertains only to demographic responses in the whole of Bengal. But the Reports used here allow us to re-examine the demography of the famine at a much more detailed level.

3. Excess Mortality During the Bengal Famine: A Reassessment

Table 4.1 summarizes the main estimates of excess famine mortality which have hitherto been made. It shows that the estimates vary greatly, depending upon the use of diverse sources of data, methods and assumptions. While some of the estimates are based on sample survey data, others are based on registration material, and still others are based on a combination of both. The sheer number of estimates by different authors reflects both the importance with which this issue has been viewed and the potential for bias in this sort of estimation exercise. However, Sen's treatment and estimates are outstanding in that he is quite clear about his assumptions and procedures. In fact, Sen's estimates have been particularly influential in shaping the recent course of this debate about the scale of mortality and in casting doubt on previous estimates. Sen's own conclusion that 'we may be inclined to pick a figure around 3 million as the death toll of the Bengal Famine' has been so widely cited that it can probably be safely described

---

[27] Census of India 1951, vol. VI, part 1B, *Vital Statistics, West Bengal 1941–50* (New Delhi, 1952).

[28] See Dyson (1991b), especially p. 284, and footnote 38, p. 280.

[29] Government of Bengal, Health Directorate, *Bengal Public Health Report*, Alipore: Government Press (for the years as stated in the text). We discovered these reports in the Secretariat Library, Writers' Building, Calcutta.

TABLE 4.1

Summary of Previous Estimates of Excess Mortality During the Bengal Famine of 1943–4

Authors	Excess deaths	Period	Data sources	Comment
1) Department of Public Health, Bengal.	792,854 to 1,017,600	May 1943– April 1944 (inclusive)	Vital registration for all-Bengal	No allowance made for under-registration of deaths; also employs an overestimated level of 'normal' mortality, which thus reduces the estimated level of excess deaths.
2) Famine Inquiry Commission 1945	'about 1.5 million'	Jan. 1943– June 1944 (inclusive)	Vital registration for all-Bengal	No allowance made for under-registration of deaths in 1944; baseline normal mortality fixed by deaths during 1938–42.
3) K.P. Chattopadhya	2.7 million (minimum)	1943 and first half of 1944	Vital registration and sample survey of ten famine affected districts	Probably unrepresentative for the whole of Bengal; also possible errors in calculations.
4) Bengal Public Health Report 1944	1.4 million	June 1943– Dec. 1944 (inclusive)	Vital registration for all-Bengal	Arbitrarily assumes under-registration of deaths as 40 per cent and this figure is also an underestimate.
5) Census of India 1951	1.413 million	1943 to 1945 (inclusive)	Vital registration for all-Bengal	Probable inadequate allowance for under-registration of deaths; use of a baseline 'normal' CDR of 20 per 1000 which is probably too high.

				Level of baseline 'normal' mortality
6) Census of Pakistan 1951	1942–4 (inclusive)	1,714,000 (for East Bengal only)	Probably vital registration for East Bengal	probably underestimated (see text).
7) A.K. Sen.	1943–6	2.62–3.05 million	Vital registration for West Bengal and estimate no. 6 for East Bengal	See text.
8) P.R. Greenough	1943–6	3.5–3.8 million	ISI sample survey for 1943, plus both data sources given above for estimate no. 7	See text.

Sources: 1. Memoranda no. 14, 'Note on mortality caused by the famine', submitted to the Woodhead (Famine Inquiry) Commission by the Department of Public Health and Local Self-Government (Medical) of the Government of Bengal, 1944, p. 64, Document from the Pinnell Papers.

2. Famine Inquiry Commission, Report on Bengal, New Delhi, 1945, pp. 108–110.

3. Quoted in Sen (1981), and also Greenough (1982).

4. Government of Bengal, Directorate of Public Health, *Bengal Public Health Report for 1944*, Alipore, Government Press, 1948, p. 13.

5. Census of India 1951, Volume VI, *West Bengal, Sikkim and Chandernagore*, Part 1A, Report, Delhi, 1953.

6. Census of Pakistan 1951, Volume 3, *East Bengal*, Report and Tables, Karachi, (not dated), p. 7.

7. Sen (1981), especially pp. 195–202.

8. Greenough (1982), especially pp. 299–309.

as representing the new 'conventional wisdom' as to the scale of excess mortality during this famine.[30] From these various considerations it seems reasonable for us to here critically review the estimates provided by Sen.[31] In fact we will argue that his estimates, too, are not without some problems.

Our chief criticism of Sen's estimates relates to the data he used and, relatedly, the treatment of West Bengal and East Bengal separately. Registration data for the whole of undivided Bengal are available for the period up to 1945. Table 4.2 presents these annual registered deaths for undivided Bengal for 1941–6 and subjects them to precisely the same procedures and assumptions which Sen applied to his data for West Bengal. As can be seen, the resulting total estimates are 1.8 and 1.9 million excess deaths respectively under his assumptions A and B.[32] On this basis there appear to be two main reasons why Sen's estimate of excess mortality (i.e. around 3 million) is too high. First, the registration materials for undivided Bengal do *not* support the idea that elevated mortality lasted for years after the famine. As the all-India Public Health Report for 1945 states, 'The deterioration in health conditions [in Bengal] that started with the famine in 1943 gradually disappeared by the middle of the year 1945'.[33] Second,

---

[30] For citations of Sen's estimate of 3 million excess deaths see, for example, Alamgir (1980), p. 85 and p. 92, Hugo (1984), p. 15, Uppal (1984), pp. 216–17, Arnold (1988), p. 44, and also Kane (1988), p. 20.

[31] Greenough's sometimes-cited estimate of between 3.5 and 3.8 million excess deaths is largely based on Sen's calculations; thus Greenough's estimate, in our view, does not deserve separate treatment here.

[32] According to Assumption A, the normal number of deaths is the average of deaths in 1941 and 1942, whereas according to Assumption B, it is the number of deaths in 1942 alone.

[33] See *Annual Report of the Public Health Commissioner with the Government of India for 1945*: New Delhi, 1948, p. 39. In this context, it is of some interest to compare deaths registered in undivided Bengal in the last half of 1945 (i.e. July to December inclusive) with the numbers registered during the same months in the previous years:

Year	Registered deaths	Year	Registered deaths
1940	605,619	1943	1,332,209
1941	585,708	1944	735,943
1942	680,658	1945	565,933

It is perhaps relevant to remark that the population in mid-1941 was similar in size to that in mid-1945 (see Table 4.4 below).

TABLE 4.2
Registered Deaths in Undivided Bengal, 1941–6:
A Re-estimation of Excess Famine Deaths Using Sen's Method

Year	Deaths	Excess deaths	
		Estimate A	Estimate B
1941	1,184,850		
1942	1,222,164		
Average			
1941–2	1,203,507		
1943	1,908,622	705,115	686,458
1944	1,726,870	523,363	504,706
1945	1,238,133	34,626	15,969
1946	1,068,996	−134,511	−153,168
Total Excess 1943–5		1,263,104	1,207,133
(Total Excess 1943–5) × 1.51		1,907,287	1,822,771

Notes: 1. For 1941, and preceding years, the registration area in Bengal covered
72,514 square miles. The data from 1942 onwards relate to an area
of 72,435 square miles. Here and subsequently we have not adjusted
for this very small difference.

2. Registered vital events for 1946 were designated 'provisional' and are
thus likely to *understate* whatever were the true final numbers. In
this context, it is noteworthy that some of the numbers of registered
deaths given above are marginally higher than the numbers which
appear in the Famine Inquiry Commission's *Report on Bengal* (Delhi:
Government Press, 1945). For example, the Report cites 1,873,749
deaths registered in 1943. This figure may well have been the 'provisional' number. If so, then the suggestion is that provisional numbers were not severe understatements of final numbers, i.e.
1,873,749/1,908,622 = 0.9817.

Sources: Dyson and Maharatna (1991). The original sources are the *Annual
Report of the Public Health Commissioner with the Government of India
for 1943 and 1944*, New Delhi, 1946; *Statistical Appendices to Annual
Reports of the Public Health Commissioner with the Government of
India for the Period 1940–4*, New Delhi, 1947; and *Statistical Appendices to Annual Report of the Public Health Commissioner with the
Government of India for the Year 1945*, New Delhi, 1948. The
provisional numbers of registered vital events in undivided Bengal
in 1946 are available in *Annual Report of the Public Health Commissioner with the Government of India for 1946*, New Delhi, 1948,
pp. 4–5.

while the West Bengal data showed a sharp decline in deaths from 1941 to 1942, the all-Bengal data instead show a slight increase, which viewed in historical perspective is perhaps not surprising (see Table 4.2). Obviously, the low number of deaths indicated for 1942 influences in an upward direction both the A and B series of excess deaths made by Sen.

Our present use of the all-Bengal registration data in Table 4.2 is straightforward. But Sen's separate treatment of material for West Bengal and East Bengal (as necessitated by his use of census publications) is subject to difficulties. This is primarily because of errors introduced by the carving out of registered deaths for the districts which were split at the time of partition (namely Nadia, Malda, Dinajpur, and Jalpaiguri districts). In fact, in order to reconstitute data for the period before 1946 to accord with the new district jurisdictions of West Bengal, simple proportions of the vital events registered in the old districts of Bengal were taken by the 1951 Census of India publication. Indeed, there are clear indications that these census publication figures, though presumably originally derived in some way from the registration data, were also subjected to very heavy statistical manipulation (for more on this and a detailed evaluation of the data contained in the 1951 Census of India publication, see Appendix B).

On the other hand, the data on registered deaths in undivided Bengal also invalidate the figure of 1.714 million excess deaths for East Bengal which was used by Sen and is given in a 1951 Census of Pakistan Report.[34]

A serious problem arises with the statistics on deaths given in this report for there is no sound basis for setting the normal average annual number of deaths in East Bengal at only 540,000. During 1938–42, for example, the average annual number of registered deaths in undivided Bengal was 1,184,903. As about two-thirds of these deaths were registered in East Bengal the normal annual number of deaths on this basis alone should be about 790,000. The origins of the number of 540,000 normal deaths may never be known; but undoubtedly it represents a gross underestimate of normal mortality, and thus an *overestimate* of famine mortality in

---

[34] Census of Pakistan 1951, *Volume 3, East Bengal, Report and Tables*, Karachi, (undated).

East Bengal.[35] It therefore seems clear that the estimate of excess mortality, based on the separate data for East Bengal and West Bengal (as contained in the respective census publications) is unsatisfactory. Moreover, given the possibility of migration and other demographic fluctuations, separate treatment of the statistics for East Bengal and West Bengal may well distort conclusions drawn for the whole of Bengal. For example, the existence of a prolonged elevated mortality at least up to 1946 in West Bengal (as shown by the statistics used by Sen) contrasts with our finding of an earlier recovery of mortality to normal level for undivided Bengal—a point to which we will return later. While this may well be related to population movements—among other things—determining the duration of famine mortality for Bengal on the basis of West Bengal's experience—as Sen did—is fraught with difficulties. Thus the foregoing discussion implies that for estimating excess deaths during the famine, it is probably more appropriate to use the registration data for *undivided* Bengal.

Perhaps the most difficult issue involved in estimating famine mortality relates to the determination of an appropriate correction factor for under-registration of deaths.

Table 4.3 presents a summary of several studies (including our own) which have assessed registration coverage at different times, and for different jurisdictions, in Bengal.

In view of the difficulties confronted by any demographic analysis for Bengal during 1941–5, especially due to the limited publication of the 1941 census results, boundary changes and also migration flows, perhaps the strongest case can be made for S.K. Jain's correction factors. His analysis, based partly on the 1951 census results and also on the migration data for West Bengal, appears to have been notably thorough. However, it should be observed that his correction factors for 1941–50 not only relate to West Bengal (rather than to undivided Bengal), but they may also have been unduly influenced by poorer registration in the latter part of the 1940s. Therefore, given the particular efforts made for improving death registration coverage in 1944 and also the possible deterioration of registration during the late 1940s,

[35] For example, if we use 790,000 as the average annual normal number of deaths then the excess deaths for 1942–4 in East Bengal amount to 965,000 which, of course, then has to be adjusted *upwards* for death under-registration.

TABLE 4.3
Estimates of Vital Registration Completeness for Bengal

| Analyst(s) | Period | Territory covered | Method(s) of assessment | Births | | Deaths | |
				Level of registration	Correction factor	Level of registration	Correction factor
1. A.E. Porter	1921–30	Undivided Bengal	Differencing method	65.5	1.53	70.0	1.43
2. S.R. Chowdhury	1931–40 (births) 1930–2 (deaths)	Undivided Bengal	Reverse survival (births) and growth balance (deaths)	61.7	1.62	76.0	1.32
3. Present author	1940–2	Undivided Bengal	Growth balance	n.a.	n.a.	74.7	1.34
4. S. Sengupta	1941–50	W. Bengal	Reverse survival	50.4	1.98	69.0	1.45
5. S.P. Jain	1941–50	W. Bengal	Differencing method and reverse survival	57.9	1.73	66.1	1.51

| 6. | P.G. Chowdhury | 1948 | Six districts of W. Bengal | Comparison of district vital returns with survey figures | 62.3 | 1.61 | 68.3 | 1.46 |

Notes: 1. The correction factor (CF) is the reciprocal of the estimate of the proportion of events registered.

2. The level of registration completeness figures given for the study by P.G. Chowdhury were obtained by comparing the number of events (i.e. births and deaths) recorded in the district vital *returns* with the number of events recorded by a special survey.

Sources: 1. Census of India 1931, *Vol. 5, Bengal and Sikkim, Part I, Report*, Calcutta, 1933, p. 127.

2. S.R. Chowdhury 'The Unprecedented Growth of Population in Bengal in the 1930s: an Effort to Find Out the Real Mechanism', M.Sc. Demography Thesis, London School of Economics, September, 1989.

3. See Appendix C.

4. Census of India 1951, *Volume VI, West Bengal, Sikkim and Chandernagore, Part IA–Report*, Delhi, pp. 329–31.

5. See Jain (1955).

6. Census of India 1951, *Volume VI, Part IB, Vital Statistics, West Bengal 1941–50*, Delhi, 1955, Appendix B.

Jain's correction factor which relates to average conditions during 1941–50 may conceivably over-correct for death under-registration during the main famine period.

It seems reasonable to follow Sen in using Jain's correction factors for under-registration and also provide estimates of excess mortality for a *range* of assumptions relating to the level of death registration completeness. Accordingly, we have adopted three sets of assumptions as follows:

Assumption 1: The correction factors of 1.62 (births) and 1.32 (deaths) as estimated by S.R. Chowdhury apply; note that this correction factor for deaths is very close to our own estimate for 1940–2 which is made in Appendix C (see especially Table 4.3).

Assumption 2: S.P. Jain's correction factors of 1.73 (births) and 1.51 (deaths) apply.

Assumption 3: Correction factors of 1.90 (births) and 1.70 (deaths) apply. These factors were chosen arbitrarily to represent an even greater degree of under-registration than is implied by Jain's work.

Given these assumptions, the basic calculations employed in order to estimate excess mortality are presented in Table 4.4. Panel A addresses the question of what the death rate would have been in the absence of the famine. Assuming a constant rate of population growth (of 1.88 per cent per annum) between 1931 and 1941, we calculated the crude death rates (CDRs) for the years 1931–42 inclusive. Then we fitted a least-squares regression line to these CDRs for 1931–42 in order to determine the CDRs during 1943–6 that would have prevailed in the absence of famine (given the downward trend in the CDRs of 1931–42). Given this fitted line, the derived 'extrapolated' CDRs for 1943–6 have all been adjusted upwards by the correction factors implied by assumptions 1–3 in order to allow for under-registration of deaths (see Panel A of Table 4.4).

Next the actual crude death rates for each of the years 1943–6 have been estimated by using the registered numbers of births and deaths adjusted upwards under assumptions 1–3 and also by calculating the corresponding mid-year populations on the basis of the adjusted births and deaths (see Panel B of Table 4.4). Now the differences between the actual CDRs and the 'extrapolated' CDRs during this period represent the excess death rates which,

TABLE 4.4

Estimation of Excess Famine Deaths in Undivided Bengal Under Assumptions 1–3

PANEL A

Year	Registered deaths	Estimated mid-year population (000's)	Registered CDR	Registered CDR adjusted upwards by CF =			Registered infant mortality rate (IMR)
				1.32	1.51	1.70	
1931	1,113,312	50,046	22.25	29.37	33.60	37.83	174.0
1932	1,022,219	50,996	20.05	26.47	30.28	34.09	178.9
1933	1,197,885	51,964	23.05	30.43	34.81	39.19	200.1
1934	1,176,887	52,950	22.23	29.34	33.57	37.79	189.2
1935	1,131,427	53,955	20.97	27.68	31.66	35.65	158.5
1936	1,222,724	54,979	22.24	29.36	33.58	37.81	170.9
1937	1,232,971	56,022	22.01	29.05	33.24	37.42	176.2
1938	1,315,886	57,086	23.05	30.43	34.81	39.19	184.1
1939	1,090,530	58,169	18.75	24.75	28.31	31.88	146.6
1940	1,111,082	59,273	18.75	24.75	28.31	31.88	159.3
1941	1,184,850	60,398	19.62	25.90	29.63	33.35	115.7
1942	1,222,164	61,544	19.86	26.22	29.99	33.76	154.3

(cont.)

Table 4.4 (cont.)

PANEL A

Year	Registered deaths	Estimated mid-year population (000's)	Registered CDR	Registered CDR adjusted upwards by CF =			Registered infant mortality rate (IMR)
				1.32	1.51	1.70	
			CDRs extrapolated on linear time-trend				
1943	1,908,622	—	19.44	25.66	29.35	33.05	195.4
1944	1,726,870	—	19.19	25.33	28.98	32.62	207.9
1945	1,238,133	—	18.94	25.00	28.60	32.20	143.2
1946	1,068,996	—	18.69	24.67	28.22	31.77	n.a.

PANEL B

Year	Assumption 1			Assumption 2			Assumption 3		
	Mid-year population (000's)	CDR	Excess deaths	Mid-year population (000's)	CDR	Excess deaths	Mid-Year population (000's)	CDR	Excess deaths
1943	62,107	40.57	926,015	62,019	46.47	1,061,765	62,013	52.32	1,194,991
1944	60,634	37.59	743,373	60,213	43.31	862,852	59,934	48.98	980,520
1945	60,580	26.98	119,948	60,014	31.15	153,036	59,656	35.28	183,740

| 1946 | 61,528 | 22.93 | – | 60,917 | 26.50 | – | 60,602 | 29.99 | – |
| | Total: 1.8 million | | | Total: 2.1 million | | | Total: 2.4 million | | |

Notes:
1. The estimated mid-year populations for 1931 and 1941 (underlined) were based directly on census results pertaining to the areas under registration. In using them to derive estimates of mid-year populations for non-census years during 1931–42 (on the assumption of regular compound growth), account is explicitly being taken of probable net in-migration in the period. However, in the absence of data, allowance cannot be made for migration after 1941. Note that between 1931 and 1941 the population was growing at the fast rate of 1.88 per cent per annum.

2. The registered CDRs given above are lower than the official rates published annually in the *Bengal Public Health Report*. This is because the official rates were unable to adequately take account of population growth during the intercensal years. The least-squares regression line derived from the registered CDRs for 1931–42 was CDR = 506.098–0.25052 (YEAR).

3. The trend line, and its extrapolation to years 1943–6 under assumption 2, are shown in Figure 4.1. As can be seen, it gives a reasonable representation of the downward trend in the death rate during the 1930s.

4. The infant mortality rates (IMRs) are infant deaths per thousand livebirths registered in the same year. The IMRs given for 1943–5 inclusive, are those registered in those years (i.e. they are not extrapolated).

Sources: For the years before 1946, data have been taken from *Bengal Public Health Report*, Alipore, Government Press, various years; the data for 1946 are from *Annual Report of the Public Health Commissioner with the Government of India for 1946*, New Delhi, 1948.

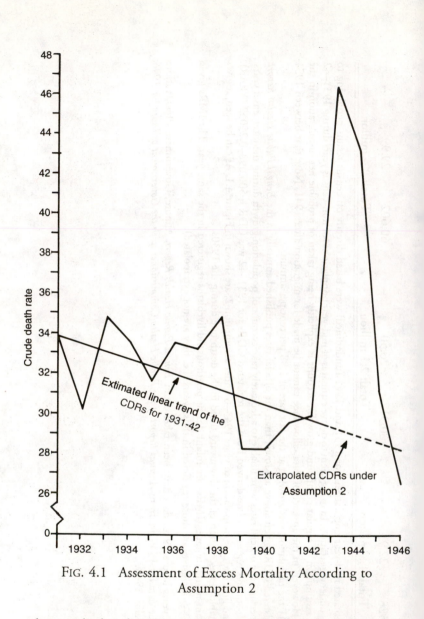

FIG. 4.1   Assessment of Excess Mortality According to
Assumption 2

when applied to the estimated mid-year populations, give the total number of excess deaths (see Panel B of Table 4.4). Figure 4.1 illustrates the basic process with reference to assumption 2. Essentially the volume of excess deaths is being evaluated as the area *under* the CDR curve, yet *above* the extrapolated CDR line.

Of course, the above estimates of famine mortality are not

entirely beyond dispute. First, the estimated extrapolated normal level of mortality during the famine period, based on the trend of 1931–42, would be different if we used a different reference period to fix the pre-famine trend in the death rate. Second, the period of famine mortality itself is not entirely an objective matter. Thus the crude death rate in 1945, being below that for 1938, can arguably be considered as representing a non-famine year. On the other hand, the below trend death rate for 1946 might partly be a reflection of the changed age structure of the population after the famine and thus could well still represent some excess famine mortality. Third, we cannot be sure that the provisional number of registered deaths for 1946 used here represented only a modest underestimate of the true final number of deaths for that year.

However, while we are not in a position to evaluate these issues, we can probably safely conclude that they are relatively minor and that their effects probably at least partly offset each other. Therefore, the implied range of famine mortality is between 1.8 and 2.4 million *excess* deaths. The upper estimate of 2.4 million is based upon an arbitrary assumption regarding the level of registration completeness (i.e. assumption 3). We know of no strong grounds for considering that the average level of death registration in 1943–4 was less than 60 per cent (as required by this assumption). Thus it seems reasonable to conclude that the rough figure of 2.1 million excess deaths arising from assumption 2 (and embodying precisely the same correction factor for death under-registration as was used by Sen) is probably as good as any.

4. The Time Path of Famine Distress and the Fertility and Mortality Responses

As for the Indian famines considered in Chapters 2 and 3, it is of interest to examine the time path of short-run mortality and fertility effects in relation to the development of the famine in Bengal. There is a dearth of direct monthly data on food availability or consumption which might help capture directly the time path of famine distress. Most previous research on food price movements in the Bengal famine has used the weekly rice price for the Calcutta market, published in the *Indian Trade Journal*. But these Calcutta prices may not adequately reflect provincial food prices. Moreover, even the Calcutta prices are unavailable

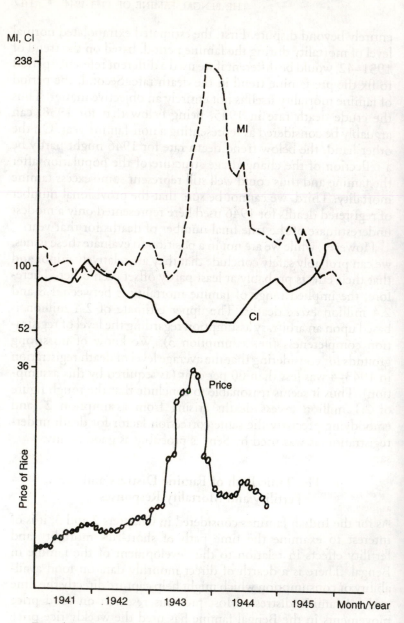

FIG. 4.2 Food Price, Mortality Index (MI) and Conception
Index (CI), by Month, Bengal 1941–5

Data Sources: See text.

from October 1943 onwards. However, fortunately, a monthly series of provincial average prices of coarse rice from July 1943 until October 1944 has been found in the personal papers of L.G. Pinnell which are lodged in the India Office Library in London.[36] Comparison of these with the monthly Calcutta prices suggests that they chime in well with—and significantly extend—previous price data (see Appendix D).

Consequently we have used the Calcutta prices up to September 1943, and we have then plotted Pinnell's provincial averages until October 1944 (see Fig. 4.2).[37] Monthly conception and mortality indices (CI and MI) are here constructed as *ratios* of monthly conceptions and deaths respectively as in the preceding chapters.[38] It is seen from Figure 4.2 that food prices were rising from early 1941, and that conceptions then were already below normal probably in response to this. The main excess mortality peak can roughly be said to have lasted for twelve months, from mid-1943 to mid-1944. Although conceptions declined substantially before the start of the mortality rise, the additional negative effects of excess mortality (and presumably morbidity) on conceptions are perhaps also discernible from Figure 4.2. Rice prices declined rather sharply during late 1943 but still remained quite high during 1944. Both conceptions and mortality returned to their pre-famine levels only in the middle of 1945 (see Fig. 4.2).

Famine relief, which started at very modest levels in late 1942, took three main forms: agricultural loans, test works and gratuitous relief. Figure 4.3 shows monthly movements in money sanctioned by the Government of Bengal under these three heads.

---

[36] Indeed, the Pinnell Papers also contain the weekly wholesale prices of rice as prevailing in the different markets throughout Bengal (i.e. about 70 markets including Calcutta) but only from January to August of 1943 (see Appendix D).

[37] For the Calcutta market, we have used the price quotations for dates near the middle of the month. No quotation was available for July 1942. These are wholesale prices, and they are expressed in terms of rupees per maund. Until February 1943 the prices are for Ballam No. 1 variety rice; thereafter they relate to Kalma No. 1 variety, since the price of Ballam is not generally available. From October 1943 onwards prices refer to the province as a whole, and they relate to coarse rice (for details see Appendix D).

[38] As was assumed previously, monthly conceptions here are taken to be monthly births displaced backwards by nine months. For the monthly distributions of average annual births and deaths during the baseline period 1936–40, see Appendix E.

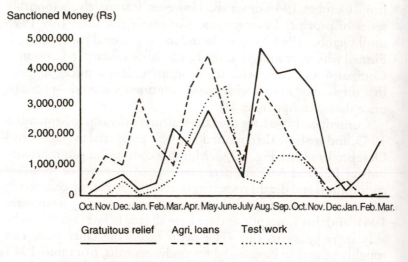

FIG. 4.3 Monthly Sanctioned Money on Three Relief Heads,
Bengal October 1942–March 1944

Sources: Pinnell Papers, (Confidential), *Memorandum on the Economic Condition of Bengal prior to the Famine of 1943*, p. 44.

It shows considerable fluctuation in money allotted, especially
during the early phase of the famine; and gratuitous relief was
relatively small during that period too. The total money sanctioned under these three heads combined reached a maximum in
May 1943—when there was no excess famine mortality at the
all-Bengal level (see Figs 4.2 and 4.3).[39] In the following two
months official relief expenditure declined; but it rose abruptly in
August when the largest sum allotted was for gratuitous relief, and
test relief was given only in small amounts (see Fig. 4.3). Gratuitous relief continued to be high (and mostly spent on the
provision of food) in the following three months, while excess
mortality was mounting. However, relief expenditures by the
Government declined drastically in December—the month in
which the number of deaths reached its maximum.

Figure 4.4 plots monthly deaths from five major causes during

[39] The relief measures, especially the test works, during this period were
inefficient, and entailed considerable wastage of money; see Famine Inquiry
Commission (1945a), p. 73.

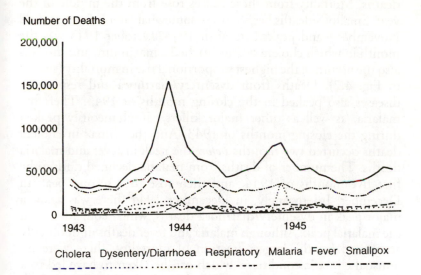

Number of Deaths

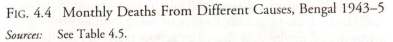

Cholera Dysentery/Diarrhoea Respiratory Malaria Fever Smallpox

FIG. 4.4 Monthly Deaths From Different Causes, Bengal 1943–5

Sources: See Table 4.5.

1943–5. In earlier famines we have examined, our conclusions about the role of malaria in famine mortality were bound to have been in the nature of inferences, as malarial deaths—presumably included in the 'fever' category—were not recorded as a separate cause. However, from 1921, the *Bengal Public Health Report* started to provide a breakdown of fever deaths into several other causes including malaria. Malaria was certainly one of the dominant constituents of the fever group.[40] The quality of death reporting in Bengal, as elsewhere, was far from perfect. But our major concern here is not so much with the actual malarial death rate as with its change and its seasonal distribution during the famine.

Figure 4.4 shows that a somewhat similar time path, especially in the latter half of 1943, was shared by cholera, malaria and fever

[40] The constituents of the fever group, and their respective percentage shares to total registered fever deaths in 1942 were: malaria (54.53), kala-azar (1.95), influenza (0.21), the enteric group of fevers (1.10), measles (0.21), relapsing fever (0.0004), typhus (0.68), blackwater fever (0.04), cerebrospinal fever (0.08) and other fevers (41.20).

deaths. Mortality from these causes rose from the middle of the year. Smallpox deaths began to rise somewhat later—from around November—and peaked in April 1944. October 1943 was the month in which cholera deaths reached a maximum, and this was also the month of the highest proportional rise in mortality (shown in Fig. 4.2). Deaths from dysentery/diarrhoea and respiratory diseases also peaked in the closing months of 1943. Therefore malaria, as well as other major killers, simultaneously peaked during the closing months of 1943. And the climax in cholera deaths occurred two months *before* the peak in fever and malaria deaths. The number of deaths from malaria declined during the first five months of 1944, and then rose to a second peak in December. Interestingly, in December 1944 there was again a major peak in dysentery/diarrhoea deaths, which coincided with the malarial peak. Although malaria and fever deaths undoubtedly accounted for the largest fraction of mortality, there were no unusual climatic conditions which can be taken to have led to a particularly virulent malaria epidemic in Bengal during the famine.[41] Indeed, the basic time pattern of rising mortality during the prime period was broadly shared by several major specified causes. This, as in several earlier famines (see chapter 2 above), indicates that a period of acute nutritional stress and social disruption led to a period of increasing mortality from several different diseases, while the exact timing of peak mortality from a particular disease was partly shaped by environmental and other factors.

In this connection, the hypothesis of 'malaria refeeding' may be considered apropos the huge malaria and fever mortality peak which occurred after September 1943 (see Fig. 4.4). The beginning of relief arrangements (which presumably led to an improved nutritional state) in September is hypothesized to have dispelled the latent state of malaria infection among undernourished hosts, and thus contributed to the rise in malaria mortality in the following months. However, the *proportion* of total victims covered by the relief kitchens was very low; probably never exceeding 5 per cent of Bengal's population.[42] While government-supported kitchens were

[41] See Famine Inquiry Commission (1945a), p. 122, Zurbrigg (undated), p. 71, and also Dyson (1991b), p. 294.

[42] See Greenough (1982), footnote 122, p. 130. In a memorandum to the Famine Inquiry Commission the Communist Party reported that relief kitchens

the main source of rural food relief, the gruel offered had 'few nutritive benefits'.[43] According to the *Report on Bengal*, it 'did not at best supply more than 600–800 calories [per day] for adults and about half this number for children'.[44] Moreover, malaria infection and mortality does not seem to have been suppressed before the start of the supposed improvement in nutrition in September. For example, total mortality from fevers (including malaria) was 45 per cent *higher* during June–August 1943 compared with the corresponding average for 1937–41. The available clinical evidence on malaria during the Bengal famine suggests that although refeeding may have caused parasites to be more numerous in famine victims, 'its effect on actual mortality is at best unclear, and quite possibly negligible'.[45] Indeed, as has been argued before, the available evidence on the malaria refeeding hypothesis suggests that even though the attack rate rises with refeeding the mortality rate probably depends considerably on the previous level of undernutrition. Although class-specific malaria mortality rates are not available for the Bengal famine, higher mortality among the most undernourished sections of the population has clearly been indicated in the surveys we have referred to above.[46]

Table 4.5 suggests that the percentage share of cholera deaths in total excess mortality was highest in 1943. Smallpox showed a similar contribution to total excess mortality in 1944. However, malaria remained far and away the single most important cause of death. And, notably, its relative contribution in excess mortality was far higher in 1944 than in both 1943 and the baseline

---

fed 1.7 to 1.9 million people, while the number in need of relief was about 20 million; see Bhatia (1967), p. 338.

[43] See Greenough (1982), pp. 131–2.

[44] See Famine Inquiry Commission (1945a), p. 128. Brennan in the context of Midnapore—one of the most affected districts—found that '[t]here was often not enough nutritional value in the gruel to do more than prolong starvation; at times, it brought death . . . Moreover, some of the worst-hit people were too weak and ill after a year's deprivation to reach the kitchens'; Brennan (1988), p. 552.

[45] See Zurbrigg (undated), p. 76.

[46] Examining the whole issue of 'refeeding malaria' in the context of the Bengal famine, Zurbrigg states that '[the] distinction between malnutrition and infection as cause of death therefore may be a technical extravagance when practically speaking it is the underlying hunger which makes the infection lethal on an epidemiological scale'; see ibid., p. 76. On this, see also Maharatna (1991).

reference period. Thus, elevated malaria mortality was relatively persistent over an extended period.

TABLE 4.5
Cause-specific Death Rates and Relative Importance of Different Causes of Death During Pre-famine and Famine Periods in Bengal

Causes of death	Cause-specific death rates		
	1937–41	*1943*	*1944*
Cholera	0.73	3.60	0.82
	(3.72)	(23.88)	(0.99)
Smallpox	0.21	0.37	2.34
	(1.06)	(1.30)	(23.69)
Fever	6.14	7.56	6.22
	(31.08)	(11.83)	(0.91)
Malaria	6.29	11.46	12.71
	(31.82)	(43.06)	(71.41)
Dysentery/Diarrhoea	0.88	1.58	1.08
	(4.47)	(5.83)	(2.27)
Respiratory diseases	1.52	1.30	1.39
	(7.67)	(−1.82)	(−1.44)
Injury	0.37	0.33	0.27
	(1.86)	(−0.33)	(−1.05)
All other	3.32	5.57	3.91
	(18.32)	(16.26)	(3.23)
All causes	19.46	31.77	28.75
	(100.00)	(100.00)	(100.00)

Notes: 1. All cause-specific death rates are based on a constant denominator—being the enumerated population in the 1941 census.
2. For the period 1937–41, the figures in parentheses are the respective percentage shares to total average annual deaths, while for both 1943 and 1944 they are the percentage shares to total *excess* deaths. The excess deaths from each of the above diseases were calculated over the respective average deaths registered during 1937–41.

Sources: Government of Bengal, Health Directorate, *Bengal Public Health Report*, Alipore, Government Press, various years.

From Table 4.6 we can note that government expenditure on the 'public health establishment' did not increase until 1944–5;

in fact during 1942–4 it was *lower* than the 1941–2 level.[47] Expenses on epidemic diseases, however, increased during 1943–4; although they (together with other expenditures) reached a maximum in 1944–5—a period in which mortality had returned close to its pre-famine level (see Fig. 4.2). Like food relief, medical relief also seems to have been supplied rather late. It thus seems plausible to suggest that greater public health expenditures during the prime excess mortality period would probably have contributed towards a lowering of the famine death toll.[48]

TABLE 4.6

Expenditure on Public Health, Bengal 1941–2 to 1944–5

Year	Public health establishment (Rs)	Expenses in connection with epidemic diseases (Rs)	Total expenditure (Rs)
1941–2	650,985	726,496	3,929,486
1942–3	614,585	942,122	3,595,021
1943–4	626,616	2,706,933	6,025,472
1944–5	735,977	7,146,172	10,929,958

Notes: 1. Expenditures on the 'Public Health Establishment' include those on the established permanent health centres and hospitals.
2. The other major heads of health expenditures include grants, public health works (e.g. conservancy, water supply and drainage).

Sources: *Statistical Appendices to Annual Reports of the Public Health Commissioner with the Government of India for the period 1940–4*, Delhi: Government Press, 1947. The corresponding figures for 1945–6 onwards are not available for undivided Bengal.

[47] Mukherjee provides evidence to show how inadequate were the government health measures adopted during the famine; reviewing the relevant statistics, he writes that 'not even one bed per village, which ought to be the lowest desideratum of a health rehabilitation plan, was provided'; see Mukherjee (1947), p. 146.

[48] As the Public Health Commissioner in his report for 1943 and 1944 noted, 'Due to a variety of causes the civil medical organisation in Bengal was quite unable to deal with the health problems that arose in connection with the famine'; see Government of India (1946), p. 3. The delay and inadequacy of health measures was also noted by the *Report on Bengal* which stated that 'some of the mortality which occurred could have been prevented by more vigorous and timely [health] measures'; see Famine Inquiry Commission (1945a), p. 142.

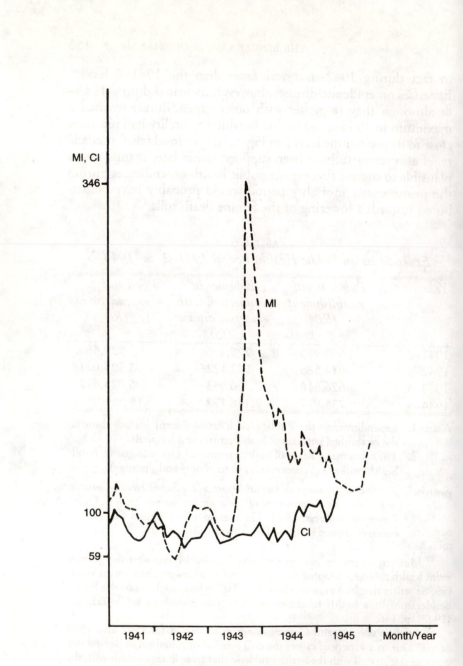

FIG. 4.5   Mortality Index (MI) and Conception Index (CI),
by Month, Urban Bengal 1941–5

Sources: See Table 4.5.

Figure 4.5 shows monthly movements of the CI and MI in urban Bengal. The reduction in conceptions in urban Bengal was much less than that which occurred in the province as a whole. Also, the urban data do not suggest a correspondence between reductions in conceptions and increases in mortality (see Fig. 4.5).

Interestingly, however, the time pattern of movements of the urban MI broadly coincides with that for the whole of Bengal (see Figs 4.2 and 4.5). Note also that the peak proportionate excess in urban mortality was *much* greater than for the whole of Bengal (and, by implication, for rural Bengal).[49] A lesser reduction in conceptions and a higher mortality increase in urban than in rural areas may both be indicative of *migration* to urban areas by rural destitutes.

5. Rural–Urban Differentials in the Fertility and Mortality Responses

Table 4.7 shows clearly that during normal years registered birth and death rates were higher in rural areas. Lower urban than rural death rates in normal times seem plausible because of better public health, sanitation and nutrition in urban areas.[50] But such a low urban birth rate may at least partly reflect the fact that industrial towns (which accounted for most of the urban population) normally had a disproportionately large number of adult males. According to the 1941 census, in the industrial towns of Bengal there were only 487 females per 1000 males. And this urban imbalance in the sex ratio was particularly acute in the reproductive age groups.[51]

[49] Slightly more than 90 per cent of total registered deaths and births occurred in villages. This corresponds to the fact the about 90 per cent of the total population lived in rural areas.

[50] For example, the number of persons vaccinated per 1000 population during 1940–1 was 343 in urban Bengal, while the corresponding figure for rural areas was only 146.

[51] The 1951 census results give the following age compositions (%) of male and female populations in Calcutta and other industrial towns:

	0–14		15–54		55+	
	M	F	M	F	M	F
Calcutta	22	36	73	57	5	7
Other towns	29	36	64	56	7	8

See Census of India 1951, *Vol. VI, West Bengal, Sikkim and Chandernagore, Part IA-Report*, Delhi, 1953, pp. 420–4.

TABLE 4.7

Crude Birth and Death Rates in Rural and Urban Areas During Pre-famine and Famine Periods in Bengal

Period	Rural	Urban	All Bengal
Pre-famine: 1936–40			
CBR	28.51	14.94	27.24
CDR	20.51	13.76	19.89
CRNI (=CBR–CDR)	8.00	1.18	7.35
Famine			
1943			
CBR	20.00	11.14	19.17
(% change in births)	(–29)	(–25)	(–29)
CDR	32.69	22.91	31.78
(% change in deaths)	(+59)	(+66)	(+59)
1944			
CBR	16.42	11.29	15.93
(% change in births)	(–42)	(–24)	(–41)
CDR	29.46	21.85	28.75
(% change in deaths)	(+43)	(+58)	(+44)
1945			
CBR	22.51	13.44	21.67
(% change in births)	(–21)	(–10)	(–20)
CDR	21.05	16.37	20.62
(% change in deaths)	(+2)	(+18)	(+3)

Notes: 1. All CBRs and CDRs are calculated on constant denominators—being the respective enumerated rural and urban populations in the 1941 census.
2. The CRNI—crude rate of natural increase—represents the change in population size, per 1000 persons, due to the balance of births and deaths, in a given year; it thus does not include the effect of migration on the change in population.
3. The percentage changes in registered deaths and births have been calculated over the respective average numbers during 1936–40.

Sources: See Table 4.5.

We have already noted that while the percentage rise in famine mortality was higher in urban areas, the percentage decline in urban births was less pronounced. These facts seem to be consistent with the hypothesis that there was a considerable inflow of destitute people to the towns where relief was believed to be more available.[52] In this connection rural–urban differentials in the provision of preventive health measures are perhaps worth noting. The number of vaccinations performed in 1943 compared with 1942 rose by 1 per cent in rural Bengal and 55 per cent in urban areas. However, in 1944 the increases were 532 and 287 per cent respectively. It is notable from Table 4.7 that rural–urban differences in the proportional decline in births and rise in deaths were far greater during 1944–5 than in 1943. This perhaps indicates that the greatest movement of people to the towns occurred during the later epidemic phase of the famine, especially 1944.

Table 4.8 presents rural–urban differentials in causes of death. What is striking about urban Bengal during the pre-famine period is the relative unimportance of malaria and fever mortality, and conversely the pre-eminence of respiratory diseases. The notably lower urban incidence of malaria may reflect better availability of anti-malarial medicines (e.g. quinine) and less monsoon surface water build-up, which is conducive to mosquito breeding. However, the much higher share of deaths in the 'all other' category in the towns may be suggestive of rural–urban differentials in reporting biases.

Most of the registered excess famine mortality in the towns was *not* due to malaria—although deaths from this disease did increase (see Table 4.8). Instead the 'all other' category was prominent. The drastic fall in the relative importance of respiratory diseases in the towns during the famine is also rather striking.[53] Given that towns attracted destitutes during the famine, many starvation deaths may have been recorded in this unspecific category. The Public Health Commissioner for India in his report for 1943 and 1944 gave the recorded number of deaths of 'destitutes' in Calcutta—'those persons who died and whose bodies were disposed of by public arrangement'—as follows: 3000 deaths between June 1942 and May 1943; and 19,000 deaths between June 1943 and May 1944.[54]

[52] See Greenough (1982), pp. 143–4.
[53] Sen also commented upon the fall in the registered deaths from respiratory diseases during the famine; see Sen (1981), p. 205.
[54] See Government of India (1947), p. 2.

TABLE 4.8
Rural–Urban Differentials in the Relative Importance of Different Causes of Death During the Pre-famine and Famine Periods in Bengal

Cause of death	Cause-specific death rates		
	1937–41	1943	1944
Rural			
Cholera	0.76	3.80	0.83
	(3.72)	(24.74)	(0.76)
Smallpox	0.17	0.36	2.32
	(0.85)	(1.52)	(23.66)
Fever	6.55	8.00	6.54
	(32.12)	(11.75)	(−0.16)
Malaria	6.89	12.51	13.84
	(33.80)	(45.67)	(76.63)
Dysentery/Diarrhoea	0.87	1.45	0.95
	(4.29)	(4.69)	(0.82)
Respiratory diseases	1.35	1.13	1.19
	(6.60)	(−1.74)	(−1.69)
Injuries	0.37	0.32	0.26
	(1.82)	(−0.42)	(−1.23)
All other	3.42	5.12	3.53
	(16.79)	(13.79)	(1.20)
All causes	20.38	32.69	29.46
	(100.00)	(100.00)	(100.00)
Urban			
Cholera	0.51	1.69	0.79
	(3.73)	(12.73)	(3.65)
Smallpox	0.57	0.42	2.53
	(4.16)	(−1.54)	(25.62)
Fever	2.17	3.35	3.18
	(15.88)	(12.82)	(13.21)

Cause of death	Cause-specific death rates		
	1937–41	1943	1944
Malaria	0.41	1.28	1.67
	(3.01)	(9.33)	(10.43)
Dysentery/Diarrhoea	1.40	2.88	2.44
	(10.28)	(15.91)	(12.53)
Respiratory diseases	3.15	2.89	3.25
	(23.10)	(−2.80)	(1.32)
Injuries	0.32	0.39	0.39
	(2.36)	(0.74)	(0.91)
All other	5.11	10.01	7.59
	(37.47)	(52.81)	(32.33)
All causes	13.75	22.91	21.84
	(100.00)	(100.00)	(100.00)

Notes: 1. All cause-specific death rates are expressed per 1000 population, using constant denominators—being the respective rural and urban populations according to the 1941 census.
2. The figures in parentheses for the period 1937–41 are the respective percentage shares to total average annual deaths, whereas they are the respective percentage shares to total *excess* deaths for both 1943 and 1944. The excess deaths for each cause have been calculated over the respective average numbers during 1937–41.
3. The fever deaths are exclusive of malaria.

Sources: See Table 4.5.

It is interesting that while the time paths of the monthly MI in rural and urban areas were roughly similar, the composition of deaths responsible for such mortality differed quite markedly. Putting on one side the possibility of rural–urban differences in death reporting, this may imply that the seasonal pattern of famine mortality was less a matter of the seasonality of one or two specific epidemic diseases. In other words, such a common time pattern from several diseases is likely to be determined largely by the general course of economic distress and its lagged effects on human health, being only partly mediated by weather and environmental forces.

6. Rates of Stillbirth and Mortality Rates of Children Aged 1–12 Months, by Sex

Table 4.9 presents stillbirth and infant mortality rates for both pre-famine and famine years. It is striking that the rate of stillbirths seems to have *declined* slightly during the famine. This and other changes may partly be due to a deterioration in registration efficiency. The neo-natal mortality rates for both sexes also declined slightly during the famine period. The higher rate of stillbirths as well as neo-natal mortality males is quite clear.

TABLE 4.9

Rates of Stillbirths and Mortality Rates of Children Under One Year of Age, by Sex, Bengal 1936–45

		1936–40	1942	1943	1944	1945
Bengal						
a) Stillbirths per	M	4.6	3.9	3.6	3.6	3.3
100 livebirths	F	4.1	3.5	3.2	3.2	2.9
b) Deaths per 1000 livebirths						
below one month	M	100	87	92	96	81
	F	87	77	84	87	71
1–6 months	M	49	48	67	71	47
	F	46	45	67	73	44
6–12 months	M	25	24	39	42	21
	F	26	25	40	46	22
below one year	M	174	159	198	210	149
	F	159	147	192	205	137

		1939–41	1943	1944	1945
Rural Bengal					
a) Stillbirths per 100 livebirths		3.94	3.19	3.20	1.80
b) Deaths per 1000 livebirths					
below one month	M	92.5	90.6	95.8	79.5
	F	79.8	82.1	84.9	69.4

		1939–41	1943	1944	1945
1–6 months	M	46.4	66.1	70.4	45.6
	F	42.5	66.1	71.1	42.7
6–12 months	M	22.2	37.9	40.5	19.8
	F	22.6	38.7	43.4	21.0
below one year	M	161.1	194.6	206.7	144.9
	F	144.9	186.9	199.3	133.2

Urban Bengal

		1939–41	1943	1944	1945
a) Stillbirths per 100 livebirths		5.07	5.31	5.5	5.3
b) Deaths per 1000 livebirths					
below one month	M	88.0	127.1	127.8	102.9
	F	76.5	127.2	113.0	91.9
1–6 months	M	42.8	77.0	90.4	64.4
	F	42.9	87.1	97.5	68.9
6–12 months	M	39.6	54.5	70.5	38.6
	F	39.6	61.0	84.8	43.3
below one year	M	170.3	258.6	288.8	205.8
	F	163.2	275.5	295.3	204.1

Notes: 1. The mortality rates for female infants aged 1–6, 6–12 months and below one year for 1941 are excluded in the calculations of the respective rural and urban averages during 1939–41 because of some inconsistencies in the published figures.

2. The stillbirth rate for the towns was not available for 1939 or earlier years. They are only available from 1940. Also stillbirths for 1943–5 were expressed per 100 live + stillbirths.

Sources: See Table 4.5.

In contrast to stillbirth and neo-natal mortality, there was a considerable *rise* in mortality for infants of both sexes aged over one month during the famine. However, the possible partial effect of better registration operations in 1944 compared to 1943 should also be recognized. There is some suggestion that the mortality of older infants was most affected by the famine. And this was particularly true for females.[55]

[55] Recent research has provided evidence to support the existence of discrimination against female children in different parts of Bengal during both

Table 4.9 also includes data on rural–urban differentials. The registered stillbirth rate during both pre-famine and famine periods was much higher in the towns. Moreover, note that the *urban* stillbirth rate during the famine rose somewhat from its pre-famine level. Since a fall in the stillbirth rate during a famine is difficult to explain, this possibly reflects better registration of stillbirths in the towns and is indicative that stillbirths *do* increase in times of famines. Although the neo-natal mortality rates for both sexes during the pre-famine period were somewhat higher in rural areas than in towns, the extent of the pre-famine female neo-natal mortality advantage seems to be of similar magnitude. But during the famine while the rural neo-natal mortality rates showed a slight rise, the corresponding urban rates rose substantially. Again, this may be indicative that neo-natal mortality rates are indeed adversely affected by famines. The registered mortality rates of infants were higher in the towns compared to rural areas during both the baseline and famine periods. During the baseline period this differential appears to be the result of significantly higher recorded urban mortality for infants aged 6–12 months. Such rural–urban differentials probably have something to do with differential registration efficiency. But during the famine period urban infants of all age groups exhibit higher registered death rates than those in the rural areas. A part of the explanation probably lies in the migration from rural to urban areas of a large number of people—many of whom were mothers with their newborn children; deaths of such migrant infants may have contributed to our above rural–urban discrepancy.

We also examined the proportional rises in mortality rates of infants by age and sex in 1943 and 1944 for rural and urban areas. The proportionate rise in female, compared to male, neo-natal mortality seems to have been most pronounced in urban areas. But the proportional rise in neo-natal mortality for both males and females was relatively small in both towns and villages. This confirms our view that neo-nates are relatively protected from famine conditions. Infants aged 6–12 and 1–6 months seem to be more vulnerable; and female infants of these ages experienced

normal and crisis periods; see Chen et al. (1981), Bairagi (1986a, 1986b) and Sen and Sengupta (1983).

higher proportional rises in mortality than males, the sex differential being more pronounced in urban Bengal.

7. Differentials by Religion

Table 4.10 shows that the death rate in the pre-famine period was highest for Muslims, followed by Hindus, Buddhists, Christians and other classes in that order. A similar order holds for the pre-famine birth rates (save for a slightly higher CBR for Christians than for Buddhists). The registration data for 'other classes' (which include different tribes) were relatively deficient (see Table 4.10).[56] In 1944 the Hindu–Muslim differential in proportional mortality rise was relatively small. Thus, the Muslim community—having the most adverse mortality in normal times—appears to have experienced a smaller rise in famine mortality compared to Hindus.

As Table 4.10 suggests, while the Muslim community experienced a somewhat higher proportional rise in IMR during 1943–4 than did the Hindus, the highest proportional rises during 1944–5 were recorded for Christians. Moreover, except for Christians, recorded stillbirth rates for all communities appear to have declined during the famine. But the Christian stillbirth rate rose substantially. The reduced famine stillbirth ratios for most of the major communities probably reflects a deterioration in registration efficiency. Lower IMRs in 1945 than during 1940–1 for all communities (except Christians) could also reflect a decline in registration coverage. The greatest decline in births was recorded in 1944 for all religions—reflecting the reduction in conceptions in 1943, the year of maximum famine severity. It is notable that the Muslim community (having the highest birth rate during pre-famine period) experienced the greatest reduction in births, followed by the Hindus.

8. Age and Sex Differentials in Famine Mortality: The Rural–Urban Contrast

Table 4.11 presents age–sex specific death rates during both pre-famine and famine years for rural and urban areas. The normal

---

[56] In terms of proportional increases in the number of deaths in 1943 the Hindu community seems to have been the most vulnerable, followed successively by Muslims, Buddhists, and Christians.

TABLE 4.10

Vital Rates by Different Religious Communities, Bengal 1940–5

Period	CBR	Index	CDR	Index	Stillbirths per 1000 births	Index	IMR per 1000 livebirths	Index
HINDUS								
1940–1	31.5	100	21.5	100	33.1	100	148.8	100
1943	20.5	65	31.0	145	27.5	83	176.5	119
1944	17.4	55	28.4	132	28.6	86	192.0	129
1945	22.5	69	20.9	97	25.0	76	138.6	93
MUSLIMS								
1940–1	33.3	100	23.8	100	45.8	100	164.9	100
1943	18.0	54	32.6	137	38.0	83	212.6	129
1944	15.5	47	30.6	129	37.8	83	223.1	135
1945	22.3	67	21.6	91	33.0	72	146.7	89
CHRISTIANS								
1940–1	26.9	100	13.9	100	24.8	100	128.6	100
1943	21.4	80	22.9	165	32.9	133	161.7	126
1944	16.1	60	18.6	134	30.4	123	200.8	156
1945	21.3	79	15.6	112	30.0	121	180.7	141

		BUDDHISTS				
1940–1	25.0	100	21.1	100	42.3	100
1943	25.9	104	38.2	181	20.3	48
1944	18.4	74	27.0	123	26.9	64
1945	27.7	107	21.3	101	59.0	139
		OTHER CLASSES						
1942	16.6	100	10.9	100	27.9	100	150.4	100
1943	14.4	87	14.6	134	28.1	101	184.4	123
1944	10.5	63	13.0	119	27.8	100	168.8	112
1945	11.3	68	10.9	100	25.0	90	139.6	93

Notes: 1. All CDRs and CBRs (expressed per 1000 population) are calculated on the respective estimated mid-year populations.
2. For 'other classes' the years 1940 and 1941 could not be considered because of some inconsistencies in the published data.
3. The infant deaths in the Buddhist community were included in the Hindu community.

Sources: See Table 4.5.

TABLE 4.11

Death Rates by Age and Sex During the Pre-famine and Famine Years, Rural and Urban Bengal 1939–44

	Rural Bengal					
	1939–41		1943		1944	
Age	Male	Female	Male	Female	Male	Female
IMR	161.1	145.0	194.6	187.7	204.3	199.3
0–4	26.3	25.1	43.4	40.5	42.7	39.7
5–9	9.7	9.4	21.2	20.5	19.6	19.1
10–14	6.3	5.5	15.5	12.7	13.3	10.7
15–19	7.4	10.2	16.3	17.8	13.7	14.9
20–29	8.4	12.2	17.4	21.6	15.3	19.3
30–39	11.5	12.1	25.0	25.2	20.8	22.3
40–49	18.1	15.6	40.2	32.9	32.2	30.3
50–59	29.4	26.3	61.6	50.6	51.0	48.1
60+	77.9	66.2	125.6	108.2	116.2	107.5
CDR	19.5	19.2	35.7	31.6	30.1	29.1
Ratio*	1.0		1.1		1.0	
	Urban Bengal					
IMR	170.3	163.2	258.6	275.5	288.8	295.3
1–4	11.7	16.2	26.8	38.6	25.0	38.0
5–9	4.6	6.5	10.6	15.8	8.2	13.6
10–14	3.8	5.8	7.8	11.0	5.7	6.4
15–19	5.4	8.9	8.8	12.5	8.5	13.6
20–29	9.4	12.8	12.7	16.3	13.1	15.6
30–39	8.7	12.7	14.1	19.6	14.6	17.9
40–49	11.7	16.8	21.7	28.7	21.0	26.4
50–59	18.1	24.3	32.6	43.9	32.7	40.5
60+	36.9	60.4	80.6	127.7	75.5	130.3
CDR	11.6	16.6	19.8	28.4	19.3	26.4
Ratio*	0.70		0.70		0.73	

Notes: 1. All age-specific death rates have been calculated on constant denominators. As rural–urban breakdown of population by age and sex is not given in the 1941 census, the respective populations have been estimated on the basis of age distribution of the total sample population as per census of 1941. These estimated populations have been used as the constant denominators for calculating the above rates.

    * Ratio of male CDR to female CDR.

Sources: See Table 4.5.

age pattern of mortality in Bengal appears to have had the expected features, and they are shared by both rural and urban areas. However, the registered mortality for females, as compared to males, in urban areas seems strikingly high; note that for all age groups (except infants in the pre-famine period) in urban Bengal the registered female death rates were higher than the corresponding male death rates.

We have examined age and sex differentials in mortality in both 1943 and 1944 (compared with the average figures for 1939–41) separately for urban and rural areas (see Fig. 4.6). The results for rural Bengal are broadly in conformity with Dyson's findings for the whole of Bengal.[57] But some additional points arise. Considering rural areas, while in all age groups except infants, the male population experienced larger proportional mortality increases compared to females in 1943; in 1944 the female population over age 30 experienced larger increases *vis-à-vis* males (see Figs 4.6 (A) and (B)). Thus in 1943 there was a slightly higher overall proportional mortality rise for males, while in 1944 the rise in overall mortality was the same for both sexes. It may also be noted that for children aged 1–9 years no significant sex differential in proportional mortality rise was recorded in either 1943 or 1944. Nor was there any sex differential in mortality rates for these age groups during normal times. Moreover, the smaller proportional female mortality increase especially in the ages 15–30 in the famine years was probably a reflection of the reduced fertility and consequent drop in maternal and related deaths during the crisis.[58] Thus the overall age–sex pattern of proportional mortality increases in the Bengal famine broadly coincides with what we have previously found for the south, west and central (*vis-à-vis* northern) Indian famines. Like the famines in large parts of southern, central and western India (and, particularly unlike north-Indian famines), the Bengal famine does not appear to have been particularly harsh (in terms of proportional increase in mortality) towards young children and the female population.

[57] See Dyson (1991b), p. 284.

[58] The number of registered maternal deaths in rural Bengal indeed declined from an average of 13,490 during 1941–2 to 10,129 in 1943, and further to 9230 in 1944, although the maternal mortality rate per 1000 births rose from a pre-famine average of 8.75 during 1941–2 to 9.0 in 1943 and to 10.0 in 1944; see *Bengal Public Health Report*, relevant years.

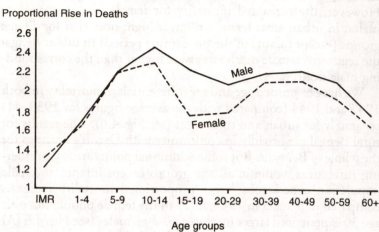

Rural Bengal 1943

Proportional Rise in Deaths

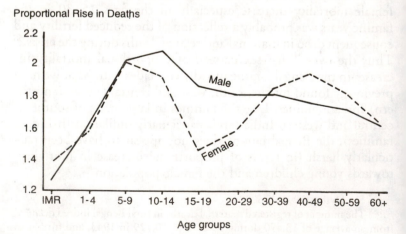

Rural Bengal 1944

Proportional Rise in Deaths

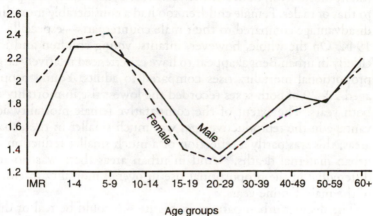

Urban Bengal 1943

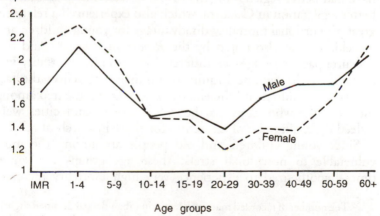

Urban Bengal 1944

FIG. 4.6 Ratios of Deaths in Famine Years to Reference Years,
by Age and Sex, Rural and Urban Bengal

Sources: See Table 4.11.

Interestingly, however, the pattern in urban areas seems to have been very different. Figures 4.6 (C) and (D) show that female infant mortality in both famine years rose considerably compared to that of males. Female children too had a considerable mortality disadvantage compared to their male counterparts—especially in 1944. On the whole, however, infants, young children and the elderly in urban Bengal appear to have experienced relatively large proportional mortality rises compared to adults. Young people aged 20–29 of both sexes recorded the lowest rise in mortality in both years. The extent of the comparative female mortality advantage in the reproductive ages was much smaller in the urban areas; this was partly a reflection of a much smaller reduction in urban maternal deaths.[59] And in urban areas there was no sex differential in the proportional rise in overall mortality in either of the main famine years.

The distinct urban pattern in Figure 4.6 could be real or due to data deficiencies. Although the *Bengal Public Health Reports* routinely comment upon differential registration between districts and between municipal towns, they do not provide any generalizations about relative registration completeness in rural and urban areas. If our interpretation of the IMR and stillbirth rates in Table 4.9 can be accepted, then urban areas seem to have had better registration than rural circles. The possibility of better registration in Calcutta, which also experienced a relatively great proportional mortality disadvantage for young children and the elderly, was also noted by the *Report on Bengal*.[60] And this Calcutta pattern of age–sex differentials in famine mortality was thought by the Famine Inquiry Commission to reflect the fact that young children and the elderly were over-represented among the migrants who came to the city.[61] Towns and cities were indeed the main poles of attraction for those in search of relief.[62]

Since young children and old people are among the most vulnerable to nutritional stress, these age groups are sometimes hypothesized to experience very high mortality increases

[59] The number of recorded maternal deaths in urban Bengal declined slightly from an average of 663 during 1941–2 to 603 in 1943, and then increased to 738 in 1944.

[60] See Famine Inquiry Commission (1945a), p. 113.

[61] Ibid., p. 113.

[62] See Greenough (1982), pp. 143–4.

compared to adults during famines.[63] But, on the other hand, these age groups also have relatively high mortality rates in normal times. And there is a considerable amount of evidence of lower proportionate rises in famine mortality among young children.[64] However, apropos the Bengal famine, Greenough provided an elaborate cultural explanation for such a pattern of age–sex mortality increase. He argues that females, young children and the elderly, who were generally dependent for their survival on the support of adult males, were ultimately 'abandoned' by the latter during the crisis. Greenough views this process as resulting largely from a moral impulse to maintain familial continuity through the preservation of the patrilineage. Critically, this depends upon the survival of the adult males, and this is the justification for 'the intentional exclusion of the less valued members (women and children) from domestic subsistence'. He adds that 'the favoured famine position of women' in adulthood results from the requirement of their giving birth to 'male descendants in the aftermath of the famine'.[65] All this is forwarded as an explanation for the relatively favoured mortality position of adults *vis-à-vis* children and elderly people.[66] But as a corollary one can suggest that females, young children and old people—all normally dependent for their livelihoods ultimately on adult males—were probably over-represented among destitutes who left home to seek relief in the towns. This probably accounts, at least, partly for the observed urban age–sex pattern of famine mortality shown in Figures 4.6 (C) and (D).[67]

[63] See, e.g. Greenough (1982) especially pp. 239–45.

[64] See chapter 2 above, Dyson (1991a and 1991b), and also Drèze and Sen (1989), especially p. 80 and the references cited there.

[65] See Greenough (1982), p. 251.

[66] The 'abandonment' of women and children has also been viewed as 'an effort to maximize the life chances of each and every member of the family in circumstances where co-residence was clearly not feasible'; see Appadurai (1984). As another alternative explanation, Agarwal has recently argued that smaller mortality increase (in absolute terms) for the adult males—*vis-à-vis* women and children—seems to relate to men's larger resource-bundles and more numerous 'fall-backs' at the beginning of the crisis, and moral codes (favouring adult males on the ground of familial continuity) may have been an ideological cover; see Agarwal (1990), pp. 384–92; see also Greenough (1992).

[67] The following sentences quoted from the *Report on Bengal* succinctly describe the familial crisis during the famine: 'Famine and migration led to

9. Conclusions

The Bengal famine was undoubtedly a great catastrophe. Its special significance in the history of Indian famines lies in the fact that it broke a fairly long spell of freedom from major famines. Although the existing literature on the demographic consequences of the famine is substantial, our use of the hitherto unutilized detailed demographic data (e.g. the registration materials for undivided Bengal) have brought to light several important findings.

This famine certainly occurred under a unique set of circumstances largely related to war-induced inflation, and very inefficient management of prices and food distribution. Since this crisis, unlike some earlier famines, was not directly caused by a drought and food shortage as such, it is a classic example of what is often termed a 'class famine'.[68] Prices were elevated in as early as 1941; and still higher prices in 1942 led to a further deterioration in economic conditions. Prices rose dramatically from the beginning of 1943, and reached a maximum in August (see also Appendix D). Mortality began to rise above its normal level from the middle of 1943; *proportional excess* mortality peaked in October (see Fig. 4.2). The main famine mortality peak was roughly of 12 months duration: July 1943 to June 1944. However, the mortality level did not return to 'normal' until the middle of 1945 (see Fig. 4.2).

While the quantum of excess deaths in the Bengal famine has been an issue of long-standing debate, Amartya Sen's recent estimate, based on the 1951 census publications for both West Bengal and East Bengal, appears to have been most influential.

---

much family disintegration. Husbands deserted wives and wives husbands; elderly dependents were left behind in the villages; babies and young children were sometimes abandoned. According to a survey carried out in Calcutta during the latter half of 1943, some breaking up of the family had occurred in about half the destitute population which reached the city'; see Famine Inquiry Commission (1945a), p. 68.

[68] See, e.g. Alamgir (1980), p. 14. The *Report on Bengal*, attributing the famine primarily to an 'enormous' rise in the rice price, states that '[l]arger landholders benefitted from the situation, since they could sell most of their rice at an enormous profit. . . . The famine thus principally affected one section of the community—the poor classes in rural areas'; see Famine Inquiry Commission (1945a), pp. 67–8. Emphasizing the Government's non-priority in tackling the crisis, Arnold labels it as a 'political famine'; see Arnold (1988), p. 97.

However, our newly found registration materials for undivided Bengal cast doubt on these previous data. Applying Sen's procedures to the new data for undivided Bengal yields estimates of 1.8 to 1.9 million excess deaths. But taking account of the pre-famine declining trend in the death rate, a figure of about 2.1 million seems more correct.

As Figure 4.2 suggests, the nature of short-term fertility responses during the Bengal famine was broadly similar to that found in former Indian famines. However, in the case of the Bengal famine a considerable reduction in conceptions occurred remarkably early especially compared to the prime period of famine mortality. This probably matched the prolonged period of rising prices and other disruptions brought about by the war.

While malaria and fever together accounted for the largest part of total mortality in normal times, malaria increased its dominance still further during the famine. However, epidemics of cholera and smallpox were also quite important in famine mortality. The cholera mortality peak preceded the malaria (and fever and dysentery/diarrhoea) peak by two months (see Fig. 4.4). The sequence of mortality peaks from cholera and fever seen here (Fig. 4.4) has been found in most of the earlier Indian famines (see especially chapters 2 and 3 above). Peak cholera mortality is often thought to occur in the phase of maximum social disruption from famine (e.g. wandering, congregations in relief camps, etc.). In the Bengal famine, relief works and camps were far from significant, and wandering in search of work was also very limited. However, movement of destitutes towards towns and cities was considerable—especially after September 1943 when relief policy began to shift towards food distribution. Thus it is notable that cholera deaths culminated during the period of maximum provision of food relief (October–November), which at the same time marked the maximum (proportionate) rise in overall mortality. It should be stressed here that food relief became significant only after famine mortality was already very high.[69]

---

[69] As the *Report on Bengal* notes, 'Distribution of food on a large scale was not begun, except in isolated areas as a result of local initiative, until September—several months after the need for it had arisen. With prices of rice soaring to unheard of levels, relief in the form of small payments of money, whether given gratuitously, as agricultural loans, or as test relief in return for work, could

While post-monsoon environmental factors (e.g. increased surface water), which contributed to the usual elevation of malaria (and fever) mortality in the later months of normal years, may have helped to aggravate excess malaria mortality in late 1943, the overall dimensions of malaria mortality during the prime famine period cannot be dissociated from the basic fact of acute nutritional deficiency on a mass scale.

The urban cause composition of excess deaths differed from the rural pattern partly as a result of differences found even in normal times, and partly due to the fact that urban Bengal recorded the deaths of large numbers of migrant destitutes. Despite rural–urban differences in the cause composition of deaths, the time pattern of excess mortality was similar between rural and urban areas. This reinforces our view that the general course of mortality increase was largely determined by the effects (somewhat lagged) of large-scale nutritional stress and debilitation on human health, while the exact timing of peak excess mortality was partly shaped by both the usual seasonal influences and the various social disruptions (e.g. population movements).

The Muslim community—normally having the highest death rate—appears to have experienced a relative advantage in terms of proportional rise in mortality (especially compared with the Hindus). However the Muslim community—having the highest fertility in normal times—experienced the greatest reduction in births.

While rural registration data exhibit no adverse effects on stillbirth rates during the famine, there has been a very marginal rise in the urban rate of stillbirth. The suggestion is that famine's effect on stillbirths is, though probably adverse, not pronounced. Neo-natal mortality appears to have been relatively protected compared with the mortality of infants beyond the neo-natal stage (see Table 4.9).[70] As has been noted earlier the rise in infant mortality may be related to both 'pre-natal exposure' to famine

---

do little to relieve distress. Food was required'; see Famine Inquiry Commission (1945a), p. 99.

[70] A similar conclusion has also been reached in the context of the Bangladesh famine of 1974–5; see Razzaque et al. (1990) and Chen and Chowdhury (1977). Remember that present-day Bangladesh was included in undivided Bengal until partition in 1947.

(e.g. through maternal nutritional stress) and post-natal conditions (e.g. through nutritional deficiencies, poor care etc.).[71] In this context, a greater proportional rise in female infant mortality seems to indicate an anti-female discriminatory bias in both food and parental care during the Bengal famine.[72] However, compared to other ages, infants of both sexes in rural areas seem to have constituted the least vulnerable group. We have also found a relative mortality advantage in the famine for young children of both sexes in rural Bengal, while older children and adults appear to have experienced comparatively large proportional increase in mortality. But, interestingly, this was not so in urban Bengal (see Fig. 4.6). Urban infants appeared to be more vulnerable than adults, and female infants seemed to be most vulnerable. Young children and elderly people in urban Bengal experienced relatively large proportional rises in mortality, while adult mortality was least affected by famine. But this urban pattern probably also reflects the influence of rural–urban migration on the numbers of registered deaths by age.

[71] See Stein et. al (1975), especially pp. 153–63.

[72] A similar pattern of sex discrimination among infants during the Bangladesh famine of 1974–5 has also been indicated; see Razzaque et al. (1990). See also D'Souza and Chen (1980).

5

Regional Variation in the Demographic Impact of the Bengal Famine and Famine Effects Elsewhere

1. Introduction

In the last chapter we analysed the demography of the Bengal famine at an aggregate provincial level. But data contained in the *Bengal Public Health Reports* enable an examination of effects at much lower levels of disaggregation. Accordingly, this chapter focuses on the regional demographic dimensions of the famine, with particular emphasis on the district level. It also examines broad demographic experiences in two other affected provinces, namely Orissa (an adjoining territory) and Madras.

An inter-district analysis is useful because it throws light on the relative importance of various factors which are commonly thought to shape the demographic consequences of the famines (e.g. the extent of crop failure, food availability, relief provision, ecology, migration and so on). The famine in Orissa was caused in much the same way as in Bengal (i.e. through war-induced inflation and sharp increase in food prices). Yet Orissa was affected 'to a much less serious extent'.[1] Moreover, as an adjacent province, Orissa felt some of the indirect effects of the famine in Bengal (e.g. through inter-provincial migration). The famine in Madras during 1943–4 also occurred largely because of war-related circumstances (e.g. disruptions in food availability and inflation). But again the Madras crisis did not develop into a mortality crisis of a scale comparable to that in Bengal. Thus it is of some interest to compare the broad demographic experiences of Bengal, Orissa, and Madras.

[1] See Famine Inquiry Commission (1945a), p. 1.

2. A Pre-famine Profile of Regional Demographic Variation in Bengal

An examination of pre-famine regional demographic variation and related conditions in Bengal is a useful background for an understanding of the spatial demographic consequences of the famine. For example, district-level changes in deaths and births, particularly if examined in proportional terms during the famine, may be partly dependent on the pre-famine baseline levels of the death and birth rates: the higher the baseline level, the lower may be the scope for a further proportional rise. More importantly, pre-existing regional differentials in ecology, environment and socioeconomic conditions can be expected to have played some role in determining the spatial dimensions of the famine. However, district-level detailed data on many relevant variables are lacking. Table 5.1 provides averages of several demographic measures in

TABLE 5.1

Some Pre-famine Demographic Measures for the Four Natural Zones of Bengal, 1940–1

District/ Division	CDR	CBR	IMR	CDR from malaria	CDR from fever	Male death rate as % of female death rate
Western Bengal (Burdwan division)						
Burdwan	20.9	28.8	162.1	8.2 (62)	13.2	101
Birbhum	22.9	35.7	162.8	8.2 (51)	16.1	106
Bankura	20.9	30.7	151.7	4.7 (38)	12.6	107
Midnapore	17.1	28.2	126.6	4.8 (48)	10.1	103
Hooghly	16.7	28.8	142.0	5.1 (66)	7.7	94
Howrah	11.5	22.0	125.2	0.7 (22)	3.3	93
Division	**18.2**	**28.9**	**145.1**	**5.3 (48)**	**10.6**	**100**
Central Bengal (Presidency division)						
24-Parganas	15.3	27.6	125.4	2.0 (26)	7.6	93
Nadia	26.0	35.1	178.4	17.3 (86)	20.1	100
Murshidabad	19.5	36.3	134.5	9.1 (66)	13.9	99

(*cont.*)

Table 5.1 (*cont.*)

District/ Division	CDR	CBR	IMR	CDR from malaria	CDR from fever	Male death rate as % of female death rate
Jessore	25.3	27.0	194.1	17.5 (86)	20.5	101
Khulna	17.7	26.3	143.8	5.2 (52)	9.7	100
Division	**20.2**	**29.9**	**155.2**	**9.3 (71)**	**13.6**	**98**
Northern Bengal (Rajshahi division)						
Rajshahi	25.3	32.3	219.3	16.8 (83)	20.3	98
Dinajpur	19.1	26.2	191.3	8.8 (63)	14.0	100
Jalpaiguri	26.3	33.4	169.8	7.7 (51)	15.1	87
Darjeeling	29.5	32.4	129.5	7.4 (44)	16.7	95
Rangpur	22.9	32.2	169.3	10.9 (60)	18.2	99
Bogra	19.6	26.2	198.9	10.4 (72)	14.5	98
Pabna	25.4	25.8	217.7	14.5 (72)	20.2	100
Malda	12.8	19.3	178.3	8.8 (82)	10.8	111
Division	**22.1**	**28.5**	**184.3**	**11.2 (66)**	**16.6**	**98**
Eastern Bengal (Dacca and Chittagong divisions)						
Dacca	16.5	29.2	142.5	2.5 (26)	9.4	108
Mymensingh	19.4	27.0	168.1	7.7 (54)	14.2	99
Faridpur	22.7	29.4	170.9	8.9 (58)	15.5	104
Bakarganj	20.3	27.0	164.6	3.6 (33)	10.9	104
Chittagong	22.6	26.8	130.2	4.3 (24)	17.9	106
Noakhali	17.5	26.4	120.2	2.0 (18)	11.0	98
Tippera	16.8	30.9	134.2	1.9 (21)	8.3	102
Division	**19.1**	**28.2**	**147.2**	**4.7 (35)**	**12.2**	**103**

Notes: 1. All data relate to rural areas.
2. All death and birth rates, expressed per 1000 population, are based on the constant denominators—being the respective populations according to the 1941 census.
3. The fever deaths include malaria.
4. The figures in parentheses are the respective percentage shares of malarial deaths to total deaths from fever.

Sources: Government of Bengal, Health Directorate, *Bengal Public Health Report*, Alipore, Government Press, various years.

1940–1 for 26 districts. It will be noticed that these districts were traditionally classified into four natural divisions of Bengal.[2] Since 1942 was itself a year of partial calamity, and is often considered as marking the start of the famine, we have not included it in calculating these pre-famine average measures.

It is clear from Table 5.1 that there was considerable regional variation in the registered pre-famine vital rates. At the divisional level, western and eastern Bengal appear to have been relatively favoured regions in mortality terms. Death rates were significantly higher in northern Bengal. Divisional variation in the CBR, however, was much smaller than that for the CDR. The average registered IMRs for the four divisions quite distinctively show their classification in terms of relative mortality levels.

The divisional vital rates, of course, conceal much intra-divisional variation. While the district of Darjeeling registered the highest CDR (29.5), Howrah recorded the lowest (11.5); the coefficient of variation of the CDR across the 26 districts is 0.21. The degree of variation in the CBR is much smaller; the corresponding coefficient of variation being only 0.14. Notice that the IMR in Darjeeling is very low in view of the fact that it recorded the highest CDR. Conversely, the registered IMR in Malda is strikingly high given that it was the district with the second lowest CDR (see Table 5.1). Such non-correspondence between IMR and CDR variation may have resulted partly from differential biases in death registration. However, we cannot exclude the possibility that such discrepancies may have been partly real, reflecting for example regional variations in the age structures of the populations.

Table 5.1 also provides data on death rates from both malaria and fevers (inclusive of malaria). Despite likely imperfections in death reporting, these data seem useful as a guide to regional variation in the malaria ecology of Bengal. There appears to have been a very significant degree of variation in death rates from malaria which probably broadly reflected regional variation in malaria endemicity. Given the possibility that in some districts

---

[2] Throughout this chapter the district-level demographic data refer to rural areas; so, the city of Calcutta, which constituted another district, is not shown. As indicated earlier (in chapter 4), since most of Bengal's population lived in rural areas, conclusions drawn for rural Bengal should remain unaltered if towns (the majority of which were very small) are included.

malaria deaths may have been more likely to be classified as 'fevers', the proportions of malaria to total fever deaths may serve as a better indicator of malaria endemicity. Table 5.1 suggests that the zones which experienced relatively adverse mortality were also heavily malarious. Both the malarial death rates and the shares of malaria in total fever mortality were significantly higher in the central and northern divisions.

TABLE 5.2
Correlation Coefficient Matrix with Some District-level Demographic Measures for Bengal, 1940–1 (As Presented in Table 5.1)

	CBR	CDR from malaria	CDR from fever	% of malaria to fever deaths	IMR	Male CDR as % of female CDR
CDR	0.59*	0.65**	0.87**	0.38#	0.44*	–0.16
CBR		0.27	0.41*	0.11	–0.02	–0.17
CDR from malaria			0.85**	0.89**	0.82**	0.00
CDR from fever				0.60*	0.66**	0.09
% of malaria to fever deaths					0.76**	0.02
IMR						0.08

Notes: ** significant at 0.01 per cent level.
* significant at 1 per cent level.
# significant at 5 per cent level.

Sources: For data used see Table 5.1.

It is useful to examine the degree of association between these different measures, taking all the districts together. In this context Table 5.2 presents the correlation matrix for all these district-level measures which are given in Table 5.1. It generally confirms our previous conclusions. First, there are very strong positive correlations between the levels of the CDR and the death rates from both malaria and fevers. Again, there are somewhat lower positive correlations between the share of malaria to total fever mortality, and the CDRs and IMRs. All this suggests that the differential pattern of malarial incidence was indeed an important determinant of the overall regional pattern of mortality during normal times. Moreover, a positive correlation is found between the CDR and the CBR. While malaria is known to produce fertility reducing effects, this positive relation may partly be the reflection of inter-district differentials in registration coverage.

In view of the very prominent part played by malaria during the famine (as we have seen in the last chapter), inter-regional differences in malaria ecology are worth considering. As far back as the 1910s and 1920s the eastern part of Bengal—being 'a land of open drainage and active rivers'—was identified as a less malarious zone. This contrasted with the relatively more malarious central and western divisions which were characterized by the poorly drained moribund delta of the Ganges, and large flood plains including that of the Damodar river. The Himalayan foothills in the north were generally considered 'the most intensively malarious zone'.[3] The favoured malaria ecology of eastern Bengal is clearly reflected in the very low registered malaria mortality during 1940–1 in the districts such as Chittagong, Tippera, Dacca and Bakarganj (see Table 5.1).

In 1925, in his celebrated work on the relationship between agriculture and malaria, Bentley noted that 'as a broad fact only between 58 and 60 per cent of the cultivable area in Central and West Bengal is under cultivation while in the less malarial eastern portion the percentage is 90'.[4] However, an examination by Klein of malarial cycles in different districts of Bengal at different times suggests that 'the prevalence of malaria was related to economic, geological, and ecological conditions, all of which interacted on each other'.[5] Overall, Bengal experienced a significant decline in mortality during the 1930s, and this has been shown to have been largely due to improving malaria mortality. Interestingly, however, during the 1930s the significant fall in recorded malaria mortality was restricted largely to endemic malarious zones (i.e. western, central and northern Bengal). But there was no real decline in malaria in the eastern parts which were already less malarious and

---

[3] See Chowdhury (1989), p. 28, and Dutta and Dutta (1978), p. 77.
[4] Quoted in Famine Inquiry Commission (1945b), p. 170.
[5] See Klein (1972), p. 143.

relatively favoured in terms of mortality.[6] Thus, while the decline in mortality at the all-Bengal level during the 1920s and 1930s seems to have conformed to the general downward trend in all-India mortality[7] there were differential rates of decline across the different divisions of Bengal. This fact produced a departure from the earlier regional pattern of mortality. In particular, by 1940–1 the *western* division appears to have been a relatively favoured mortality zone compared to the *eastern* and the other divisions. A close comparison of Bentley's map of malaria endemicity for Bengal in 1916 with a similar map constructed for 1948 indicates a significant reduction in malaria endemicity in western Bengal.[8] Note also from Table 5.1 that in both the central and northern divisions (i.e. those with the highest death rates) there seem to have been a male mortality advantage which was not present in the two other zones. With all this as background, we now examine the regional variation in the demographic impact of the famine.

3. Inter-district Variation in Mortality Effects

The Bengal famine was widespread. In fact, no district entirely escaped distress. However, as we shall see, all regions were not affected uniformly in respect of both timing and severity. Some districts began to endure famine distress earlier than others, while some experienced a lesser degree of famine severity. Regional diversity in the demographic impact results from a complex set of interactions between local economic, environmental, ecological and infrastructural factors, and also from the effects of migration. Thus, while inter-relationships between measures of famine distress (e.g. undernutrition, starvation, etc.) and mortality can be, and indeed have been, relatively easily examined using household- or individual-level data,[9] an attempt to establish such relations at the district level is fraught with difficulties.

Our prime concern here is to examine the regional *pattern* of mortality rise (rather than to estimate district-level excess deaths). In doing so, averages of 1940 and 1941 are taken to be the

[6] See Chowdhury (1989), Table 11, p. 30.

[7] See Davis (1951).

[8] For Bentley's original map for 1916, see Dutta and Dutta (1978), p. 81; for the 1948 version, see Akhtar and Learmonth (1986), p. 109.

[9] See, e.g. Mahalanobis et al. (1946), Mukherji (1965) and also Sen (1981).

reference levels for calculating the increases in mortality. Table 5.3 presents districtwise percentage rises in deaths for the six half-yearly sub-periods between January 1943 and December 1945. As can be seen, during the first half of 1943 most districts experienced little change in mortality—there were even improvements in some districts (see Table 5.3). But the predominantly coastal districts of Midnapore, Chittagong, Khulna and Noakhali—which were hit by the October cyclone in 1942—did experience early rises in mortality during the first half of 1943, as too did Tippera (which is adjacent to Noakhali). On the whole, the east of Bengal appears to have experienced a comparatively early rise in mortality. However, it was only during the last half of 1943 that all the districts experienced mortality rises and in many the proportional increases were huge. In the first six months of 1944, the mortality elevation continued but with some moderation. During the last six months of 1944 there was a further reduction in excess mortality—save in a few districts, particularly the two adjacent districts of Malda and Dinajpur. In the first half of 1945 some districts experienced rises in mortality, while some showed a further decline. Consequently, in percentage terms, the overall rise in excess mortality in Bengal stayed much the same between the last half of 1944 and the first half of 1945 (see Table 5.3). However, in the last half of 1945 most districts experienced a considerable decline—with the notable exception of Malda. While in some districts (e.g. Howrah, Murshidabad and Birbhum) elevated mortality, though declining, continued up to the end of 1945, only Malda and Dinajpur actually experienced a major mortality peak during the last half of 1944.

The eastern division on the whole appears to have experienced a relatively fast recovery (see Table 5.3). Indeed, a fairly sharp improvement in mortality in the eastern zone during the last half of 1945 is particularly noticeable. The main famine death peak in most districts of Bengal seems to have lasted from about July 1943 to about June 1944 (see Table 5.3). At the divisional level, the highest proportional mortality increase during this prime period of mortality was actually recorded by eastern Bengal—followed by the western, central and northern divisions in that order.

The ranks of the districts in terms of percentage mortality rise during the six half-yearly sub-periods (i.e. January–June 1943 to July–December 1945) are quite similar. A matrix of Spearman's

TABLE 5.3

Inter-district Variation in Mortality Rise in Bengal, January 1943–December 1945

Districts	Percentage rise in deaths over the average of 1940 and 1941						
	1943		1944		1945		July 1943–
	Jan.–June	July–Dec.	Jan.–June	July–Dec.	Jan.–June	July–Dec.	June 1944
Burdwan	−14.68	72.48	48.00	20.12	6.53	−7.73	60.35
Birbhum	−10.19	164.71	107.78	56.18	33.34	31.35	136.64
Bankura	−13.33	119.21	33.29	9.55	13.42	−12.04	77.74
Midnapore	37.14	229.44	73.99	28.91	16.15	2.92	155.70
Hooghly	−14.05	63.92	34.02	30.76	35.39	2.62	49.24
Howrah	14.84	203.76	137.49	92.77	58.36	57.56	168.76
Western Bengal	**4.30**	**150.70**	**67.60**	**32.40**	**21.61**	**6.00**	**110.11**
24-Parganas	−6.16	177.10	100.61	24.80	17.37	−5.67	138.13
Nadia	−2.43	140.77	70.49	14.68	35.91	−6.72	109.28
Murshidabad	−1.21	212.93	105.87	64.19	77.66	37.53	161.54
Jessore	−10.74	27.19	39.57	−12.34	5.58	−32.89	32.74
Khulna	21.38	34.34	41.00	1.18	13.58	−7.73	37.18
Central Bengal	**−1.19**	**111.32**	**71.46**	**15.01**	**27.71**	**−6.43**	**92.89**
Rajshahi	5.46	71.72	36.14	6.71	44.50	−0.38	55.18
Dinajpur	1.17	25.85	59.68	81.25	55.03	44.69	42.67
Jalpaiguri	5.69	61.62	25.93	47.69	29.51	15.57	44.66

Darjeeling	-4.18	20.21	7.47	12.81	8.45	5.40	13.83
Rangpur	20.53	121.26	145.99	47.86	16.41	7.57	132.76
Bogra	3.62	62.68	91.18	42.43	59.62	23.23	75.30
Pabna	-12.68	56.41	60.83	16.01	26.82	-42.72	58.37
Malda	-46.72	69.16	100.66	184.25	57.58	111.11	87.58
Northern Bengal	**1.44**	**71.52**	**77.51**	**39.73**	**35.76**	**9.92**	**74.36**
Dacca	0.39	216.35	139.57	18.85	19.38	-12.81	178.02
Mymensingh	12.75	92.91	114.13	35.02	39.16	-9.74	102.64
Faridpur	-11.48	110.87	63.13	-17.61	-11.29	-41.89	88.59
Bakarganj	1.27	77.70	52.77	-3.08	-4.12	-16.38	64.93
Chittagong	37.26	193.90	28.38	-3.03	-8.14	-29.65	110.76
Noakhali	31.25	138.73	83.28	1.16	7.96	-22.08	112.62
Tippera	29.02	231.39	118.02	15.23	10.33	-16.60	176.42
Eastern Bengal	**12.14**	**142.82**	**90.14**	**10.52**	**11.02**	**-19.64**	**117.40**
All-Bengal	**6.07**	**121.04**	**80.39**	**21.66**	**21.42**	**-6.25**	**101.62**

Sources: See Table 5.1.

rank correlation coefficients for these sub-periods is presented in Table 5.4. The coefficients between adjacent sub-periods are respectively 0.36, 0.60, 0.51, 0.79, and 0.74. Note that correlations become even stronger during the later phase of famine. And there is some suggestion that the relationship extended beyond immediately adjacent periods; thus, for example, districts which experienced relatively high mortality increases in July–December 1944 also tended to experience relatively great mortality increases during July–December 1945. However, the ranks are not significantly correlated beyond one year. This probably reflects the fact that with the passage of time the pattern of epidemics tended to reorder districts in terms of mortality.

TABLE 5.4

Rank Correlation Coefficients (Spearman) Matrix for the Districts in Terms of Proportional Mortality Increases in the Six Half-yearly Sub-periods, January 1943–December 1945

	Jan.–June '43	July–Dec. '43	Jan.–June '44	July–Dec. '44	Jan.–June '45
July–Dec. '43	0.36#				
Jan.–June '44	0.19	0.60*			
July–Dec. '44	−0.07	0.10	0.51*		
Jan.–June '45	−0.07	−0.02	0.37	0.79**	
July–Dec. '45	−0.03	−0.05	0.22	0.84**	0.74**

Notes: ** significant at 0.1 per cent level.
    * significant at less than 1 per cent level.
    # significant at less than 5 per cent level.

Source: For data used see Table 5.3.

Since there is evidently significant inter-district variation within each division in Table 5.3, it is useful to classify the districts into groups in terms of their proportionate increases in mortality during the prime famine period. Accordingly the districts have been classified as follows:

Group A (very severely affected): Those experiencing more than 150 per cent rise in mortality during the period July 1943 to June 1944: Midnapore, Howrah, Murshidabad, Dacca, and Tippera.

Group B (severely affected): Districts experiencing 100–150 per cent rise in mortality: Birbhum, 24-Parganas, Nadia, Rangpur, Mymensingh, Chittagong, and Noakhali.

Group C (moderately affected): Districts experiencing 50–100 per cent rise in mortality: Burdwan, Bankura, Rajshahi, Bogra, Pabna, Malda, Bakarganj, and Faridpur.

Group D (slightly affected): Districts experiencing less than 50 per cent rise in mortality: Hooghly, Jessore, Khulna, Dinajpur, Jalpaiguri, and Darjeeling.

Using this classification Figure 5.1 illustrates the regional distribution of deaths during the peak mortality period from July 1943 to June 1944. It may be noted that the same fourfold classification as used above in terms of percentage rise in mortality during July–December 1943 as compared to the corresponding period during 1938–42 was employed in an official memorandum submitted to the Famine Inquiry Commission by the Department of Public Health and Local Self-Government (Medical) of the Government of Bengal.[10] Although these two classifications do not match with each other exactly, they are reasonably close and comparable.

It is of interest to compare the above classification with the subdivisional classifications that were provided separately at the time by two official departments of the Bengal Government, namely the Departments of Industries and Revenue.[11] The precise criteria used (or the exact time period referred to) for their fourfold classifications of districts in terms of severity are not explicitly mentioned in either of these Departments' reports.[12] However, in general, the 'most severely affected' category in both reports roughly corresponds to our classification (except for Murshidabad which emerges as a very severely affected district only in our classification). However, those districts classed as

[10] See Pinnell's Papers, Memorandum No. 14, p. 63.

[11] Government of Bengal (1944a, b).

[12] For example, as Greenough has remarked, 'The criteria adopted by the Industries Department in determining the impact of famine on the subdivisions were not stated clearly in the Plea for Rehabilitation (1944), but mortality was not the only or even the main criterion; apparently subdivisional officers and other district officers and other district officials were asked to form personal estimates of famine severity'; see Greenough (1982), p. 142.

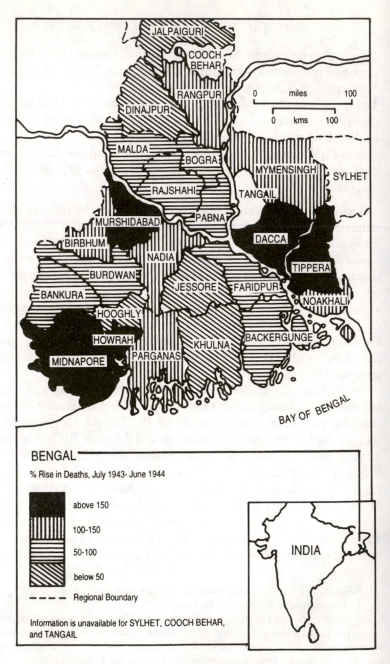

FIG. 5.1 Regional Pattern of Percentage Rises in Deaths in
Bengal: July 1943–June 1944, Districts of Bengal

Sources: See Table 5.3.

'severely affected' do not correspond well between the various classifications. Mymensingh, for example, is considered as a 'severely affected' district according to both the Industries Department's report and our classification, but not according to the Revenue Department's report. Again, Khulna and Jessore were classed as 'severely affected' districts only by the Industries Department report whereas they were not so labelled according to both the Revenue Department report and our grouping. All this indicates that the criteria for identifying district-level severity were not solely based on excess mortality.[13] On the whole the impression one derives from the classification made by the Industries Department is that famine severity in eastern Bengal was more widespread and acute than in western Bengal. But neither our classification (based exclusively on excess mortality) nor that of the Revenue Department support such a conclusion.

In this connection, it seems appropriate to examine the issue of whether there was a genuine difference in the post-famine time span of elevated mortality between West and East Bengal. We have already seen (from Fig. 4.1 in the preceding chapter) that the registration data for the whole of the province do not indicate any excess mortality beyond 1945. However, the data from the 1951 West Bengal census report used by Sen did show elevated mortality for West Bengal up to at least 1946. Since the procedure by which deaths in divided districts (i.e. those which were partly allocated to West Bengal) were carved out by the 1951 West Bengal census report, was unsatisfactory (see section 3 of chapter 4 above, and also Appendix B), we can simply ignore the division of these districts in deriving registered deaths for West and East Bengal. The numbers of annual registered deaths so derived are given in Table 5.5 on the basis of excluding the four divided districts (Nadia, Dinajpur, Jalpaiguri and Malda) from the calculations. In view of Sen's use of data for 1941 and 1942 to represent the pre-famine situation, it is interesting that West Bengal indeed recorded a reduction in registered deaths from 1941 to 1942. Yet, East Bengal (and the province as a whole) experienced an increase. Also, Table 5.5 shows that in

---

[13] Sen also found significant discrepancy between these official 'diagnoses' of famine severity and excess mortality rankings of districts in West Bengal; see Sen (1981), p. 208.

TABLE 5.5
*Number of Registered Deaths in Bengal, East and
West Bengal 1941–6*

Year	Bengal	West Bengal	Index	East Bengal	Index
1941	1,184,850	316,102		743,031	
		(381,934)			
1942	1,222,164	285,493		820,955	
		(343,568)			
Average					
1941–2	1,203,507	300,797	100	781,993	100
		(362,751)	(100)		
1943	1,908,622	530,813	176	1,204,146	154
		(622,235)	(172)		
1944	1,726,870	471,324	156	1,056,859	135
		(577,757)	(159)		
1945	1,238,133	360,696	120	711,094	91
		(447,130)	(123)		
1946	1,068,996	–	–	–	–
		(414,687)	(114)		

Notes: 1. The numbers of deaths for West and East Bengal above have been calculated by ignoring four districts (namely Nadia, Dinajpur, Jalpaiguri, and Malda) which were split in 1947.

2. The figures in parentheses are the respective numbers of deaths for West Bengal as given in the Appendix to the 1951 census of India publication. These figures, however, do include deaths in the above four divided districts falling in West Bengal, but they differ from those given in the main text (which were used by Sen) (for details see Appendix B).

3. The numbers of deaths in West and East Bengal do not add up to those for undivided Bengal because the latter are inclusive of deaths in the above four districts.

4. The registered deaths for undivided Bengal in 1946 were designated as 'provisional'; and the number of registered deaths in the districts of undivided Bengal in 1946 are not available because the *Bengal Public Health Report* published for 1946 covered only *West* Bengal.

Sources: For total registered deaths in Bengal and in West and East Bengal (with above four districts being excluded) from 1941 to 1945, Government of Bengal, Health Directorate, *Bengal Public Health Report*, Alipore, various years; for registered deaths in Bengal in 1946, *Annual Report of the Public Health Commissioner with the Government of India for 1946*, New Delhi, 1948. For the figures in parentheses, see Appendix IV Census of India 1951, vol. VI, part 1B, *Vital Statistics, West Bengal 1941–50*, New Delhi, Manager of Publications, 1952, pp. 67–8.

West Bengal registered deaths did not return to pre-famine levels even by 1946, whereas East Bengal experienced an improvement in 1945. So, although the data for West Bengal used by Sen were defective, as we have already indicated, his finding of a prolonged post-famine mortality tail in West Bengal appears to be correct. So too may have been the suggestion from the data which he used that registered deaths in West Bengal actually *fell* between 1941 and 1942.[14] On the other hand, these data in Table 5.5 also suggest that the proportional rise in registered deaths in West Bengal during the famine was higher than in East Bengal.[15] This poses an interesting problem.

Among Bengal's four natural divisions during the pre-famine decades, eastern Bengal was a relatively favoured mortality zone (particularly compared to northern Bengal) (see Table 5.1). As we have seen this was at least partly due to a comparatively low incidence of malaria in eastern Bengal.[16] But these pre-partition natural divisions (into 'eastern Bengal' and 'western Bengal') do not correspond geographically to the East–West political partition of Bengal in 1947 (which forms the basis of Table 5.5). Several districts (or more precisely large parts of districts) of post-partition East Bengal (or what became East Pakistan) came from the pre-partition 'Northern' and 'Central' divisions of Bengal.[17]

Before the famine, post-partition East Bengal generally did not experience either favoured mortality or a lower malaria incidence compared to West Bengal. For example, excluding (as above) the four split districts from our calculations, the average death rate during 1940–1 was actually higher in East Bengal (23.3) than in West Bengal (18.2). Moreover, the average death rate from malaria during 1938–42 was, in fact, much higher in East Bengal (7.8 per 1000 population) than in West Bengal (4.9).

[14] See Dyson and Maharatna (1991), Table 1, p. 283.

[15] The lower mortality rise in East Bengal where Muslims were a majority (70.3 per cent of the total population according to the 1941 census) appears to be consistent with our finding that the Muslim community experienced a relatively low proportional rise in mortality compared to Hindus (see Table 4.10).

[16] See Chowdhury (1989) and Klein (1972).

[17] Since 1947 (the year of independence and partition) the eastern wing of Pakistan was officially called East Bengal until the constitution of Pakistan, passed in March 1956, designated it as the Province of East Pakistan.

Indeed, large parts of both moribund deltaic areas (which were very malarious) and the endemic malarious northern division (of undivided Bengal) became a part of East Pakistan (or East Bengal). So historically, while a close relationship was found between river deterioration and the incidence of malaria, in fact, a substantial area of decaying rivers was actually included in post-partition East Bengal.[18] Thus we suggest that East Bengal's lesser rise in famine mortality was at least partly related to its greater pre-famine malaria endemicity. In other words, highly endemic malaria in much of East Bengal (or what became East Pakistan from 1947) in the pre-famine period probably left relatively little scope for a large proportional increase in malaria mortality. Conversely, lower pre-famine malarial death rates in West Bengal probably made a relatively large proportional rise in death rates possible in the wake of the famine.[19] But this can hardly be an explanation for East Bengal's *earlier* post-famine recovery (see Table 5.5). Improved mortality in East Bengal in 1945 (and by implication, 1946) might be viewed as consistent with the operation of some kind of demographic 'Darwinian' selection.[20] The problem, then, is to explain the observed contrast between West and East Bengal.

Migration may have played a role in accounting for this East–West contrast. In particular, a net inflow of people into West Bengal during the post-famine period might have produced an artificial elevation of deaths for several years. At the time, war, famine, the freedom struggle and communal riots were all sources of population movement. But evidence about migration to settle

[18] Areas of decaying rivers in East Bengal were designated as follows around the time of the famine: (a) moribund delta: Kushtia, Jessore, north-west Faridpur, and north-west Khulna; (b) north Bengal: Dinajpur, western Rangpur, western Bogra, western Pabna, and all of Rajshahi district; see Ahmad (1958), pp. 38–9.

[19] Application of this principle was also noticed in the context of differential decline in malaria mortality from the 1920s to the 1930s in different divisions of Bengal. The eastern division, having very low malaria mortality, experienced little change while the western, central, and northern divisions with a higher malarial death rate experienced relatively large proportional falls; see Chowdhury (1989), p. 30. In fact, the role of malaria endemicity in the regional variation of famine mortality will be discussed later in greater detail.

[20] See, e.g. Bongaarts and Cain (1982).

the issue is scanty.[21] However, on the whole it appears reasonable that West Bengal probably experienced a net population inflow in the wake of both pre-partition Hindu–Muslim tensions and the partition of Bengal. For example, according to census information, the percentage of Hindus in the population of West Bengal rose by 15 points between 1941 and 1951, while there was a corresponding 10-point decline in the percentage of Muslims. In contrast, in East Bengal the rise in Muslim composition and fall in that of Hindus were both about 6 points.[22]

4. The Late Mortality Peak Districts: Malda and Dinajpur

The very delayed nature of the mortality peaks in the two adjacent districts of Malda and Dinajpur merits particular attention (see Table 5.3). Figure 5.2 presents monthly mortality indices and deaths by cause for Malda and Dinajpur. In both districts there was a mortality peak in conformity with that of the whole of Bengal during the final months of 1943. But the *major* mortality peak in both districts occurred in the closing months of 1944, when mortality in Bengal was only a little above normal. It seems that the major mortality peak around November 1944 was due to fresh outbreaks of epidemic diseases. In Malda the maximum malaria deaths occurred in January 1943 whereas the highest MI happened nearly one year later (see Figs 5.2 (A) and (B)). Moreover, two cholera mortality peaks (of almost the same magnitude) occurred in the month of November in both 1943 and 1944. In Dinajpur, on the other hand, the heavy mortality of late 1944 seems to have been associated with a huge peak from malaria mortality (although deaths from respiratory diseases and fever also peaked). The elevation of registered mortality from respiratory

[21] According to the 1951 census, in 1946 alone, 44,624 persons left East Pakistan (or East Bengal) and settled in West Bengal. However, non-availability of data on the number of persons migrating out of West Bengal and settling in East Bengal in 1946 prevents us from making an estimate of the net flow of people; see Census of India 1951, *Volume VI, Part II-Tables* (Delhi: Manager of Publications, 1953), p. 498.

[22] See Census of India 1951, *Volume VI, Part 1C* (Delhi: Manager of Publications, 1953), pp. 4–5, Census of Pakistan 1951, *Volume I, Pakistan, Report and Tables* (Karachi: Manager of Publications (undated)), chapter 2, p. 27.

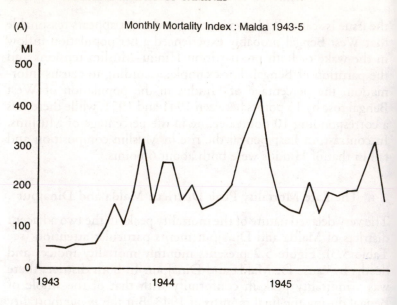

(A)   Monthly Mortality Index : Malda 1943-5

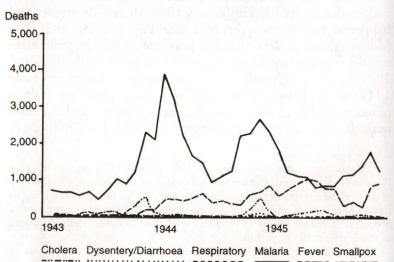

(B)   Monthly Deaths by Cause: Malda 1943-5

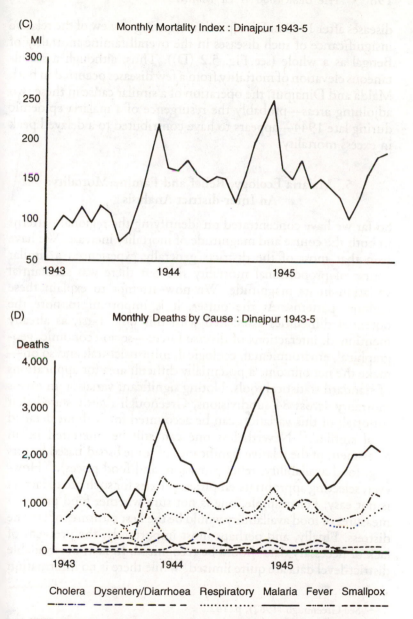

(C)

MI

Monthly Mortality Index : Dinajpur 1943-5

300

250

200

150

100

50

1943   1944   1945

(D)

Monthly Deaths by Cause : Dinajpur 1943-5

Deaths

4,000

3,000

2,000

1,000

0

1943   1944   1945

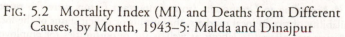

Cholera   Dysentery/Diarrhoea   Respiratory   Malaria   Fever   Smallpox

FIG. 5.2   Mortality Index (MI) and Deaths from Different
Causes, by Month, 1943–5: Malda and Dinajpur

Sources: See Table 5.1.

diseases after 1943 in Dinajpur is interesting in view of the relative insignificance of such diseases in the overall famine mortality of Bengal as a whole (see Fig. 5.2 (D)). Thus, although a simultaneous elevation of mortality from a few diseases occurred in both Malda and Dinajpur, the operation of a similar cause in these two adjoining areas—probably the resurgence of a malaria epidemic during late 1944—appears to have contributed to a delayed peak in excess mortality.

5. Malaria Ecology, Relief and Famine Mortality: An Inter-district Analysis

So far we have concentrated on identifying the regional patterns in both the course and magnitude of mortality increase. We have seen that most of the districts generally experienced a similar course of proportional mortality rise but there was substantial variation in its magnitude. We now attempt to explain these regional patterns. At the outset, it is important to note the potential difficulties associated with this task. First, as already mentioned, interactions of diverse forces—socio-economic, geographical, environmental, ecological, infrastructural, and so on— make the net outcome a potentially difficult area for applications of standard statistical tools. Noting significant variation in excess mortality across 84 subdivisions, Greenough rightly stated that '[n]ot all of this variation can be accounted for without detailed local studies'.[23] Nevertheless one can still be interested in an assessment of the relative significance of some broad-based factors (e.g. food availability, relief provision, and food prices).[24] However, selecting appropriate empirical proxies for such broad factors is not easy. For example, one is not sure whether food prices or measures of food availability would be the best measures of famine distress. Finally, and perhaps most importantly, the problem of lack of necessary data should be recognized. In fact, the available district-level data are quite limited. While there is no information

[23] See Greenough (1982), p. 142.

[24] According to Greenough, 'some important factors were the price and availability of rice in local markets, the surplus or deficit status of the locality, the wage-rate offered to labour as well as the opportunities for employment, and the extent of public and private relief'; see Greenough (1982), p. 142.

on food availability or food production, data on the 'harvest prices' of autumn and winter rice and cultivated area under this crop for the districts of Bengal do exist for the years up to 1942–3. After 1942–3 these data are available only for the districts of West Bengal. In any case, in the absence of any major drought as a precipitating factor we should not necessarily expect changes in area under cultivation to reflect scarcity or famine distress.

Table 5.6 provides district wise data on CDRs during the main twelve-month period of elevated mortality, CBRs during 1944, changes (proportional) in the harvest price of autumn and winter rice and the cultivated area under it in 1942–3, and also statistics on gratuitous relief during the period October 1942–March 1944. It appears that variation in divisional CDRs during the prime famine period was less than during the pre-famine period. However, there seems to have been some changes in the ranks of four divisions during the prime famine period (compared to the pre-famine years) (see Tables 5.1 and 5.6). For example, the eastern region, which was third in the rank of mortality in the years preceding the famine, appears to have recorded the highest death rate during the famine. Thus, in terms of proportional rise in mortality, the eastern and western divisions—relatively favoured mortality zones in the pre-famine period—experienced a relative mortality disadvantage compared to the two other divisions. It is notable that the eastern division experienced both the highest proportional rise in mortality and the greatest proportional reduction in births.[25] Again there does not seem to be a clear correspondence, particularly at the divisional level, between mortality increases and changes in the price of winter rice and area cultivated under it in 1942–3.

However, there are indeed some significant intra-divisional variations. Therefore, it may be useful to proceed by examining the correlations among the demographic and other measures. Table 5.7 provides the correlation matrix with district-level data on several such factors. Since estimates of simple correlations can be influenced by extreme values we have calculated both ordinary and rank (Spearman) correlation coefficients (the ordinary coefficients are not given in Table 5.7 but the results obtained with

[25] There has been a rise in coefficient of variation in the district-level CBRs of 1944 (0.21) from the pre-famine level (0.14).

TABLE 5.6
Inter-district Differentials in Demographic and Other Measures: Bengal

District	CDR 1943–4 (July–June)	CBR 1944	Despatches of food-grains in 1943 (tonnes)	Ratio of price of rice in 1942–3 to the average for 1938–40	% change in area under rice in 1942–3 compared with 1938–40	Grant for gratuitous relief (Rs) Oct. '42–Mar. '44
Burdwan	33.4	19.9	14,978	3.38*	−15.82	1,899,010 (49)
Birbhum	54.2	21.9	1,729	5.14	−03.62	747,560 (40)
Bankura	37.1	19.7	4,710	3.07	+01.97	902,500 (48)
Midnapore	43.7	21.5	20,498	4.85	+09.90	12,844,004 (48)
Hooghly	25.0	21.7	9,752	2.00	+03.88	1,145,470 (48)
Howrah	30.9	20.8	17,174	5.47	+110.23	888,970 (47)
Western Bengal	**38.3**	**21.0**	**68,841**	**4.11**	**+17.76**	**18,427,514 (48)**
24-Parganas	36.5	14.7	19,795	5.03	+06.86	1,840,500 (46)
Nadia	54.5	19.4	3,612	3.29	−01.00	217,710 (33)
Murshidabad	51.0	18.4	4,579	3.74	−00.18	243,660 (23)
Jessore	33.6	15.9	1,138	n.a.	+04.75	77,760 (35)
Khulna	24.3	18.8	13,278	2.18	+15.38	238,360 (82)

Central Bengal	39.0	17.3	42,402	3.56	+5.16	2,617,990 (42)
Rajshahi	39.3	20.2	654	2.82	+21.58	113,480 (17)
Dinajpur	27.2	25.8	631	4.76	−02.72	185,920 (31)
Jalpaiguri	38.1	21.3	2,947	2.95	−09.88	104,300 (41)
Darjeeling	33.6	21.2	5,802	3.60	−00.32	13,060 (29)
Rangpur	53.2	17.0	3,919	2.00	+04.51	565,800 (52)
Bogra	34.3	18.8	425	2.68	00.00	181,020 (41)
Pabna	40.3	9.8	6,764	4.61	−00.39	331,000 (42)
Malda	24.0	19.2	202	3.73	+26.47	9,300 (39)
Northern Bengal	38.4	18.8	21,344	3.39	+4.91	1,503,880 (39)
Dacca	46.0	10.0	26,577	3.80	+13.66	1,535,760 (54)
Mymensingh	39.4	13.5	8,908	4.50	+08.79	640,320 (39)
Faridpur	42.7	12.4	16,493	n.a.	+08.05	1,539,970 (24)
Bakarganj	33.5	16.9	5,248	4.00	−02.56	1,171,820 (37)
Chittagong	47.5	13.7	23,366	1.00	−00.63	986,710 (63)

(*cont.*)

Table 5.6 (cont.)

District	CDR 1943–4 (July–June)	CBR 1944	Despatches of food-grains in 1943 (tonnes)	Ratio of price of rice in 1942–3 to the average for 1938–40	% change in area under rice in 1942–3 compared with 1938–40	Grant for gratuitous relief (Rs) Oct. '42– Mar. '44
Noakhali	37.2	16.6	6,754	5.97	−09.46	1,172,095 (48)
Tippera	46.6	13.2	10,932	2.70	+22.31	700,835 (39)
Eastern Bengal	41.6	13.5	98,278	3.66	+5.73	7,747,510 (39)
All-Bengal	39.9	16.5	230,865	3.52	+05.30	30,296,894 (44)

Notes: 1. The CDRs and CBRs are based on constant denominators—being the respective populations according to the 1941 census.
 2. The figure marked * refers to 1943–4.
 3. The year to which the data on price and area relate ends on 30 June.
 4. The figures in parentheses are the respective percentage shares of gratuitous grant of money to total grants.
 5. The change in the price of, and area under, rice for 1942–3 is calculated with reference to the averages for the years 1938–9 and 1939–40.

Sources: For births and deaths: *Bengal Public Health Report*, Alipore, relevant years; for data on sanctioned money on different forms of relief: the Pinnell Papers, Confidential, *Memorandum on the Economic Condition of Bengal Prior to the Famine of Bengal 1943*, p. 44; for the data on food despatches in 1943, see Famine Inquiry Commission (1945a), Appendix V, p. 223; for price and area data, see Government of India, Ministry of Agriculture, *Indian Agricultural Statistics*, vol. 1, relevant years.

TABLE 5.7
Correlation Matrix with District-level Data on Different Demographic and Other Measures During the Famine

	X_2	X_3	X_4	X_5	X_6	X_7	X_8	X_9	X_{10}	X_{11}	X_{12}	X_{13}
X_1	0.16	0.17	0.47#	0.40#	0.43*	0.27	0.17	-0.40#	-0.55*	0.22	0.43*	0.23
X_2		0.13	0.24	0.15	0.07	-0.02	-0.32	-0.29	-0.12	-0.23	-0.05	-0.23
X_3			-0.10	-0.18	0.18	0.04	-0.12	-0.56*	0.05	-0.10	0.03	-0.23
X_4				0.87*	0.80*	0.69*	0.45*	-0.35#	-0.62*	0.29	0.12	0.00
X_5					0.63*	0.72*	0.51*	-0.21	-0.51#	0.04	-0.03	0.05
X_6						0.87*	0.59*	-0.36#	-0.64*	0.33#	0.26	-0.13
X_7							0.62*	-0.26	-0.51*	0.05	0.05	-0.08
X_8								-0.28	-0.51*	0.00	-0.09	-0.24
X_9									0.37#	0.18	0.33	0.47#
X_{10}										-0.35#	-0.12	0.09
X_{11}											0.50*	0.05
X_{12}												0.50*

* P ≤ .01, # P ≤ .05

X_1: percentage rise in deaths during July 1943–June 1944 over the averages of 1940 and 1941;
X_2: ratio of price of rice in 1942–3 to average 1938–40;

(cont.)

Table 5.7 (*cont.*)

X_3: percentage change in area under rice cultivation in 1942–3 compared with 1938–40;

X_4: government grant on gratuitous relief during Oct. 1942–Mar. 1944;

X_5: Government grant on gratuitous relief per capita during Oct. 1942–Mar. 1944;

X_6: despatches of foodgrains in 1943;

X_7: despatches of foodgrains per capita in 1943;

X_8: percentage share of gratuitous grant to total relief grant of money;

X_9: average CDR during 1940–1;

X_{10}: share of malaria mortality to total fever mortality during 1940–1;

X_{11}: number vaccinated per 1000 population in 1943;

X_{12}: percentage decline in births in 1944 from average of 1940–41;

X_{13}: average CBR during 1940–41.

Notes: 1. These are all rank (Spearman's) correlation coefficients. We also calculated ordinary correlation coefficients; they were found to be broadly consistent with these rank correlation coefficients.

2. It seemed appropriate to exclude few extreme figures (e.g. very large gratuitous relief for Midnapore which began to receive relief much earlier than other districts owing to the cyclone of 1942; also excluded was the extremely large proportional rise in area under rice cultivation in Howrah).

Sources: See Table 5.6.

them are broadly consistent with those shown). It is of interest to examine the direction and strength of correlations of those variables which might be thought to have a causal relation with X_1 (the percentage rise in deaths during July 1943–June 1944). The positive correlation between X_1 and X_2 (the proportional rise in the price of rice in 1942–3) is consistent with the view that the degree of rise in food prices was a determinant of famine distress and associated mortality. But the association is extremely weak (see Table 5.7). This may well partly stem from the relative uniformity in price rises across districts, reflecting the integration of the market. However, the observed positive correlation between X_1 and X_3 (the percentage rise in the area under rice cultivation in 1942–3) is interesting; this seems contrary to our expectation in the context of a drought-related Indian famine in which reduction in area under cultivation is a well-known route to distress for a large section of the population. But the Bengal famine was not associated with any significant drought. On the whole, variation in the area under rice cultivation does not appear to have had any significant role in determining the regional pattern of mortality increases across the districts of Bengal.[26]

The positive correlations of X_1 with X_4 (grant on gratuitous relief during Oct. 1942–Mar. 1944) and X_5 (the *per capita* grant on gratuitous relief) are of interest. This seems contrary to our general expectation that relief should reduce distress, and thus help minimize mortality. Although government grants on gratuitous relief are for a period which does not strictly coincide with that of the prime mortality increase, this should not cause much difficulty in interpreting our results. This is because gratuitous relief (of which the dominant form was food distribution) did not assume significance until September 1943; very few districts actually received gratuitous relief before that time.[27] Similarly, most of the grain despatches in 1943 occurred during the last four months of the year.[28] Again, a significant positive correlation of X_1 is found with government despatches of foodgrains to the

[26] The finding of a positive relation—though rather weak—may partly be due to the influence of migration: i.e. people may have been drawn to areas where above-normal farming activity caused an increased demand for labour, and this may have inflated the number of deaths in such areas.

[27] See Brennan (1988).

[28] See Brennan (1988), Fig. 5, p. 559.

districts in 1943 (expressed in both absolute and per capita terms, X_6 and X_7) (see Table 5.7).[29] This relation may, indeed, have an important implication both *vis-à-vis* the criteria by which the official allocation of food relief was made and also for the role that such relief played in shaping the regional pattern of mortality increase. Several possible mechanisms behind such a positive relation may be suggested: first, the allocation of gratuitous relief in the districts may have been determined partly by the proportional rises in death rates rather than vice versa. It is amply evident that gratuitous food relief (being the most appropriate form of relief in the famine) was provided very late (see chapter 4 above). Therefore, food relief distributed during the epidemic phase ultimately may not have helped reduce excess mortality. Instead its distribution over different districts *followed* the criterion of excess mortality itself. Thus, our hypothesis is that the distribution of gratuitous relief reflected mortality increases across districts and not vice versa.[30]

Now one implication of this hypothesis is that the administration was fairly efficient in collecting information about mortality rises, and in organizing the distribution of food on the basis of that information. This may seem to be in conflict with Sen's finding (based on the data for West Bengal) that 'the Bengal government's diagnoses of the relative severity of the famines in the different districts differed quite substantially from the excess mortality rankings for 1943–6 as well as for 1943 itself'.[31] And considering all the districts of undivided Bengal, we have already indicated that the two official subdivisional classifications of

[29] Much of the government grants on gratuitous relief were presumably for purchasing foodgrains and for running relief kitchens; strong correlations found between foodgrain despatches and gratuitous expenditures lends support for this view (see Table 5.7). We have also estimated the correlations of percentage rise in deaths during July–December 1943 with X_4, X_5, X_6 and X_7; they are respectively 0.42**, 0.41**, 0.54** and 0.16.

[30] It may be noted that the absolute (rather than proportional) rises in death rates during July 1943–June 1944 have also been found to have significant positive correlations with X_4 (0.42**), X_5 (0.41**), and X_6 (0.54**). Interestingly, the finding of a much smaller correlation of mortality rise with X_7 may be suggestive that the allocation of food despatches was based more on an index of mortality increase than on the number of potential or actual victims in the various districts of Bengal.

[31] Sen (1981), p. 208.

famine severity—which were also referred to by Sen—do not seem to have been based on exclusive or even primary considerations of regional mortality increases.

However, Sen states that 'relief operations were strongly influenced by these diagnoses'.[32] In this context the timing of these 'diagnoses' is important. In fact, both the official diagnoses of famine severity were made for the purpose of post-famine rehabilitation. Such official classifications, if made during the early part of a famine, can be supposed to have influenced the distribution of relief according to regional priorities. However, *delayed* distribution of relief food (as was the case during the early epidemic phase of the Bengal famine)—when famine-induced mortality had already assumed an alarming scale—is likely to be more influenced by information about the regional pattern of excess mortality. The balance of evidence suggests that the Bengal famine fitted the latter scenario. Although official awareness about relative mortality in different districts may have required a certain amount of administrative efficiency, this does not seem implausible, especially during the epidemic phase.[33] However, the significant negative correlation found between the malarial share in fever mortality during 1940–1 (X_{10}) and food despatches (represented by both X_6 and X_7) may raise the question as to why despatches of foodgrains were relatively more in the districts which were relatively less malarious. Nor is it clear whether larger supplies of food were despatched to the normally deficit districts. In fact, there are several difficulties—both conceptual and statistical—with the notion of a 'normally deficit or surplus district'. The *Report on*

---

[32] Ibid.

[33] Indeed there is evidence in the context of famines of the late 19th century that monthly (sometimes even fortnightly) mortality data (death rates) for individual districts were collected by respective district administrations during peak famine period. For example, a Memorandum submitted by the Sanitary Commissioner for the North-Western Provinces and Oudh (United Provinces) on the public health during the famine of 1896–7 states that 'To ensure early recognition of distress in any locality, special arrangements were made. The health and condition of the general population was reported fortnightly to this office by all Civil Surgeons, and from these reports a general statement was compiled and submitted to Government. District officers also telegraphed the death-rates of their districts month by month'; see Government of North-Western Provinces and Oudh (1898)), vol. I, p. 132.

Bengal, however, characterized some districts as 'normally deficit', and it also mentioned some districts as being 'buying areas' according to the Bengal government early in 1943. However, the *Report on Bengal* itself is quite doubtful whether these 'buying' districts—as regarded by the Government of Bengal—'were genuinely surplus'.[34] Moreover, relevant data to enquire about any inverse connection between food deficit and malaria endemicity are lacking.

Another possible explanation of a positive relationship between mortality rise and the extent of provision of food relief across districts centres around the 'refeeding hypothesis'. It might be suggested that refeeding a district through food relief actually produced relatively high malaria mortality. However, as we have already argued (see chapter 2), even if refeeding enhances the chance of malarial attack, the actual risk of death depends on nutritional state prior to the nutritional improvement.[35] We have also seen in the preceding chapter that the food provision not only covered a very small proportion of affected population, but it probably caused rather insignificant nutritional improvement. Moreover, this hypothesis is hardly consistent with the observed negative relationship between food relief provision and previous malaria endemicity shown in Table 5.7. In other words the question remains as to why food relief provision appears to have been smaller in districts which had a higher level of malaria endemicity in the pre-famine period—a question which does not seem answerable in terms of any direct causal connection between them.

Finally, inter-district migrations could also produce a positive relationship between mortality rise and the provision of relief. A district favoured with comparatively more food relief may have attracted destitutes from neighbouring areas, and this could inflate the number of deaths registered in the receiving district. But then the question of what actually determined the allocation

---

[34] Famine Inquiry Commission (1945a), p. 114.

[35] Brennan has shown that official food policy during the famine appears to have depended on the private market. Even considerable parts of the government food despatches were sold through the market, resulting in a smaller amount of grain being available for running free kitchens; see Brennan (1988).

of relief provision remains open. Relatedly, this explanation should also take account of a negative relationship found between relief provision and malaria endemicity. Although information about famine-induced population movement between districts of Bengal is very scanty, some inferences may be drawn about the influence of migration on the regional variation of mortality—a point to which we will return.

We now turn to consider the influence of environmental and ecological variables. These can be partly represented by both the pre-famine CDRs for 1940–1 and the shares of malaria deaths in total fever mortality during 1940–1 (variables X_9 and X_{10} respectively). The proportional rise in deaths (X_1) during the prime mortality period appears to be negatively correlated with both X_9 and X_{10}. In the case of X_9, this may be of no surprise in a statistical sense; since the lower the base the greater the scope for proportional increases. However, district-level proportional rises in deaths during July 1943–June 1944 are very strongly (r= 0.90) correlated with the corresponding *absolute* rises in death rates. We have already indicated that malaria ecology probably played a key role in determining pre-famine inter-district variation in mortality (see Table 5.1). Thus, our results in Table 5.7 also suggest that the lower the malaria endemicity in a district (X_{10}), the greater its mortality increase during the famine (X_1). Indeed, as we have already analysed, a large part of the increased overall mortality during the famine was accounted for by malaria epidemics. Taken together, these considerations imply that the severity of malaria epidemics was probably less in those districts which were already heavily malarious—a point to which we will return.

In Table 5.7, district-level public health measures—represented by the number of persons vaccinated in 1943 (X_{11})—show a weak positive association with X_1. This suggests that public health measures played little role in reducing mortality increase, and supports the notion that public health measures were not only inadequate but also very late—a view which has already been argued at the all-Bengal level (see chapter 4 above).[36]

---

[36] Taking the number of vaccinated infants per 1000 births in 1943 as an index of public health provision in each district, we found a similar positive

Thus, we have considered roughly four groups of variables in relation to the explanation of inter-district variation in mortality increase during the famine: the economic variables (X_2 and X_3); relief variables (X_4 to X_8); environmental and ecological variables (X_9 and X_{10}); and public health variable (X_{11}). In order to better understand the causal mechanisms involved, estimation of a multiple regression equation may also be useful. However, formulating such an equation requires some consideration about the selection of dependent and independent variables. First, mortality increase in districts may be measured in both absolute and proportionate terms. So far we have concentrated on the percentage rise in deaths (X_1). However, as mentioned above, it is very strongly and positively correlated with the absolute rise in the number of deaths per 1000 population during the prime famine period (a variable we can denote by X'). Accordingly, we can use both X_1 and X' as separate dependent variables.

But correlations also exist between several of the above (supposedly) explanatory variables. For example, X_4 appears to be positively and rather strongly correlated with both X_5 and X_6. And X_6 is also fairly strongly correlated with X_7. In fact, these correlations are all to be expected, since the different measures all relate to roughly the same variable, namely provision of gratuitous relief. Therefore, we include only one independent variable to represent gratuitous relief in the regression; X_6 seems to be the most appropriate. On similar grounds, we select X_{10} to represent the ecological (mainly malarial) dimension.

Thus we estimate the following two multiple regression equations:

$$(1) \quad X_1 = a + bX_2 + cX_3 + dX_6 + eX_{10} + fX_{11}$$

$$(2) \quad X' = a' + b'X_2 + c'X_3 + d'X_6 + e'X_{10} + f'X_{11}$$

The results are presented in Table 5.8. The signs of the regression coefficients for equation (1) are all consistent with the estimated correlations presented in Table 5.7. But none of the independent variables seems to be statistically significant, and together they

correlation with mortality increase, whether expressed in proportional (0.25) or absolute (0.32) terms.

TABLE 5.8

Results of Estimated Multiple Regression Equations of Mortality Increases During the Prime Famine Period

Independent Variable	Coefficients	t-values
Equation (1)		
X_2	6.069	0.784 (0.44)
X_3	0.526	1.195 (0.24)
X_6	1.260×10^{-3}	0.850 (0.41)
X_{10}	−0.441	−0.697 (0.50)
X_{11}	0.107	0.400 (0.69)
Constant	77.310	1.220 (0.24)
$R^2 = 0.36$, Adjusted $R^2 = 0.18$		
Equation (2)		
X_2	0.228	0.142 (0.89)
X_3	8.583×10^{-3}	0.094 (0.93)
X_6	1.325×10^{-4}	0.431 (0.67)
X_{10}	−0.028	−0.215 (0.83)
X_{11}	0.040	0.718 (0.48)
Constant	15.320	1.166 (0.26)
$R^2 = 0.11$, Adjusted $R^2 = -0.14$		

Notes: 1. Figures in parentheses are the respective significance levels.
2. The statistic, 'adjusted R^2', (denoted as R_n) corrects R^2 to more adequately reflect the goodness of fit of the model in the population. R_n is given by

$$R_n = R^2 - \frac{p(1 - R^2)}{N - p - 1}$$

where p is the number of independent variables in the equation being estimated, and N is the number of observations. However, it should be remembered that R^2 is a measure of linear relationship between the variables; so, low value of R^2 indicates, strictly speaking, weak *linear* causal relationship rather than low association.

Sources: For data used see Table 5.7.

explain only a small percentage of the inter-district variation in X_1. For equation (2), the explanatory power is even lower.[37] These poor results probably partly reflect the fact that the regional pattern of variation in mortality increase during the famine was far more complex than our explanatory variables can capture. In addition, our regression equation captures only linear relationship.

However, in order to identify the most significant factors in explaining variation in mortality increase, we also attempted a stepwise regression. This method first selects the variable with the highest correlation with the dependent variable. Then a criterion, namely, a minimum probability level (0.05) of the F statistic, is set to be fulfilled for entry of that variable. If the variable fails to meet this entry requirement, the procedure terminates with no independent variable in the equation. If it passes the criterion, a second variable is selected, based on the highest partial correlation. If the second variable passes the entry criterion, it also enters the equation, and so on. Applying this stepwise procedure we found that the share of malaria to total fever deaths (i.e. variable X_{10}) was the only significant independent variable.[38] The resulting estimation equation is as follows:

$$X_1 = 155.47 - 1.05\ X_{10}, \quad R^2 = 0.23, \text{ Adjusted } R^2 = 0.20$$
$$(0.00) \quad\ \ (0.01)$$

[37] It may be noted that the different R^2 values obtained for X_1 and X'—which are highly correlated—may well be the result of the fact that these are being measured on two different scales, and hence are not strictly comparable; on this see Scott and Wild (1991), also Kavalseth (1985). We also tried a semi-logarithmic form of the regression, but it too provided a negligible overall explanatory power.

[38] No independent variable satisfied the minimum significance criterion to be included in the model when stepwise regression was tried on the absolute change in the death rate (i.e. X') as the dependent variable. However, the estimated regression equation of X' on X_{10} is as follows:

$$X' = 24.19 - 0.11\ X_{10}, R^2 = 0.08.$$

The fact that X_{10} explains less of the total variation of X' than of X_1, while both X_1 and X' are highly correlated, may seem surprising. But this is not implausible in view of the following considerations: first, while R^2 is a measure of strength of the linear relation, X' and X_1 are non-linear transformations of each other. Second, the fact that the correlation between X' and X_1 is, though high, not perfect may mean that sample variability partly accounts for this discrepancy.

Thus it appears that pre-famine malarial endemicity is the most important factor (among those considered) in explaining inter-district variation in increase, although it still leaves much of the total variation unexplained. This suggests that the regional pattern of famine mortality was shaped through a complex interaction of diverse forces, and also that our formulation of different measures is largely unable to capture this.

However, the finding that the regional pattern of malaria eco-logy partly shaped the regional dimensions of famine mortality can be thought of as consistent with the positive relationship found between mortality rise and the provision of gratuitous food relief if we accept the view that the allocation of food relief was determined, to a certain degree, by the criterion of mortality rise. In other words, the pre-famine variation in malaria endemicity in the districts seems to have partly determined the variation in mortality increase, which in turn probably became an overriding consideration behind the allocation of food relief—a form of relief which, though appropriate under the circumstances, proved to be of little help in reducing the mortality cost of the famine.[39] Indeed, the realization that the provision of food was to be the only effective form of relief, came rather late (in the middle of August 1943) when the revenue minister had no way but to admit that 'there was no question now of saving the lives of all the destitutes in Bengal, but only of saving as many as could possibly be saved'.[40] The decision then was taken in favour of 'gruel' relief rather than 'cash or uncooked grains'. Even after this decision was adopted by the Revenue Department (which was responsible for relief) there was further delay associated with the policy of collecting rice locally—a policy which proved to be a failure.[41] But meanwhile

[39] In this connection it is worth noting that grain supplies (or despatches) in most districts constituted a rather small part of the effective gratuitous relief effort of the district administrations. This is mainly, as Brennan has convincingly argued, because of 'the competitive structure built into the provision of grain and relief in the districts'—a fact that held the economically weakest (in terms of shortfall in purchasing power) at a relative disadvantage; see Brennan (1988), p. 559. Brennan provides strong indication that a large part of the apparently 'massive' relief expenditures by the government failed to favour the most vul-nerable sections of the population.

[40] Quoted in Greenough (1982), p. 129.

[41] See Greenough (1982), p. 130.

'mortality rose alarmingly in September'. In response, the Revenue Department began to depend more and more on 'gruel kitchens', which it opened in large numbers both in towns and villages and which it kept in operation until the end of the year.[42]

Thus, while evidence is fairly clear about the government's delayed response in food provision, we do not have any direct evidence to say that the government distributed food across districts, following the criterion of respective mortality rises. Furthermore, the correlations between the mortality rises and measures of food relief are far from perfect. Indeed, the scatter-plot of district-level ranks in terms of mortality increase and food despatches in Figure 5.3 (A) shows that a cluster of six districts received relatively large amounts of foodgrains—namely Dacca, Howrah, Midnapore, Chittagong, 24-Parganas and Tippera (in fact, these districts received more than 50 per cent of the total food despatches in 1943). These districts also appear to have experienced relatively large mortality rises. Interestingly, exclusion of these six districts reduces the rank correlation coefficient close to zero. Now, Howrah, 24-Parganas and (probably Midnapore) are all relatively close to Calcutta—the centre from where food was being despatched. Also, Chittagong is an important port. Finally, Tippera is next to Dacca (which is also an important centre in eastern Bengal)—and note too that Faridpur (which received the sixth highest amount of foodgrain despatches) is just across the river Padma from Dacca. It is plausible that the amount of food despatch received by a district was at least partly determined by its locational proximity to the main centres of communications. And the suggestion is that food tended to be despatched via the main foci of communications —namely Calcutta, Dacca and Chittagong. Conversely, as Figure 5.3 (A) shows, a cluster of districts in north-western Bengal (e.g. Malda, Bogra, Dinajpur) received relatively few food despatches probably due to poor communications. Relatively large food provision received by the relatively favourably located districts probably in turn caused a large inflow of victims, many of whom died there.

There seems to have been a geographical basis, too, for the negative relationship between food despatches and the previous malaria endemicity. The scatter-plot in Figure 5.3 (B) suggests

[42] Ibid., p. 130.

Foodgrain Ranks

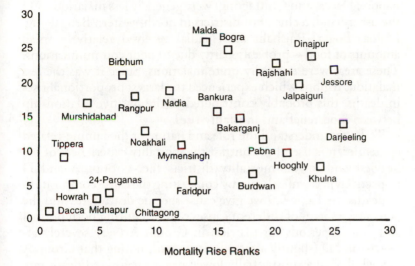

FIG. 5.3 (A)   Scatter-plot of District-level Mortality
Increases (X_1) and Food Despatches (X_6)

Foodgrain Ranks

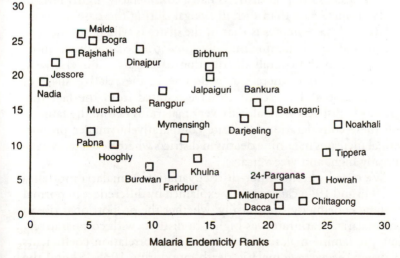

FIG. 5.3 (B)   Scatter-plot of District-level Food Despatches (X_6)
and Malaria Endemicity (X_{10})

that districts which were proximate to the main foci of communications (e.g. Calcutta, 24-Parganas, Howrah, Tippera, Midnapore, Dacca, and Chittagong) were generally less malarious. On the other hand, a cluster of districts in north-western Bengal (e.g. Malda, Bogra, Rajshahi and Nadia) received relatively small amounts of food—probably partly due to poor communications. These areas were normally quite malarious. Since it was the less malarious regions which experienced the largest proportional rises in deaths, this probably contributed to the positive relationship between food relief and mortality rises.

To better understand the role and nature of the famine-related epidemics, it is useful to contrast the mortality experiences of the heaviest and lowest mortality districts (i.e. Groups A and D respectively). We may begin by contrasting the cause composition of deaths. In Table 5.9 we give cause-specific death rates and the percentage shares of different causes of death during both normal and famine periods for districts in Groups A (very severely affected) and D (slightly affected). It is worth noting that Group A as a whole had a substantially lower average registered death rate in the pre-famine period than did Group D. In Group A malaria does not seem to have been the most dominant killer during normal times, whereas it certainly was in Group D (see Table 5.9). Indeed, Group D districts had a considerably higher level of malarial incidence than did all-Bengal during the baseline years 1940–1. What emerges is that in the districts which experienced the greatest excess famine mortality, *malaria* became much more important in the overall distribution of deaths. Conversely, in Group D districts there was a decline in the relative share of malaria deaths. This seems to have resulted from the fact that Group D districts were already very malarious before the famine. All these considerations indicate comparatively smaller proportional increases in famine deaths in districts where death rates were already high, and vice versa.

We tested whether inter-district variation in malaria mortality in 1943 and 1944 can be partly explained by differences in normal malaria endemicity; specifically, whether the proportional rise in the malarial death rate was higher in districts with comparatively low pre-famine malaria death rates. The correlation coefficients between the average malaria death rate during 1938–42 and the percentage rise in malaria deaths in 1943 and 1944 were respectively –0.41 and –0.48 (both being statistically significant at the 5 per cent level). The implication is again that inter-district variation in malaria during the famine was partly determined by variation in the normal level of malaria endemicity. The most heavily hit districts—in terms of famine excess mortality—were those which were usually relatively malaria free.

TABLE 5.9
Cause-specific Death Rates and Percentage Shares of Different Causes of Death During Normal and Famine Periods in the Heaviest and Lowest Famine Mortality Districts (Groups A and D)

	Cause-specific death rates		
Cause of death	1940–1	1943	1944
	Group A		
Cholera	0.57	3.18	0.85
	(3.52)	(13.19)	(0.72)
Smallpox	0.17	0.39	2.13
	(1.01)	(1.76)	(18.76)
Malaria	3.89	11.90	12.76
	(23.79)	(40.19)	(69.75)
Fever	5.37	8.34	6.68
	(32.86)	(21.64)	(14.10)
Dysentery/Diarrhoea	1.03	2.09	1.47
	(6.27)	(5.40)	(1.74)
Respiratory diseases	0.93	0.82	0.87
	(5.69)	(–0.73)	(–1.77)
Injuries	0.34	0.40	0.32
	(2.06)	(0.08)	(–0.78)
All other	4.06	7.00	4.00
	(24.80)	(18.47)	(–2.52)
All causes	16.35	34.08	29.07
	(100.00)	(100.00)	(100.00)
	Group D		
Cholera	0.54	2.11	0.66
	(2.41)	(18.18)	(1.49)

(*cont.*)

Table 5.9 (*cont.*)

Cause of death	Cause-specific death rates		
	1940–1	*1943*	*1944*
Smallpox	0.08	0.03	0.39
	(0.38)	(–0.26)	(5.77)
Malaria	9.64	12.30	12.78
	(43.19)	(7.88)	(35.19)
Fever	4.82	10.28	12.00
	(21.61)	(65.99)	(45.96)
Dysentery/Diarrhoea	0.86	1.51	1.37
	(3.87)	(3.94)	(1.65)
Respiratory diseases	2.26	2.75	3.22
	(10.15)	(1.41)	(5.29)
Injuries	0.34	0.34	0.43
	(1.52)	(–0.34)	(0.27)
All other	3.76	4.39	4.63
	(16.87)	(0.76)	(4.39)
All causes	22.31	33.71	35.48
	(100.00)	(100.00)	(100.00)

Notes: 1. All death rates above (expressed per 1000 population) are based on constant denominators being the respective populations according to the 1941 census. For the period 1940–1, the figures in parentheses are the respective percentage shares to total deaths, whereas for both 1943 and 1944 they are the percentage shares to total *excess* deaths. Excess deaths by cause in 1943 and 1944 were calculated over the respective averages for 1940 and 1941.

2. All data refer to rural areas.

Sources: See Table 5.1.

This issue is probably better illustrated in Figure 5.4 which compares the seasonal patterns of fever and malaria deaths in Groups A and D. District-level registration data on the monthly distribution of malaria mortality for the pre-famine period are not available. But Figure 5.4 makes fairly clear the contrast between these two extreme groups of districts in terms of both pre-famine malaria ecology and its implications for the nature of epidemics associated with the famine. It is notable that seasonal patterns of fever mortality in both groups of districts during the pre-famine years (1940–1) exhibited a peak in the later months of the year. But the Group A districts appear to have experienced relatively evenly

Deaths

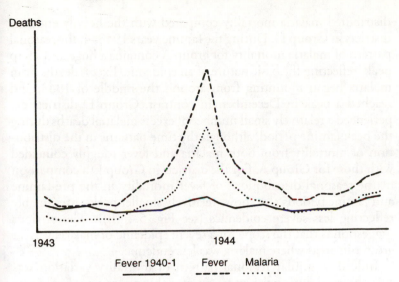

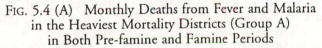

FIG. 5.4 (A) Monthly Deaths from Fever and Malaria
in the Heaviest Mortality Districts (Group A)
in Both Pre-famine and Famine Periods

Deaths

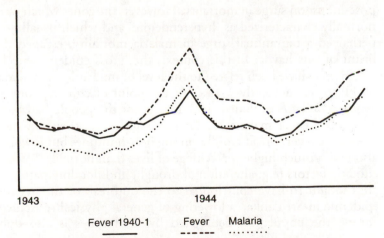

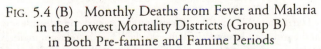

FIG. 5.4 (B) Monthly Deaths from Fever and Malaria
in the Lowest Mortality Districts (Group B)
in Both Pre-famine and Famine Periods

Sources: See Table 5.1

distributed malaria mortality compared with the heavily endemic districts in Group D. During the famine years 1943–4, the seasonal pattern of malaria mortality for group A contains a huge and sharp peak, reflecting the basic nature of an epidemic. Excess deaths from malaria began mounting from around the middle of 1943, and reached a peak in December. In contrast, Group D districts experienced a relatively small number of excess malarial deaths during the peak famine period, although the time patterns in the distribution of mortality from both malaria and fever roughly coincided with those for Group A. For the districts in Group D a comparison of the seasonal distributions of fever mortality in the pre-famine and famine periods also shows relatively smaller peaks, presumably reflecting less severe epidemics (see Fig. 5.4 (B)). The obvious suggestion is that the scope for a severe epidemic of malaria was far greater in areas where malaria was less endemic.

Indeed, a similar regional pattern of mortality variation was also observed during the 'most catastrophic malaria epidemic ever recorded'—that in Sri Lanka in 1934–5.[43] Basically the epidemic —which followed 'an extraordinary drought' in 1934—swept devastatingly through the south-western area of the island which was normally least malarious, experiencing in most years a small post-monsoon surge in mortality. However, the zones which were normally characterized as 'hyperendemic' and which usually experienced a big annual surge in malaria mortality, escaped the brunt of this havoc. In this context, the 'gross epidemic mechanism' may have been related to the level of immunity to malaria. As Harrison succinctly writes, 'At the point of climatic convergence *culicifacies* exploded. If at that point the people had been relatively free of malaria for long enough . . . , then not only would the fever spread rapidly among non-immunes but it would also take a much higher percentage of lives than normal'.[44] While climatic factors (e.g. alteration of drought and flooding patterns) are thought to have contributed to the outbreak of the malaria epidemic in Sri Lanka, 'a lowering of general physical resistance' among the population debilitated by hard times is also duly

[43] See Harrison (1978), p. 203; this epidemic received considerable scientific interest at that time, and was meticulously studied. For the relevant major works, see the references cited in Harrison (1978), footnote 8 on p. 203.

[44] See Harrison (1978), p. 205.

recognized.[45] We have seen that the origin of the malaria epidemic in Bengal in 1943–4 was apparently not explainable in terms of climatic vicissitudes. Rather, it seems to have been largely related to the prolonged debilitation and social disruptions in the wake of the famine.[46] But once the epidemic broke out, the regional variation in the outcome of the epidemic may well have been partly influenced by pre-famine levels of immunity to malaria (measured rather crudely here in terms of proportion of malarial deaths to total fever deaths during 1940–1).

6. Regional Variation in the Fertility Effects

Unfortunately, owing to the non-availability of monthly data on numbers of births by district, it is not possible to examine variations across districts in the detailed timing of the fertility effects. However, to throw some light on variation in the overall fertility effects during the prime famine period, we may examine the percentage declines in the number of registered births in 1944 compared to the annual average numbers for 1940 and 1941. We have already seen that in the province as a whole the greatest reduction in births occurred in 1944.

Looking at Table 5.7, the correlation coefficient between the percentage rise in deaths during the period July 1943–June 1944, and the percentage decline in births in 1944 across the districts, is found to be 0.43. So, in general, districts which experienced major mortality rises tended to experience the greatest reductions in birth rate. A part of the lack of correspondence between mortality increase and fertility reduction may be due to the somewhat different time spans which have been taken when calculating these measures. Moreover, some degree of non-correspondence between mortality rise and fertility fall may result from inter-district distress migration and the independent effect of epidemics upon mortality. Out-migration of destitutes from a distressed district may have both lowered registered birth and death rates in these districts and raised registered birth and death rates in receiving districts. Besides, while

[45] See Harrison (1978), p. 205; Zurbrigg (1988) has also shown that economic distress played a part in causing malaria epidemics in Punjab.

[46] Zurbrigg has argued that acute nutritional deprivation was 'an important, perhaps key, factor underlying the epidemic of malaria mortality during the Bengal famine'; see Zurbrigg (undated), p. 73.

inter-district variation in excess mortality was explained by variation in the pattern of epidemics, a great part of the fertility reduction, caused presumably by nutritional stress and other social disruptions, occurred before the start of the epidemic phase.[47]

7. The Famine of 1943–4 Outside Bengal: Events in Orissa and Madras

The famine of 1943–4 not only affected Bengal but also some neighbouring provinces (e.g. Orissa and Bihar). Madras too was affected by a serious famine during 1943–4. Table 5.10 presents

TABLE 5.10

Average Annual Harvest Prices of Staple Crops (Rs per maund) in Orissa, Madras, and Bengal

Year	Madras		Orissa		Bengal	
	Jower	Rice	Wheat	Rice	Rice	Wheat
1938–9	2.69	3.94	3.01	2.56	3.5	3.5
1939–40	2.88	4.31	4.00	3.01	4.4	3.8
1940–1	2.75	4.75	4.25	3.63	5.1	4.1
1941–2	3.25	5.38	5.88	4.13	5.3	5.0
1942–3	5.88	8.38	11.88	6.19	14.0	15.0
1943–4	7.81	9.81	15.00	9.69	15.0	12.6
1944–5	7.25	9.44	11.75	8.25	12.5	11.7
1945–6	7.25	10.01	11.98	8.44	12.6	12.5
1946–7	7.44	10.38	11.98	9.00	12.5	14.0

Notes: 1. The provincial annual harvest prices are the respective medians of district-level average prices.

2. In both Orissa and Bengal the harvest prices of rice are those for winter rice only.

3. Years to which the above data relate end on 30 June.

Sources: Government of India, Ministry of Agriculture, Directorate of Economics and Statistics, *Indian Agricultural Statistics, Volume 1*, Calcutta: Government Press, various years.

[47] Interestingly, the correlation coefficient between district-level CBRs during 1940–1 and percentage declines in births in 1944 is positive and also statistically significant (see Table 5.7).

the average provincial prices of some staple foodcrops in Bengal, Orissa, and Madras. It is clear that in all three provinces prices showed a somewhat rising trend from 1939–40 onwards. In both Orissa and Bengal, food prices in 1943–4 were about four times the 1938–9 levels, while they were about three times higher in Madras. Thus, Madras seems to have experienced a somewhat smaller inflationary food price rise. In the post-famine years food prices continued to be very high in all these provinces (and this seems to have been particularly the case in Madras). Thus war-related inflation and consequent declines in purchasing power were a common influence in causing distress in these provinces.

In fact, Orissa was considered a 'surplus' province in rice production during 1942–3 despite the damaging effects of the 1942 cyclone in its coastal districts. During the period between 1 December 1942 and 31 October 1943, Orissa exported about 10,000 tonnes of rice. But during the rule of the free trade policy in Bengal, prices in Orissa rose steeply, 'which had the effect of placing rice beyond the reach of the poor'.[48] According to the Government of Orissa, the free trade experiment in Bengal— introduced in March 1943—'was undoubtedly the greatest factor in causing high prices, hoarding, and unavailability of foodgrains to consumers in the latter part of 1943'.[49] Serious distress, accompanied by some starvation deaths, was reported to have affected four coastal districts, namely Balassore, Cuttack, Puri, and Ganjam. And these districts were immediately adjacent to the border of Bengal. Considerable out-migration of destitutes from Bengal to these districts is known to have occurred.

The official interpretation of the Madras crisis of 1943–4, however, has tended to blame weather conditions as the precipitating factor.[50] But there is hardly any evidence of significant crop

[48] See Famine Inquiry Commission (1945a), p. 4.

[49] Quoted in Knight (1954), p. 89.

[50] For example, the annual provincial Administration Report for 1943 stated that 'there was a complete failure of the north-east monsoon in 1942 and rain was inadequate and ill-timed for the purpose of cultivation during the south-west monsoon. There was consequently a failure of crops in the Ceded districts resulting in distress which steadily became more acute and widespread'; see Government of Madras (1944), p. 13. The Famine Inquiry Commission in its *Final Report* has stated that in four districts (Bellary, Anantapur, Kurnool and Cuddapah) 'both the north-east and south-west monsoons of 1942 failed and

failure in 1942–3; indeed data on the area under different crops (particularly foodgrains) in 1942–3 do not suggest any decline compared with the preceding years.[51] Thus, as has been noted, 'in 1942–4 no climatic irregularity occurred [in Madras province] that might be held responsible for a substantial production decline of food grains'.[52] However, there does seem to have been a decline in net availability of foodgrains in 1942–3—a decline which appears to have been partly related to a reduction in imports.

There has been little research conducted on the matter of food availability in Madras during 1942–4, particularly when compared to the corresponding literature for Bengal. However, there are indications that the experiences in Madras and Bengal during the first half of the 1940s provide us with two contrasting scenarios concerning the responses of government both in terms of handling war-related inflation and disruptions in food supplies and in terms of mitigating the associated distress. In fact, Madras, like Bengal and other regions of India, experienced war-induced price rises from the early 1940s, which created distress among the grain-purchasing population. A poor harvest in the non-Tamil parts of the province in the winter of 1942–3 caused localized food shortages. Faced with limited prospects for securing food from outside the province, the Government of Madras started a scheme to move grain between surplus and deficit districts. It first offered contracts to private merchants to do this, and later, dispensing with the merchants, invested its own capital in transport services and storage godowns.[53] In view of the exceedingly high prices of food in the open market, food rationing on a card system basis was introduced in Madras in September 1943. To run this system the government even introduced measures of 'compulsory requisition' of grain from surplus cultivators and millers. All these measures of the Madras government—which essentially amounted to state

famine conditions prevailed in large areas of these districts during the greater part of 1942 and 1943'; see Famine Inquiry Commission (1945b), p. 6.

[51] See Government of India, Ministry of Agriculture, Directorate of Economics and Statistics, *Indian Agricultural Statistics*, Calcutta, Volume 1, various years.

[52] See Guilmoto (1991), p. 17.

[53] See Baker (1984), p. 48; in 1943–4 alone the Madras Government put up the capital of Rs 82.7 million for the purpose of grain distribution.

intervention in the market—contrast sharply with the indifference and non-interference of the policies of the Government of Bengal. For example, the Famine Inquiry Commission's *Report on Bengal* stated that '[t]he failure to introduce rationing at any time during 1943 added to the difficulties'.[54] In contrast, the relatively high level of state intervention in Madras appears to have been somewhat effective in protecting the interests of the province's vulnerable population.

So, in Madras the famine was dealt with relatively promptly and effectively. This was particularly true in relation to the state's handling of food distribution and relief operations. For example, 3 million rupees were spent on 'financial assistance' in 1943 alone, in the affected districts; and the total expenditure on relief operations amounted to 21.8 million rupees.[55] In 1944 'nearly 16 million workers [employed in 34 famine camps in Madras] were paid their wages in grain'.[56] Unlike the situation in Bengal (where the management both of food supplies and of distribution was very inefficient), in Madras the administration appears to have been relatively successful both in procuring rice from surplus areas in the northern and southern deltas, and in its distribution throughout the affected areas. Moreover, the existence of reserve stocks of millet in the hands of cultivators in dry areas also helped to ease the food supply situation. Higher prices especially in 1943 induced cultivators to sell part of their reserve stocks—a fact which was of some assistance in the famine-stricken areas.

With this as background, Table 5.11 provides birth and death rates in both Madras and Orissa for the pre-famine, famine, and post-famine periods. It shows that the birth rate in 1942 was below normal in both Orissa and Madras. This probably signifies a reduction in conceptions from as early as 1941. Given the increased level of food prices from around 1940 (see Table 5.11), this indicates an early (negative) response of conceptions to economic distress. Birth rates declined markedly in 1944; the decline was slightly greater in Orissa than in Madras. The implication is

---

[54] See Famine Inquiry Commission (1945a), p. 64. On the detailed evidence of Bengal's failure in the management and distribution of food, see Knight (1954), pp. 92–5 and Greenough (1982), chapter 3.

[55] Famine Inquiry Commission (1945b), p. 6.

[56] See Government of India (1946), p. 22.

TABLE 5.11A

*Crude Birth Rate (CBR) and Crude Death Rate (CDR) During
Pre-famine, Famine, and Post-famine Periods: Orissa and Madras*

	Madras		Orissa	
	CBR	CDR	CBR	CDR
Pre-famine				
1937–41	35.3	22.5	33.1	28.1
1942	33.8	22.5	31.9	25.7
Famine				
1943	31.2	25.2	31.4	31.0
1944	29.4	25.4	25.7	31.0
Post-famine				
1945	29.4	22.2	27.9	28.4
1946	31.7	18.9	28.0	24.2
1947	33.2	20.4	27.8	28.0
1948	30.8	17.8	27.2	23.3
1949	30.9	16.7	26.6	22.6
1950	29.7	18.9	27.4	20.9

TABLE 5.11B

*Infant Mortality Rate (IMR) Per 1000 Livebirths During
1937–46: Orissa and Madras*

	Average 1937–41	1942	1943	1944	1945	1946
Madras						
Rural	160.6	150.0	160.6	191.8	169.1	147.5
Urban	256.4	252.1	270.6	195.6	170.9	144.5
Orissa						
Rural	209.3	191.3	203.1	209.4	178.4	172.2
Urban	172.5	167.2	187.6	172.6	168.2	144.9

Note: 1. All CBRs and CDRs are based on the respective official estimated mid-year populations.

Sources: For CDRs and CBRs, see *Annual Report of the Director General of Health Services*, Delhi, various years; for IMRs see *Statistical Appendices to Annual Reports of the Public Health Commissioner with the Government of India for the period 1940–1944*, Delhi, Government Press, 1947.

that in Madras at least the maximum reduction in conceptions occurred in the prime famine year of 1943.

Mortality in both provinces rose significantly above normal in both 1943 and 1944 (see Table 5.11). Assuming that the main span of famine mortality in both provinces was from May 1943 to April 1944, the Director of Public Health with the Government of India calculated excess deaths over the respective annual averages during 1938–42; the resulting figures are 176,827 and 52,146 respectively for Madras and Orissa.[57] Although no account was taken of death under-registration in producing these estimates, it is clear that excess mortality, though by no means insignificant, was far from comparable to that in the Bengal famine.[58]

The Famine Inquiry Commission stated that '[although] there was great distress among the poorer sections of the people, the famine did not cause exceptional mortality [in Madras]'.[59] In this connection we may note that the information collected in the parish registers of three affected *taluks* in Travancore state indicates a 46 per cent rise in deaths during 1943–4 over the figure for 1941–2. Comparison of death rates based on parish figures with those from official registration data shows that the latter figures were about 50 per cent deficient.[60] It is notable in Table 5.11 that in both Orissa and Madras the CDRs, while generally back to their respective baseline levels in 1945, dropped still further in 1946. This conforms with the hypothesis that immediate post-famine death rates tend to be lower than during pre-famine years (partly due to age structural selection effects).[61] On the other hand, the data in Table 5.11 do not suggest any post-famine compensatory recovery in birth rates. This may have been due partly to the persistence of high food prices and partly to a possible deterioration in registration just prior to independence.

Table 5.11B shows that in Madras, as in Bengal, the urban IMR was considerably higher than that in rural areas, whereas the

[57] Ibid., p. 2.

[58] Reviewing the relevant literature, Guilmoto suggests that Madras as a whole registered a 20 per cent increase in mortality in 1943–4; p. 18; this certainly represents a very small volume of excess mortality compared to the Bengal famine; see Guilmoto (1991).

[59] Famine Inquiry Commission (1945a), p. 6.

[60] See Sivaswamy et al. (1945), pp. 81–5 and 110.

[61] See, e.g. Bongaarts and Cain (1982).

opposite held true in Orissa. In Madras, the IMR rose slightly in 1943 in both rural and urban areas. But in 1944 the IMR rose markedly in rural areas while it declined in the urban sector. However, in Orissa infants seem to have experienced no mortality rise during the famine.

Figure 5.5 portrays the monthly distribution of deaths from the four most important causes in 1943 and 1944. The time pattern of deaths from these causes in Orissa shows a remarkable similarity with that for Bengal. Deaths from different causes showed a rising trend from the middle of 1943; while cholera deaths peaked in October, the fever mortality-peak occurred just one month later (in December). Registered deaths from dysentery and diarrhoea, though peaking in late 1943, were rather persistently high until the middle of 1944; and mortality from smallpox reached a sharp climax in April 1944. Interestingly, there was a rising trend in mortality from these causes (except smallpox) from the middle of 1944; and peak mortality from cholera, dysentery and diarrhoea occurred about a month before the peak in fever mortality (in December 1944). All these patterns in Orissa fairly closely resemble those experienced in Bengal.

One should note that the prime cause of distress in Orissa, as in Bengal, was the enormous rise in food prices. Although Orissa was a surplus province in rice production, 'purchases of rice by agents and merchants from Bengal during the free trade period pushed the price almost up to the Bengal level, so that in parts of Orissa, as in Bengal, the poor could not buy enough food'.[62] The movement of famine victims from Bengal towards adjacent parts of Orissa was also of significant magnitude. Thus, whereas registered deaths in 1943 in Orissa as a whole increased by 17.9 per cent over the quinquennial average, the rise in Balassore district, bordering Bengal, was 40.7 per cent. In Balassore alone, 1105 starvation deaths were recorded; many of these victims were believed to be migrant destitutes from Bengal.[63] The Director of Public Health in Orissa attributed the increased mortality in 1943 to 'food shortage, migration within the province, and the influx of destitutes from Bengal'.[64]

In Madras, as in Orissa and Bengal, fever mortality, peaked in

[62] See Famine Inquiry Commission (1945a), p. 144.
[63] Ibid., p. 144.
[64] Ibid., p. 144.

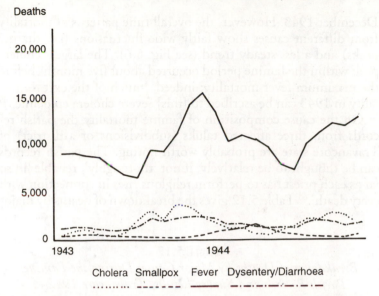

FIG. 5.5   Monthly Deaths by Major Causes: Orissa 1943–4

Sources: See Table 5.11.

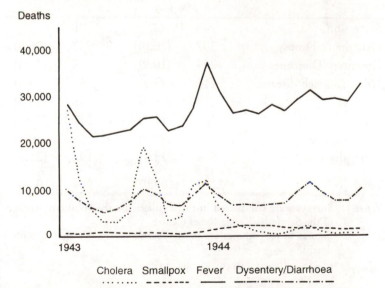

FIG. 5.6   Monthly Deaths by Major Causes: Madras 1943–4

Sources: See Table 5.11.

December 1943. However, the overall time patterns of mortality from different causes show fairly wide fluctuations (i.e. sharper peaks) and a less steady trend (see Fig. 5.6). The largest cholera peak within the famine period occurred about five months before the maximum fever mortality; indeed, 'much of the excess mortality in 1943 can be ascribed to [this] severe cholera epidemic'.[65]

On the cause composition of famine mortality the parish records from three affected taluks (subdivisions of a district) of Travancore state are probably worth noting. The parish records can be thought to be relatively, if not 'thoroughly', reliable 'in so far as each priest has to perform religious rites in connection with every death'.[66] Table 5.12 gives the breakdown of deaths by major

TABLE 5.12

Breakdown of Deaths by Major Causes During the Famine: Parish Records and Survey Results, Travancore 1942–4

Cause of death	Number of deaths			
	Parish registers 1943–4		Surveys 1942–4	
Starvation	46	(2.1)	0	
Oedema & Dropsy	597	(26.8)	242	(26.8)
Dysentery/Diarrhoea	244	(10.9)	96	(10.6)
Other stomach diseases	115	(5.2)	59	(6.5)
Scabies	411	(18.4)	48	(5.3)
Fever	260	(11.7)	211	(23.3)
Consumption	42	(1.9)	56	(6.2)
Other diseases	514	(23.1)	192	(21.2)
Total	2229	(100.0)	904	(100.0)

Notes: 1. Surveys were conducted in three villages by the voluntary workers of the Servindia Kerala Relief Centre.
2. Figures in parentheses are the respective percentage shares to total deaths.

Sources: Sivaswamy et al. (1945), pp. 94, 116.

[65] Ibid., p. 145.
[66] See Sivaswamy et al. (1945), p. 84.

causes as were recorded in the parish registers of the three taluks for 1943–4. The cause composition of deaths during the famine bears a rather distinct reflection of acute nutritional deprivation and its adverse health effects. Indeed, there was virtually no famine relief policy in Travancore state. As Sivaswamy and his associates write, 'Policies which were followed by Provincial Governments such as Madras, and Bengal in later stages, for distributing relief were hardly followed here [Travancore]'.[67]

In Figure 5.7, the proportional rises in deaths by age and sex in both 1943 and 1944 compared with the averages for 1941 and 1942 are plotted separately for rural and urban sectors of Madras and Orissa. Figures for infant deaths by sex were not available. Several points emerge. First, unlike in Bengal, there does not seem to have been any striking difference in rural–urban patterns in Orissa and Madras. This may indicate a lesser volume of rural–urban distress migration compared to Bengal. This may partly be due to relatively better distribution of relief provisions. In both provinces, older and teenaged children (i.e. those aged 5–9 and 10–14 years) generally appear to have been more vulnerable groups. In rural Orissa, older teenagers (15–19) appear to have been the most vulnerable. Young children (aged 1–4 years) seem to have been less vulnerable compared to most other age groups in 1943. However, in Madras in 1944, young children appear to have been quite vulnerable compared to adults and elderly people. In fact, young adults and middle-aged people in Madras generally appear to have experienced a distinct mortality advantage (in terms of proportional rises in mortality); in Orissa the elderly people (60+) showed relatively small rise in mortality. So what emerges from Figure 5.7 is that teenaged children generally appear to have experienced relatively adverse mortality, while adults and some-times even elderly people seem to have experienced a relative mortality advantage. This is broadly consistent with our previous analysis based on the findings from former major Indian famines. The female population aged 15–19 years in Madras and those aged 15–29 years in Orissa appear to have had a distinct mortality advantage compared with males of the same age. Part of the explanation may be the reduction in births and the consequent fall in the number of maternity deaths during the famine. Again,

---

[67] Ibid., p. IV.

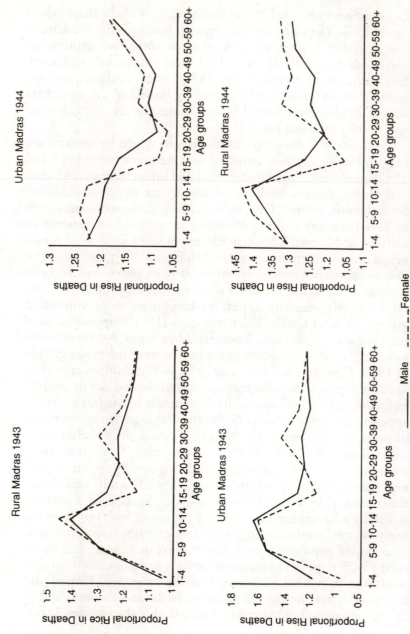

(A)

Rural Madras 1943

Proportional Rise in Deaths

1.5 · 1.4 · 1.3 · 1.2 · 1.1 · 1

Age groups: 1-4 5-9 10-14 15-19 20-29 30-39 40-49 50-59 60+

Urban Madras 1943

Proportional Rise in Deaths

1.8 · 1.6 · 1.4 · 1.2 · 1 · 0.5

Age groups: 1-4 5-9 10-14 15-19 20-29 30-39 40-49 50-59 60+

Urban Madras 1944

Proportional Rise in Deaths

1.3 · 1.25 · 1.2 · 1.15 · 1.1 · 1.05

Age groups: 1-4 5-9 10-14 15-19 20-29 30-39 40-49 50-59 60+

Rural Madras 1944

Proportional Rise in Deaths

1.45 · 1.4 · 1.35 · 1.3 · 1.25 · 1.2 · 1.15 · 1.1 · 1.05 · 1.1

Age groups: 1-4 5-9 10-14 15-19 20-29 30-39 40-49 50-59 60+

——— Male   - - - - Female

(B)

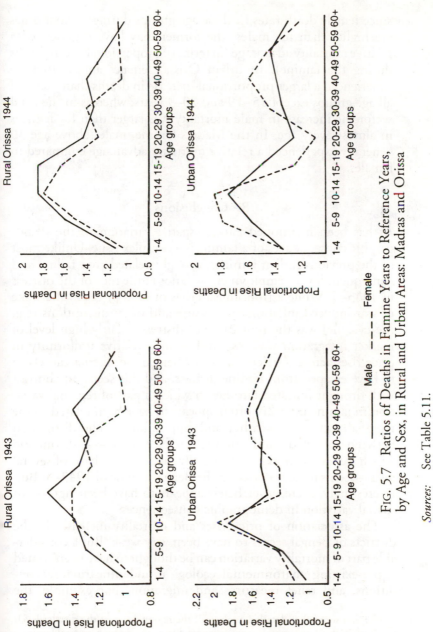

FIG. 5.7 Ratios of Deaths in Famine Years to Reference Years, by Age and Sex, in Rural and Urban Areas: Madras and Orissa

Sources: See Table 5.11.

since female death rates in these age groups during normal times are higher than for males, the former may have experienced a relative mortality advantage (in terms of proportional rise in deaths during the famine). In urban Orissa, females appear to have experienced a larger proportional increase in deaths than males in all age groups except 15–19 and 20–9 years, whereas in the rural sector the increase in male mortality was larger than for females in almost every age. In the Madras famine, males above age 30 generally experienced a relative mortality advantage compared to females.

8. Conclusions

As has been mentioned earlier, spatial variation in the demographic consequences of a famine is a complex issue. Unlike most of the previous Indian famines, drought-related crop failure and consequent loss of employment was not at the root of the distress in 1943–4. While astronomical levels of food prices in the wake of war-induced inflationary pressure and other disruptions (e.g. the cyclone) was the root cause of distress, a fairly high level of market integration was responsible for a relative uniformity in price rises across districts. Thus, in Bengal, no district can claim to have escaped from famine distress, and this seems to contrast with drought-initiated famines in which a part of regional variation in famine intensity often appears to have been related to the regional pattern of weather and crop failure.[68] The distinction between 'affected' and 'non-affected' districts—a distinction which we have seen was traditionally made on the basis of several tests—seems to have ceased in the Bengal famine of 1943–4. But, interestingly, there nevertheless appears to have been significant spatial variation in demographic consequences.

The association of price rises and mortality increases in the districts of Bengal seems to have been very weak. But a considerable part of mortality variation can be thought to have been related to pre-existing environmental, ecological, and infrastructural conditions, and relief measures and migration. For example, the

---

[68] For a somewhat detailed analysis of the regional (i.e. at the district-level) variation in the demographic consequences during the major historical famines, i.e. those which have been considered at the province-level in chapter 2 above, see Maharatna (1994b).

regional variation in malaria ecology appears to have partly shaped the regional pattern of mortality increase. Indeed, malaria endemicity (as measured by the proportionate share of malaria deaths in total fever mortality) has been found to be the most important variable in explaining regional variation in mortality increase—although its overall explanatory power is still rather small. Differences in the cause composition of deaths between the 'heaviest mortality' and 'lowest mortality' districts also suggests an intervening role for pre-existing conditions related to malaria endemicity. The greatest increases in malaria deaths in 1943 and 1944 happened in districts which normally were relatively less affected by malaria. This is consistent with our finding that West Bengal—with a lower overall pre-famine malarial incidence—registered a higher rise in famine mortality. The experiences of Malda and Dinajpur districts show that the epidemic phase of famine may extend well beyond the famine period itself. And the scale of these late epidemics may be even more severe.

The most appropriate form of relief in the crisis, namely gratuitous food distribution, was almost certainly inadequate, and more importantly, it was late. Indeed, the policy of food distribution really assumed significance only after the outbreak of the epidemic. Yet once they occur, epidemics almost by definition, seem inescapable and are likely to take their toll within a short time span. This probably explains why regional distribution of relief does not seem to have influenced the mortality variation. On the contrary, it may be that the distribution of food relief was partly influenced by the regional pattern of mortality increases.

However, the communications network and locational factors also seem to have contributed to the positive relationship between food relief and mortality increase. In fact, districts in the neighbourhood of Calcutta and a few others in the vicinity of naval connections (which mostly lie in eastern Bengal) generally appear to have received the large bulk of foodgrains; and these areas—being generally the least affected by malaria during normal times—appear to have been most affected by malaria epidemics. On the other hand, foodgrains probably flowed relatively less in the far-flung districts (in the north-western part of Bengal) with poor communications; and these happen to have normally been heavily malarious, experiencing relatively small rise in malaria mortality. Thus, the suggestion remains that the very late start of gratuitous food relief ultimately could not prove successful in mitigating excess mortality, a large part of which resulted within a relatively short span of time from the vigorous outbreaks of some epidemics.[69]

In this connection, the experience in Madras presents a somewhat contrasting episode. There relatively prompt and more active state intervention, particularly in the spheres of food collection and distribution, combined with larger relief provision. This probably puts the failure of the Bengal government into greater focus. While a large part of grain imports into the districts of Bengal was ultimately in the hands of private traders, the Madras government engaged in a serious competition with the private sector. The lower mortality cost of the Madras famine may partly be ascribed to the government's active interventions during the crisis. This view gains support from the experience of adjoining Travancore state where a much larger mortality increase coincided with a negligible provision of relief. These contrasting episodes testify to the role that a government's timely and effective intervention (especially in marketing and distribution of food) and provision of relief can play in moderating the scale of overall mortality.[70]

However, while the scale of excess mortality associated with the famine of 1943–4 was colossal only in Bengal, the broad patterns of demographic responses were somewhat similar in all these locations (i.e. Bengal, Orissa, and Madras). Fertility reduction appears to have been a common demographic response. The monthly distribution of mortality during the famine shows a somewhat common pattern; epidemics of cholera, malaria, and smallpox occurred in succession, although the exact timing of the peaks of mortality from these epidemics were partly mediated by the social disruptions and environmental factors. Evidence

[69] As Bhatia writes, 'It had been proved repeatedly in the past that, once a famine got out of hand, even a lavish expenditure on relief later would fail to save life and prevent distress. This was once again demonstrated during the famine of 1943'; see Bhatia (1967), p. 337.

[70] As the *Report on Bengal* states, 'While other Governments in India were admittedly faced with a much less serious situation than the Government of Bengal, their generally successful handling of the food problem, and the spirit in which those problems were approached, and the extent to which public co-operation was secured stand in contrast to the failure in Bengal'; see Famine Inquiry Commission (1945a), p. 105.

about starvation deaths, though relatively small in number, has been reported in each of these locations. Deaths from acute undernutrition and debility also seem to have occurred. Indeed, evidence from these provinces suggests that the course of excess mortality was largely determined by the general course of distress—with its lagged effects on human health, being also partly mediated by environmental and other factors. Some similarity has also been found in the age and sex patterns of mortality increase in these provinces during the famine. The rural–urban contrast in Bengal, which can be seen as an outcome of social crisis (e.g. abandonment of dependants and their movement towards towns in the hope of some relief) does not seem to have been prominent in Madras and Orissa. This may well reflect a lesser severity of distress in these two provinces and a relatively better distribution of relief provisions.

6

The Demography of Droughts and Food Crises in Contemporary India: A Case Study of the Maharashtra Scarcity of 1972–1973

1. Background

As has already been discussed, the occurrence of the famine of 1943–4, after about thirty-five years of absence of major famines, shattered the belief 'that famine had become a thing of the past'. Ironically, however, this disaster itself is marked as the beginning of an era in which famine has truly come to be considered as a phenomenon of India's past. Since independence in 1947, India's vast population has never experienced a major famine comparable to those of the pre-independence period.[1] This development, of course, partly reflects the expansion of India's economy in the post-independence period.

Interestingly, however, the absence of major famines in independent India does not appear to be due to improved availability of food. There is a strong indication that, since independence, India's net food availability has remained 'remarkably stagnant'.[2] Although food production has increased, this has not been translated into rising food availability per capita, because the production gains have been neutralized partly by reduced food imports and partly by increased population growth. Moreover, even the growth of food and agricultural output has been far from uniform across different parts of India. While increases in yields and output, resulting from the so-called 'Green Revolution', have largely

---

[1] Note that Bangladesh has experienced at least one major famine in the recent period (i.e. that of 1974–5).

[2] See Drèze (1990), p. 37.

been confined to the irrigated regions, large unirrigated tracts—covering around two-thirds of the total cropped area—have witnessed 'virtual stagnation'.[3] Moreover, apart from fast population growth, these regions have also experienced considerable ecological problems (e.g. deforestation, soil erosion, and lowering watertables).[4] In fact, frequent visitations of drought and crop failures in one part or the other still constitute an important element of India's reality. As Drèze writes about the period since independence, ' . . . localized crop failures (mainly due to drought) have occurred in different parts of the country almost every year'.[5] Several such weather failures and crop losses have even shown 'the potential of turning into a major famine'.[6] For example, Bihar and large parts of south India suffered from a serious drought in 1951, but this impending subsistence crisis was averted largely by 'arranging imports, controlling prices and managing distribution of supplies by the State'.[7] Crop failures of a local character have usually created conditions for arrival of food from neighbouring areas at reasonable prices, and hence the 'Famine Codes strategy' of creating purchasing power and stimulating private trade appears to have worked rather well. This, of course, does not mean that the actual will and determination with which relief has been organized has always been commendable at every stage or at every time. Indeed, some obvious failures have occurred such as in Assam in 1974–5.[8]

However, apart from such numerous local crises, India has also experienced the threat of major famine and widespread starvation on at least four occasions since independence: in 1966–7, 1972–3, 1979–80, and 1987–8. But none of these crises has developed into a large-scale famine (in comparison with major Indian famines of the past and contemporary African crises). Like most of the previous Indian famines, these recent crises have also been initiated by almost countrywide drought. Indeed, the crises of

[3] See Drèze (1990), p. 37.
[4] Drèze has argued that in all these respects India's unirrigated regions do not seem to have fared better than the African countries; see Drèze (1990), p. 37.
[5] See Drèze (1990), p. 45.
[6] See Bhatia (1991), p. 340.
[7] See Bhatia (1991), p. 344.
[8] See, e.g. Prabhakar (1975) and Baishya (1975).

1966–7 and 1972–3 both occurred in the wake of a considerable shortfall in monsoon rains for at least two consecutive years. Of course, all regions did not suffer uniformly from the drought, depending, among other factors, on the irrigation facilities (i.e. the degree of weather dependence). Bihar and Maharashtra were the worst affected states during the 1966–7 and 1972–3 crises respectively. Indeed, these two food crises were probably the most important that have occurred in India since 1947. Although neither was a huge disaster on the scale of, say, the Bengal famine of 1943–4, both events have evoked considerable attention and controversy (see below).

Although the drought of 1979–80, unlike the former two, was short-lived, 'its intensity and geographical coverage were exceptional'.[9] However, large buffer stocks of foodgrains that India had accumulated by that time were used both to prevent excessive rise in food prices and to finance public works programmes. The crisis was also well anticipated with remarkable foresight; and a massive employment programme of the 'food-for-work' type was launched. As Drèze remarks, '[t]he country seems to have taken the drought in its stride with remarkable ease'.[10] According to some authors, this event has proved that the nexus between major drought and the threat of widespread famine, that had dominated India's past, has indeed been broken.[11]

India's progress in famine prevention has also been affirmed by the experience during a severe drought in 1987. The rainfall deficiency during the 1987 monsoon was quite substantial in large parts of India,[12] but 'the decline in foodgrains production in 1987–8 from the previous year was only of the order of 3.5 per cent'.[13] This, of course, partly reflects 'the resilience that Indian agriculture has come to acquire over the years against ravages of

---

[9] See Drèze (1990), p. 46. There has indeed been a considerable reduction in foodgrain output (e.g. by 30 per cent in north India as a whole, and much more in individual states).

[10] See Drèze (1990), p. 48.

[11] See, e.g. Bhatia (1991).

[12] Indeed, the monsoon failure of 1987 followed two and, in some cases, even three consecutive low rainfall monsoon periods; see Government of India (1990), vol. I.

[13] See Bhatia (1991), pp. 366–7.

drought'.[14] Measures taken by government to minimize the drought damage to crops are also believed to have been partly responsible for this.[15] Thus, although India after independence has experienced several serious droughts and food crises, none has caused any major tragedy. A part of the explanation, of course, lies in the key political, economic, and demographic changes that had taken place by the 1960s. However, given India's persistent susceptibility to famine, the relatively effective relief provision also seems to have played a distinct role in the absence of major famines. In this context, the literature on the experiences during the Bihar famine of 1966–7 and the Maharashtra drought of 1972–3 has put the issue of the role of relief into sharper focus. Indeed, two pivotal areas of debate have been the success, or otherwise, of famine relief measures and the demographic consequences—particularly for mortality. The Bihar famine (sometimes termed a 'near famine') has often been considered a success story of India's famine prevention efforts—as indeed has the Maharashtra crisis.[16] On the other hand, apropos both events, quite

[14] See Bhatia (1991), p. 367.

[15] It is worth noting that although the drought of 1987 probably had little impact on the overall mortality level, there seems to have been a considerable reduction in the birth rate in several affected states:

	CBR			CDR		
	1983–6	1988	1989	1983–6	1988	1989
Gujarat	31.2	28.1	26.5	8.6	9.2	8.8
Rajasthan	33.6	28.4	28.5	9.6	8.7	7.7
Maharashtra	28.0	25.8	24.4	6.8	6.7	6.1

Source: Registrar General, India, Ministry of Home Affairs, Sample Registration Bulletin, December 1987, vol. XXI, no.2, New Delhi, Table 3.

[16] On the Bihar famine, Aykroyd (1974) writes that '[f]amine in Bihar was kept at bay. . . . No exceptional mortality was recorded (p. 140). . . . The scale of relief was immense (p. 141). . . . In a book about the conquest of famine the Bihar emergency of 1967 deserves a prominent and honourable place' (p. 142). On the Maharashtra drought, Drèze (1990) writes that '[t]he sufferings occasioned by the Maharashtra drought were, indeed, very much smaller than one might have expected given the almost complete collapse of agricultural incomes. . . . Mortality rose only marginally, if at all . . . (pp. 68–9). The effectiveness of relief measures largely explains why this devastating drought caused relatively little damage in terms of excess mortality' (p. 99).

contrary views have also been expressed. For example, reviewing the Bihar episode Drèze has concluded that '[t]here is precious little evidence to support the self-congratulatory statements that have commonly been made about the Bihar famine'.[17] Oughton, on the other hand, has criticized both the relief provision and the management of food during the Maharashtra drought; she also provides some evidence of mortality increase in 1973.[18] It is true that some of these contrasts may reflect differences in perspective or purpose. But there can be no doubt that the basic gist of the suggested controversy—which clearly extends to mortality—is genuine.

Indeed, Drèze's careful comparative analysis of both the events has raised the issue of the *distribution* of hardship and, relatedly, the degree to which relief measures were successfully targeted. In the case of the Bihar famine, he concludes that relief was generally not well directed; the poor suffered most and 'there appears to have been a pronounced maldistribution of hardship across areas more or less severely affected by crop failures'.[19] In contrast to the Bihar famine, the food deficit in Maharashtra was better distributed (e.g. between different socio-economic groups), and the famine relief 'strategy was eminently successful . . . in drawing food into deficit areas through the generation of purchasing power in the right hands at the right time and in the right places . . . '[20] And this, as Drèze argues, is the explanation of why 'mortality rose little if at all' during the Maharashtra scarcity. In this context our chief purpose is twofold: to assess the demographic

[17] See Drèze (1990), p. 59.

[18] The following sentences quoted from Oughton (1982) would make her assessment clear: 'Between 1970 and 1973 Maharashtra . . . suffered from a series of droughts . . . which caused considerable distress. . . . The mortality rate in rural Maharashtra rose from 13.0 per thousand in 1970 to 15.6 . . . in 1973 (p. 169). . . . The data [on relief works] suggest that coverage was not very good. . . . There are reports of many relief works being badly run [p. 186]. . . . [At the local level the famine was] a failure in the management . . . of the food system . . . the government was unable to procure grain, stocks were run down, and by the final drought year the supply coming through the public distribution system . . . was reduced to a trickle in relation to the need' (p. 193).

[19] Drèze (1990), p. 60. And this conclusion has been also corroborated by our recent systematic analysis of the available evidence on the Bihar famine of 1966–7; see Dyson and Maharatna (1992).

[20] See Drèze (1988), p. 101.

consequences (including excess deaths) during the Maharashtra scarcity of 1972–3; and to examine the geographical distribution of mortality compared with various proxy measures of agricultural production failure and relief provisions.

To assess the demographic effects of this crisis we have adopted a 'detrending' approach. That is, we have computed the ratio (times 100) of the registered death (or birth) rate in the main crisis year to that which would have prevailed if the linear (ordinary least squares (OLS)) trend of rates during the previous few years continued. This procedure—which has also been applied to some of the agricultural time series—seems appropriate, particularly in circumstances where there is evidence of a trend in the data during the period before the crisis. Moreover, it has the important advantage that it does not reflect absolute levels of registered vital rates, which we shall see are often seriously flawed.

2. The Demography of the Maharashtra Drought of 1972–3[21]

By many criteria—including the comparative maturity of its statistical base—Maharashtra, a large part of which was included in the former Bombay Presidency under British administration, is a relatively developed state. But during the early 1970s it suffered three successive years of drought. This culminated in the disastrous failure of the monsoon rains of 1972 and the associated calamitous agricultural year 1972–3, when cereal production fell to under half its 1967–8 level. At the beginning of the drought of 1970–3, Maharashtra was facing an agricultural decline as a result of stagnant area under cultivation, stagnant yields and increasing population pressure. As Drèze writes, 'By any criterion, the severity of agricultural decline in Maharashtra before the early 1970s, and the extent of crop failures during the drought, dwarf the food crises which led to dramatic famines in the Sahel over the same period'.[22] The crisis, however, was eventually broken by favourable monsoon rains during the second half of 1973.[23]

---

[21] This section draws on an earlier paper written jointly by Tim Dyson and me; see Dyson and Maharatna (1992).

[22] Drèze (1990), p. 68.

[23] For detailed background information on this crisis see, for example Drèze (1990), especially pp. 65–97, Oughton (1982) and Subramanian (1975).

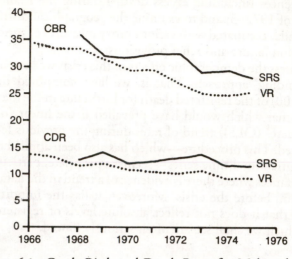

FIG. 6.1   Crude Birth and Death Rates for Maharashtra,
VR (1966–75) and SRS (1968–85)

Sources: See footnote 24.

Two independent time series of vital rates are available for this
crisis. First, there are annual CBRs and CDRs from the ordinary
system of vital registration (VR); second, there are rates produced
by the then newly instituted SRS. During the late 1960s and early
1970s the SRS was still in its formative stages and undoubtedly
experienced some changes and disruptions. Figure 6.1 compares
the VR and SRS birth and death rates for Maharashtra for the
relevant period. Because SRS rates for the whole state (i.e. rural and
urban areas combined) are unavailable for 1968 and 1969, those
shown for these two years are simply the published rural rates
adjusted slightly downwards to allow for the lack of urban rates. But
the SRS rates shown for 1970 and subsequent years are the final
official all-state figures produced by the Registrar General.[24]

[24] The SRS rates for years 1970–5 inclusive in Fig. 6.1 are taken from Mari
Bhat et al. (1984), pp. 70, 82. The rates for earlier years are derived from Office
of the Registrar General, *Sample Registration Bulletin*, vol. VIII, no. 1, April
1974. During 1970–2 inclusive the average SRS death rate for the state as a
whole was 0.905 of the published rural rate; accordingly this figure was used

Several important points emerge from Figure 6.1. There is considerable agreement between the CBR and CDR trends indicated by both the SRS and the vital registration system. Evidently, vital registration coverage in Maharashtra was quite good; for the years 1970–5 inclusive, the average VR crude birth and death rates are respectively 87 and 81 per cent of the averages of the corresponding SRS rates. Indeed, in view of (i) the longer time span for which the VR figures are available, (ii) the lack of SRS urban coverage in both 1968 and 1969, and (iii) the various other disruptions which the SRS undoubtedly suffered (especially in 1973 and 1974)[25] it may well be prudent to give greater weight to the *trends* implied by the vital registration statistics.

Figure 6.1 suggests two key demographic responses to the Maharashtra scarcity. First, both data sources indicate that the birth rate dropped during the crisis. The SRS implies that the decline occurred in 1973, while the vital registration system—in our view more plausibly—suggests quite a drop in 1972 also. Given the nine months of gestation, the implication is that some reduction in the level of conceptions took place in 1972 and perhaps even 1971. This conforms to our finding in the context of major Indian famines of the past, namely that the level of conceptions in a population experiencing famine tends to decline at the early stage (i.e. the starvation phase) when mortality is often hardly above its normal level.

Secondly, Figure 6.1 contains fairly clear evidence of excess mortality, particularly in 1973. A few simple calculations can illustrate its rough range of magnitude. A minimum estimate is obtained if we simply compare the SRS death rate of 13.6 in 1973 with the average CDR of 12.2 recorded for the adjacent years 1972 and 1974; in a population of just over 50 million in 1971 this would imply about 70,000 excess deaths (i.e. 70,577 = (13.6–12.2) × 50,412). On the other hand, a more sophisticated treatment is possible, using the VR data (with an adjustment for under-registration) and taking into account (i) the pre-crisis trend in the CDR, and (ii) the growth of population since the census

---

to obtain 'all state' CDRs for 1968 and 1969 from the published rural figures. The corresponding figure used for births was 0.967. The VR rates in Fig. 6.1 are taken from various issues of *Vital Statistics of India* cited in Table 6.1.

[25] See Mari Bhat et al. (1984), especially p. 33.

in 1971. On the basis of the OLS trend in the registered death rates for 1966–71 inclusive, the death rates in 1972 and 1973 should have been 9.5 and 8.8, respectively; in fact the registered rates were 9.9 and 10.5. If the VR crude death rate was only 81 per cent of the SRS rate, then a minimal correction factor for VR death under-reporting is 1.23 (i.e. 1/0.81). Assuming that Maharashtra's population grew at the average annual rate for the 1971–81 decade of 2.41 per cent, by early 1972 the state's population would have been 51,627,000. Thus a rough estimate is about 133,352 excess deaths (133,352 = (51,627 × ((9.9 – 9.5) + (10.5 – 8.8)) × 1.23). While the approximate nature of this figure must be emphasized, this figure may actually represent a significant achievement in 'damage limitation' in such a large population experiencing a severe and prolonged crisis. But whatever the true figure, there can be little doubt that there *was* excess mortality associated with the Maharashtra drought.

TABLE 6.1
Percentage Shares of Different Causes of Deaths,
Maharashtra 1971–3

Cause of death	Per cent shares to total deaths 1971–2	Per cent shares to total excess deaths 1973
Cholera	0.04	1.05
Smallpox	0.01	−0.04
Dysentery/Diarrhoea	4.20	13.60
Respiratory	15.10	9.80
Fever	17.46	20.60
Accident/Injury	3.70	−0.01
All other	59.50	55.00
	100.00	100.00

Note: The excess deaths by cause in 1973 have been calculated over the respective average numbers of deaths in 1971–2.

Sources: *Vital Statistics of India*, Ministry of Home Affairs, New Delhi, various years.

Table 6.1 presents percentage shares of major causes of deaths in both pre-famine and famine years. As can be seen there has been an increased importance of cholera, dysentery/diarrhoea, and

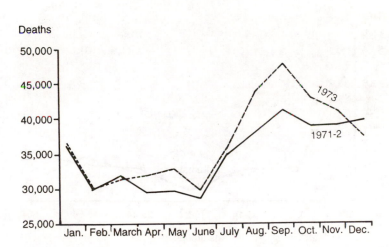

Deaths

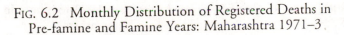

FIG. 6.2 Monthly Distribution of Registered Deaths in
Pre-famine and Famine Years: Maharashtra 1971–3

Sources: See *Vital Statistics of India* cited in Table 6.1.

fevers in accounting for the excess deaths in 1973. This is in broad
conformity with our findings on India's earlier famines. While
dysentery/diarrhoea has increased the most, respiratory diseases
have recorded a decline in their share of excess deaths from the
pre-famine level. Although there has been an increase in fever
deaths, malaria probably did not play a very significant role in the
Maharashtra crisis. However, as Figure 6.2 shows, the monthly
distribution of famine mortality appears very similar to what has
often been found during the earlier Indian famines: relatively
moderate excess deaths during the hottest months prior to the
monsoon, and the peak famine mortality after the resumption of
the monsoon (i.e. during August–October). And this timing of
peak mortality (in September 1973) exactly coincides with the
normal annual peak mortality, reflecting the influence of the usual
seasonal and environmental factors. Unfortunately, the monthly

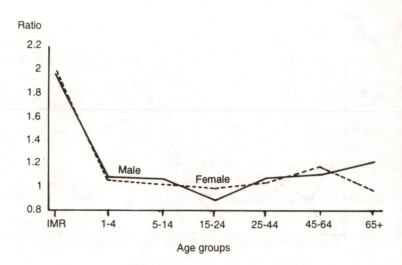

FIG. 6.3   Ratios of Registered Deaths in 1973 to Those in
1971–2 by Age and Sex: Maharashtra

Sources: Based on *Vital Statistics of India* cited in Table 6.1.

data on cause-specific deaths for 1973 are not available. From the
experiences of the earlier famines, it seems probable that much of
the excess mortality in the pre-monsoon months was due to
cholera, while dysentery/diarrhoea deaths tended to peak after the
resumption of the monsoon.

Figure 6.3 presents the age–sex pattern of proportional mortality increase in 1973 (from the average in 1971–2). It shows that
infants of both sexes experienced a significant increase in mortality. While young children and elderly people appear to have
experienced a very small elevation of mortality, the prime adult
age groups recorded a mortality improvement. Interestingly, these
results are consistent with those found for the historical famines
of lesser mortality (in chapter 3 above). This confirms our view
that when overall excess mortality associated with a famine is low
or even negligible, the greater vulnerability to nutritional stress of

infants, young children and probably the elderly becomes apparent. In other words, in the Indian context the raised mortality of infants, young children and elderly people appears to be a good index of widespread nutritional stress, even when it is not followed by a major mortality crisis. The mortality increase for infants during the Maharashtra crisis being the highest partly reflects the adverse health effect on infants of malnutrition of pregnant women. This finding may also partly reflect the fact that a relatively large number of women were on relief works, while many must have been mothers of newborn children, and so could not give adequate care to their infants. That the relief policy during the crisis provided substantial female employment, thus protecting food entitlement of the female population in a direct manner, has often been commended.[26] In any case, infants, young children and the elderly—who are the most vulnerable groups—do not seem to have received special protection within the family during the crisis. Furthermore, overall, the female population seems to have experienced a slightly higher proportional increase in mortality than the male.[27] This has also been noticed during the Bombay famine of 1911–12 which involved very low excess mortality. Thus, a relative female advantage in mortality increase (in proportional terms) that has been found in some major historical famines does not show up during lesser mortality crises.

To gain an understanding of the geographical distribution of crisis mortality requires some background information. In this context, Table 6.2 gives basic data for Maharashtra's 26 districts. The relative advancement of the state is reflected in the fact that in 1971 nearly one-third of the entire population lived in urban areas; in addition to Greater Bombay—which is entirely urban—the districts of Thana (which is adjacent to Bombay), Poona and Nagpur (which both contain major cities with these names) were all fairly urbanized. Table 6.2 also gives the average vital registration CBRs and CDRs for the period immediately preceding the main crisis year 1973 (as mentioned earlier, SRS does not provide district-level vital rates). These birth and death rates are strongly

[26] See, e.g. Drèze (1990) and Agarwal (1990). In a survey of a particular taluka during the 1972–3 drought, female labourers were found to be almost as numerous as male labourers on relief works; see Kulkarni (1974).

[27] The ratio of total registered deaths (all ages) in 1973 to those in 1971–2 was respectively 1.07 and 1.08 for males and females.

TABLE 6.2
Demographic Data for the Districts of Maharashtra

District	Population 1971 (000's) (i)	Per cent Urban 1971 (ii)	Average Reg. CBR 1967–72 (iii)	Average Reg. CDR 1967–72 (iv)
Ahmednagar	2,269	11	29.8	10.7
Akola	1,501	23	34.4	12.3
Amravati	1,541	28	38.4	13.2
Aurangabad	1,971	17	25.0	9.0
Bhandara	1,586	11	35.5	14.7
Bhir	1,286	12	22.9	8.0
Buldana	1,263	18	36.1	14.6
Chandrapur	1,640	10	37.8	14.8
Dhulia	1,662	17	34.8	14.5
Greater Bombay	5,970	100	29.4	10.2
Jalgaon	2,123	24	35.0	14.2
Kolaba	1,263	12	25.5	10.4
Kolhapur	2,048	22	29.4	9.7
Nagpur	1,943	54	34.1	12.3
Nanded	1,398	17	23.4	8.3
Nasik	2,369	29	32.1	12.4
Osmanabad	1,897	13	27.0	9.1
Parbhani	1,507	16	23.6	8.9
Poona	3,178	43	30.8	10.4
Ratnagiri	1,991	8	24.2	10.6
Sangli	1,540	19	26.7	9.2
Satara	1,727	14	30.4	11.0
Sholapur	2,254	28	31.3	11.0
Thana	2,282	36	25.3	7.9
Wardha	780	24	38.9	14.9
Yeotmal	1,424	14	41.0	15.6
Maharashtra	50,412	31	30.5	11.2

Sources: The 1971 census data in columns (i) and (ii) are taken from Census of India 1971 *Maharashtra, General Population Tables, Part II-A,* Series 11, p. 37; the registration figures in columns (iii) and (iv) are from various issues of *Vital Statistics of India* cited in Table 6.1.

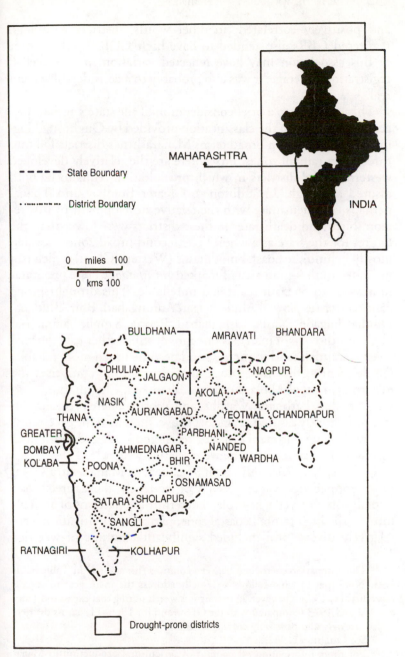

FIG. 6.4 Famine Locations

and positively correlated; in other words, districts with high registered CBRs also tended to have high CDR.[28] While some of this association may have reflected variation in the level of registration coverage, it was also probably to a considerable extent real.

This brings us to a brief consideration of the state's agricultural ecology. Following the classification provided by Oughton,[29] Figure 6.4 shows that in broad terms Maharashtra's districts fall into three main rainfall zones. First, there are the relatively developed western coastal districts in which precipitation tends to be both assured and high. In addition to Greater Bombay and Thana, perhaps commensurate with the relative development of this region, birth and death rates in these districts were lower than the figures for the state as a whole. The second broad zone—located mostly behind the coastal mountains (Western Ghats) which run north to south—is an area of marked *rainshadow*. Here precipitation tends to be both scant and unreliable. This drought-prone zone comprises *parts* of Ahmednagar, Aurangabad, Bhir, Buldana, Dhulia, Jalgaon, Nasik, Osmanabad, Poona, Sangli, Satara, and Sholapur districts. Finally, as one moves still further east, normal levels of rainfall tend to increase and become much more reliable. Consequently, the third broad agricultural zone comprises the eastern districts of Akola, Amravati, Bhandara, Chandrapur, Nagpur, Nanded, Parbhani, Wardha, and Yeotmal; here precipitation is comparatively assured. Table 6.2 shows that, with the exceptions of Nanded and Parbhani districts, registered birth and death rates throughout this eastern zone were relatively high.[30]

In the early 1970s, only about 9 per cent of Maharashtra's total gross cropped area was irrigated. Consequently, these three broad rainfall zones played a key role in determining patterns of agriculture. In the high rainfall coastal zone, patterns of cultivation were relatively diverse and included significant amounts of wet rice

---

[28] The correlation coefficient between columns (iii) and (iv) in Table 6.2 is 0.93. Note that in what follows we chiefly address the main year for excess mortality, i.e. 1973. However, in passing it is worth noting that excess mortality in 1972 and 1973 (compared with the OLS trend for 1966–71) across districts is also strongly and positively correlated (r=0.77).

[29] See Oughton (1982).

[30] For more information on patterns of agricultural production in Maharashtra, see Oughton (1982), especially pp. 175–9.

farming. But in the drought-prone zone the predominant cultivation of coarse foodgrains such as *jowar* (sorghum) and *bajra* (millet) depended almost entirely upon the lottery of the monsoon. Finally, in the eastern zone with relatively assured rainfall, cereal production was also comparatively high and, in addition, significant amounts of cotton were grown. Furthermore, this eastern zone contained the two districts (Bhandara and Chandrapur) with the highest proportions of irrigated area in the state at the time.[31]

With this as background, Table 6.3 gives key data for the districts and state, with particular reference to the main period of crisis (i.e. 1972–3). Districts have been grouped by zone; and within zones we have demarcated those districts with higher levels of urbanization, while the remainder have been ranked according to a rough index of famine provision in 1973.

The state-level statistics in Table 6.3 underscore the gravity of the situation that was faced. Even in good agricultural years Maharashtra was a cereal deficit state. But in 1972–3, per capita cereal production declined to barely 51 kg per person—only 47 per cent of the level of 1967–8, and only 71 per cent of what might have been expected even on the basis of the declining trend of the previous four years. An average of just over 6 per cent of the state's entire population were attending scarcity relief labour works during the period January–September 1973 (although the resumption of monsoon rains meant that this relief provision was sharply curtailed by October). The registered CBR in Maharashtra in 1973 was 4 per cent lower than might have been expected, while the death rate was 15 per cent above the trend of the previous years.

Table 6.3 shows that the coastal zone was comparatively protected from the crisis. Although cereal production in 1972–3 was much lower than might have been expected, per capita cereal production levels remained surprisingly high—particularly in view of the relatively low profile of agriculture in the economy of this zone. There was some limited provision of relief in Thana and Kolhapur districts. But only in Greater Bombay was the registered death rate above trend. The unweighted mean figures

---

[31] For more information on patterns of agricultural production in Maharashtra, see Oughton (1982), pp. 175–9.

TABLE 6.3

District-level Indices of Agriculture, Relief Provision, Fertility, and Mortality, by Zone, Maharashtra 1972–3

	Cereal production per capita 1972–3	Cereal production in 1972–3 as per cent of 1967–8	Cereal production in 1972–3 detrended	Per cent of population on relief Jan.–Sept. 1973	Detrended vital rates in 1973 compared to trend of 1967–72		
					CBR	CDR	IMR
	(i)	(ii)	(iii)	(iv)	(v)	(vi)	(vii)
Coastal zone							
Greater Bombay	n.a.	31	69	n.a.	112	112	101
Thana	46	42	40	2.4	113	98	109
Kolhapur	53	65	54	3.5	94	92	101
Kolaba	131	67	82	0.5	93	92	104
Ratnagiri	85	86	77	0.2	95	100	95
Unweighted mean	79	58	64	1.7	101	99	102
Drought-prone zone							
Poona*	38	43	74	6.4	100	109	108
Bhir*	27	17	32	19.8	78	105	95
Osmanabad*	61	45	129	18.1	79	112	98

Sholapur*	27	18	46	15.8	82	109	119
Ahmednagar*	47	33	67	14.7	84	94	118
Aurangabad*	31	20	57	14.5	81	112	117
Sangli*	20	18	22	12.7	92	97	111
Nasik*	32	26	44	9.3	94	110	118
Dhulia*	54	49	58	6.0	89	122	124
Satara*	45	41	44	5.9	91	98	104
Buldana	86	63	95	4.8	83	132	129
Jalgaon	72	70	152	2.8	88	121	112
Unweighted mean	45	37	68	10.9	87	110	116
Eastern assured zone							
Nagpur	49	67	108	1.9	116	131	114
Parbhani	66	41	216	7.4	90	139	165
Nanded	51	29	181	6.0	81	132	130
Yeotmal	86	85	98	3.3	85	122	144
Akola	64	61	91	2.6	89		

(cont.)

Table 6.3 (cont.)

| | Cereal production per capita 1972–3 | Cereal production in 1972–3 as per cent of 1967–8 | Cereal production in 1972–3 detrended | Per cent of population on relief Jan.–Sept. 1973 | Detrended vital rates in 1973 compared to trend of 1967–72 | | |
| | | | | | CBR | CDR | IMR |
	(i)	(ii)	(iii)	(iv)	(v)	(vi)	(vii)
Chandrapur	118	71	65	2.2	87	117	121
Amravati	62	79	161	1.9	89	134	149
Wardha	80	68	128	1.5	83	121	165
Bhandara	92	58	43	1.0	92	99	112
Unweighted mean	74	62	121	3.1	90	125	129
Total Maharashtra State	51	47	71	6.1	96	115	116

Notes: 1. The districts marked with an asterisk were designated the ten 'most acutely affected' districts by Subramanian, with the implication that this reflected the official assessment, see Subramanian (1975).

2. The detrended cereal production measures in column (iii) have been calculated relative to the trend for years 1967–8 to 1971–2.

Sources: Columns (i), (ii) and (iii) are taken or derived from Drèze (1990), p. 70. Column (iv) is based on district labour attendance statistics in Subramanian (1975), pp. 576–80. Columns (v), (vi) and (vii) are based on statistics from various issues of *Vital Statistics of India* cited in Table 6.1.

for the coastal zone as a whole imply that fertility and mortality were largely unaffected.

Turning to the districts which lie at least partly in the drought-prone zone, a more complicated picture emerges. Cereal production per capita across these districts in 1972–3 was barely 45 kg —only 37 per cent of the level of 1967–8, and well below trend. Moreover, all of what were termed the 'most acutely affected' districts were located in this zone. Labour relief provision during January–September 1973 averaged over 10 per cent of the population. And in Bhir and Osmanabad districts very nearly one person in five was recorded as receiving such relief. Perhaps not surprisingly, the drought-prone zone also experienced the sharpest decline in CBR in 1973; again Bhir and Osmanabad experiencing the most marked reductions (see Table 6.3).

However, mortality in the drought-prone zone seems to have been less severely affected than fertility. Thus the unweighted means in Table 6.3 indicate that the death rate was 10 per cent above trend while the birth rate was 13 per cent below trend. The infant death rate appears to have generally recorded a larger proportionate rise above trend than did the overall death rate. This may partly reflect the faster rate of decline in infant mortality than the overall death rate during the pre-famine period. Table 6.3 also shows that, in 1973, death rates were higher than expected in nine of the twelve districts in the zone. But in only three—a northern cluster consisting of Buldana, Dhulia, and Jalgaon—was the increase on trend higher than the all-state figure of 15 per cent. It is also noteworthy that according to most of the agricultural indices shown, these three districts escaped relatively lightly during the drought; for example, they each experienced per capita cereal production levels above the state average (very much above in the cases of Jalgaon and Buldana).[32] Indeed, within the drought-prone zone there is a strong indication in Table 6.3 that mortality rose in those districts where cereal production in 1972–3 was greatest relative to trend.

This last point is strengthened when we consider events in the eastern zone. Throughout this region cereal production was well

[32] In our view the classification of Buldana with the other districts of the drought-prone zone is particularly debatable, because for many years it was closely associated with the Akola, Amravati, and Yeotmal districts. Together, these four districts constituted the former province of Berar.

below the levels of 1967–8. It is quite clear that 1972–3 was a bad agricultural year in the east. But per-capita production figures were generally high—especially if the predominantly urban constitution of Nagpur district is taken into account. And, compared with trend, cereal production in 1972–3 in most of the districts of the eastern zone was higher than expected.[33] In general, relief provision in this zone was low, except for the two adjacent southwestern districts of Parbhani and Nanded (which we have already had cause to distinguish). Moreover, there is clear evidence that birth rates were somewhat reduced throughout most of this zone in 1973. However, the most interesting feature of Table 6.3 is the strong indication that it was the districts of the eastern zone which registered the greatest death rate rises. Only Bhandara was spared a major increase in deaths compared to trend. And across the zone as a whole the CDR was 25 per cent higher than expected. So, somewhat paradoxically, it was in many ways the favoured eastern agricultural zone which experienced the greatest rise in death rates in 1973.

Table 6.4 presents the correlation coefficients between the various measures in Table 6.3. Not surprisingly, the various cereal production indices are positively related with each other. There is also clear support for Drèze's contention that relief measures were comparatively well targeted. For example, greater proportions of the population received work relief in those districts where per capita cereal production levels were least and where the birth rate reduction (itself a powerful measure of agricultural stress) was greatest.

Finally, Table 6.4 provides support for the suggestion that, relative to their respective trends, death rates rose most in those districts where cereal production was highest. The full explanation for this relationship is almost certainly complex; it might involve for example, a district-level examination of levels of nutrition, outbreaks of disease, and patterns of rainfall. However, two

---

[33] However, of the districts in the eastern zone only Amravati actually experienced an increase in the absolute volume of cereal production between 1971–2 and 1972–3 (the only other district in Maharashtra to experience such an increase being Jalgaon). Thus, for example, the very high detrended measure for Parbhani in Table 6.3 should not obscure the fact that there was nevertheless a slight decline in the district's cereal out-turn between 1971–2 and 1972–3. For the relevant statistics, see Drèze (1990), p. 70.

TABLE 6.4
Matrix of Zero-order Correlations, Maharashtra

	Cereal production in 1972–3 as per cent of 1967–8	Cereal production in 1972–3 detrended	Per cent of population on relief	Detrended CBR 1973	Detrended CDR 1973	Detrended IMR 1973
Cereal production per capita 1972–3	0.75*	0.26	−0.64*	−0.04	0.09	0.16
Cereal production in 1972–3 as per cent of 1967–8		0.33	−0.80*	0.12	0.23	0.22
Cereal production in 1972–3 detrended			−0.24	−0.17	0.73*	0.57*
Per cent of population on relief				−0.50*	−0.19	−0.28
Detrended CBR 1973					−0.13	−0.26
Detrended CDR 1973						0.74*

Notes: * significant at one per cent level.

Sources: For the data used, see Table 6.3.

tentative explanations can perhaps be proposed. First, relief provision together with other attendant government attention (e.g. to health measures and water supplies) may have played some role in limiting death rate rises throughout much of the drought-prone zone. For example, it is noticeable from Table 6.3 that of the ten districts which were designated the 'most acutely affected', all of which received significant government attention and relief, only Dhulia registered a detrended CDR rise higher than the average for the state.[34] Indeed, the correlation between the relief provision and detrended mortality in 1973 is negative (see Table 6.4). This finding contrasts with the experiences revealed by the district-level data for India's major famines of the late nineteenth and early twentieth centuries. Because, during the earlier famines, although relief provision was generally relatively large in more severely affected districts, there was no clear indication that the larger the provision of relief the lower the proportional increase in mortality. In fact, in some cases, a positive relationship was found while in some other cases almost no relation was discernible.[35] This, as our examination of the evidence indicates, reflects deficiencies of relief policy (e.g. untimeliness, inadequacy, excessive harshness).[36] Thus, the finding of a negative relation of relief provision with mortality rise in the Maharashtra drought reflects its relative effectiveness.

The second explanation for the relationship relates to inter-district (and perhaps even interstate) patterns of migration.[37] The general tendency in the literature on the Maharashtra drought has been to play down, even deny, the existence of significant population movement. But the empirical base for the view that migration was negligible seems to consist of a few very small-scale studies.[38] On the other hand, there is considerable evidence from various

[34] It is worth noting that Dhulia is inhabited by a relatively large tribal population; according to the 1971 census, they constituted more than 37 per cent of the total population—which is indeed the highest proportion among all the districts of Maharashtra.

[35] See Maharatna (1994b) for the findings on the regional variation in the demographic consequences of major famines in late nineteenth and early twentieth-century India.

[36] Ibid. for details.

[37] On this, see also Dyson and Maharatna (1992).

[38] See Drèze (1990), p. 75 and also Subramanian (1975), pp. 463–5. Subramanian (1975) alludes to interstate migration into Maharashtra and some movement towards Bombay.

parts of India that populations in drought-prone zones have well-established strategies of migration in the event of drought and production failure.[39] Thus in the present context, it is noteworthy that the districts of Akola, Amravati, Buldana, and Yeotmal—which together formerly comprised the province of Berar—each experienced comparatively large increases in death rates. There are reports, in the case of famines in the late nineteenth century, of large numbers of people migrating into precisely these districts in search of work and food—who subsequently died there.[40] In 1972, there was a considerable rise in the registered CDRs in several districts of Madhya Pradesh (Balghat, Bastar, Chindwara, Durg, and Seoni) which lie on the eastern border of Maharashtra; and this was not matched by reductions in CBRs in those districts.[41] The suggestion may be that famine victims from Maharashtra migrated and thus raised the number of registered deaths in these adjoining areas of Madhya Pradesh. That migration played a role in the geography of the demographic response to the Maharashtra drought is also suggested by the detrended CBR and CDR measures for the more urbanized districts—especially Bombay and Nagpur—in Table 6.3. More generally, we posit that some of the more vulnerable sections of society may have moved towards areas of relative agricultural improvement in 1973, perhaps conditioned by customary routes for distress migration. There, some of them died.

One may argue that the larger increase in death rate in the eastern zone may not necessarily be real if there was considerable in-migration from drought-prone areas. Absence of appropriate adjustment in the denominator for migration in 1973 may

---

[39] See chapter 3 above and Dyson (1991a), p. 7, and also Maharatna (1993b).
[40] See Dyson's own paper in Dyson (1989b), p. 164.
[41]

District	CDR			CBR		
	1971	1972	1973	1971	1972	1973
Balghat	11.8	14.0	13.5	28.9	31.7	29.9
Bastar	9.6	12.0	11.6	21.7	21.2	22.5
Chindwara	12.9	15.8	14.8	35.1	34.8	31.8
Durg	11.5	12.6	7.3	31.4	32.1	19.1
Seoni	13.3	16.1	14.2	35.1	34.2	30.6

Sources: Registrar General, *Vital Statistics of India*, New Delhi, various years.

produce upward and downward biases in the detrended death rates for the receiving and sending zones respectively. But there are some considerations here: first, if registration of an infant death implies registration of a livebirth, calculation of infant mortality rate—being the ratio of infant deaths to total livebirths—does not require any adjustment for denominator when there is migration. And the pattern of regional variation in detrended death rate has largely been corroborated by detrended IMR data too. Second, in-migration into the eastern zone may well have increased the true death rate on the ground that migrants had a higher risk of death. Indeed, migrants are generally more exposed to disease. Finally, there was also some probable interstate migration.

3. Concluding Discussion

There is no doubt that there was considerable mortality during the Maharashtra drought—at least 70,000 excess deaths. Both the VR and the SRS reveal a similar picture of demographic response at the state level. There was a pronounced reduction in births in 1973, and probably 1972. And deaths also increased in 1973, and probably 1972. The cause composition of this excess mortality appears to have a broad similarity with what was generally observed during the earlier Indian famines: increased importance of cholera, dysentery/diarrhoea, and fevers. The seasonal pattern of mortality, too, appears to be similar to that of the previous famines, reflecting the influence of normal seasonal and environmental factors (e.g. post-monsoon unfavourable conditions) in shaping peak mortality during the crisis. Similarly, the greater vulnerability of infants, young children and the elderly has again been established, just as in historical famines with moderate excess deaths (chapter 3). In fact, malnutrition among children is often seen as one of the signs of the onset of a subsistence crisis.[42]

On the question of regional variation in the crisis, Figure 6.5 shows the contrast between the relationship of mortality and production failure in Bihar and Maharashtra. The contrary slopes largely corroborate with the arguments proposed by Drèze, i.e. 'bad' targeting of relief in Bihar and 'better' targeting of relief in Maharashtra. In fact, the relief measures in Maharashtra were

---

[42] See Government of India (1990), vol. I, p. 9.

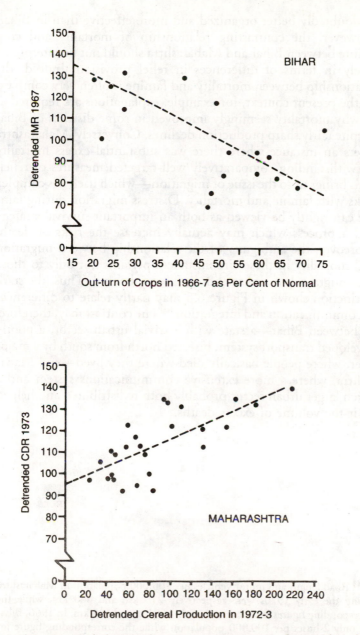

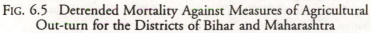

FIG. 6.5 Detrended Mortality Against Measures of Agricultural
Out-turn for the Districts of Bihar and Maharashtra

undoubtedly better organized and more effective than in Bihar. However, the contrasting relationship of mortality and crop failure between Bihar and Maharashtra should not be interpreted solely in terms of differences in relief provision. Indeed, the relationship between mortality and famine is often very complex. In the present context, for example, explanations are required as to why mortality seemingly improved in some districts of Bihar despite fairly sharp production declines. Conversely, Maharashtra offers an instance where there was substantial excess mortality notwithstanding comparatively well-targeted measures of relief. This brings us to the issue of migration—which itself has complex links with famine and mortality. Distress migration during famine can rightly be viewed as both an important survival strategy and a process which may actually increase the risks of death. Moreover, the ambiguity of the relationship between migration and mortality in these circumstances pertains not only to those who migrate, but also to those who stay behind. Thus, the stark distinction shown in Figure 6.5 may partly relate to differences in communication and integration.[43] The contrast may, therefore, be between Bihar—a state with a trivial urban sector, a poorly developed transport system, bisected north from south by a major river, where people basically died where they lived—and Maharashtra, where a more extensive communications system and a much larger urban sector probably both redistributed and helped limit the volume of excess deaths.

[43] Road length and motor vehicles per 100,000 population in Maharashtra during the early 1970s were respectively 219 km and 660 km, while the corresponding figures for Bihar were only 166 km and 135 km. In 1966, Bihar had only 2 buses per 100,000 population while the corresponding figure for the whole of India was 73; see Government of India, Central Statistical Organisation, *Statistical Abstract*, New Delhi, various years.

7

Summary and Conclusion

The present study has set out to examine demographic responses during Indian famines since the 1870s. In fact, demographic information is only available for the period after the 1860s, since the establishment of censuses and vital registration. During the closing decades of the nineteenth century and in the early twentieth century four major famines occurred, affecting large parts of the Indian subcontinent: those of 1876–8, 1896–7, 1899–1900 and 1907–8. Various estimates (including our own) suggest a declining trend in the overall number of excess deaths during these famines. Between the end of the first decade of the present century and the Second World War, India was relatively free of famine. However, in 1943–4 a further severe famine occurred, largely affecting the eastern province of Bengal. Since this crisis, India has not experienced a major famine of comparable scale, although occasional food crises and droughts have occurred in several vulnerable regions since independence in 1947. Thus, the evidence is of a long-term decline in both the frequency and severity of famines. Our chief purpose has been to exploit the fact that India with a considerable wealth of historical materials presents a good opportunity for investigating famine demography from a historical perspective.

The study began with a detailed analysis of demographic responses during the four major famines mentioned above. Although there is controversy as to the major underlying factors that contributed to the occurrence of these famines, there is no doubt that drought was the proximate cause (see Table 2.5). The major drought which actually brought famine was sometimes the culmination of deficit rainfall in one or two preceding years. During the prime famine year, i.e. the year *following* the drought, there was a substantial rise in the death rate over the pre-famine level. The birth rate was very often somewhat below the baseline level during the prime famine year, indicating the onset of fertility-reducing factors *before* the major mortality increase. In the year following the famine, there was a substantial reduction in the birth rate, reflecting the further reduction in conceptions during the main crisis year. Thus, all these famines involved a considerable loss of population during the prime famine period.

However, as hypothesized, there was a compensating rise in fertility above normal levels in the immediate post-famine period, and usually a continued elevation in the birth rate during the longer-term post-famine period. An alteration in age composition favouring the prime reproductive years, especially for females, seems to have contributed to this post-famine 'excess birth rate', although the possibility of some deliberate behavioural changes (e.g. a lowering of the female age at marriage) favouring elevated fertility should not be ruled out. In the post-famine period death rates appear to have been less stable than previously, and this seems to have been largely due to the occasional outbreak of epidemics. However in the longer-term post-famine period, the crude rate of natural increase appears generally to have exceeded the pre-famine levels, thus tending to promote recovery of the pre-famine population size. On balance, the post-famine demographic responses observed during these famines support the hypothesis of a fairly quick recovery to the pre-famine population size.

Our analysis of time-series data on food prices, conceptions, and mortality shows that the failure of the monsoon rains immediately triggered sharp food price rises, which reached a peak by the arrival of the *next* monsoon. In step with the rising prices, the level of conceptions declined fairly quickly. There is relatively little information on foetal wastage due to the onset of famine distress. And although there is some evidence of an increase in stillbirths, the effect does not seem to have been pronounced. On the whole, it seems to us that the foetus was probably rather well protected from the dire circumstances of famine. In any event, stillbirths constitute a very tiny fraction of all births. Although mortality sometimes began to rise somewhat later than the start of the fertility reduction, we nevertheless found a strong correspondence in the movements of our CI (conception index) and MI (mortality index), especially during the prime famine period. This certainly implies the existence of strong fertility-reducing effects produced by excess mortality (and presumably raised morbidity). Also, to the extent that the declining CI represents deepening nutritional stress and other disruptions (through, for example, the nutrition–fecundity link and spousal separation) the correspondingly rising MI presumably also reflects increasing distress. This view is reinforced by our finding that occasional elevations of mortality unrelated to famine conditions do not seem to have exerted a similar negative effect on conceptions. This probably also provides justification for treating the reduction in the level of conceptions as perhaps a more robust index of the existence of famine conditions than the elevation of mortality. However, information on conceptions only becomes available when the corresponding births occur nine months later. So the movement of our CI represents an *ex post facto* index of the development of famine, and it cannot really be used for predicting the crisis.[1]

Although we generally found signs of rising mortality from the early months of the year following the drought, the main MI peak usually occurred around the middle of the year—especially at the time of the resumption of monsoon rains. Again, the famine mortality peak, while dramatic, was comparatively short. In fact, peak famine mortality occurred at a time when food prices were either stabilized at a high level or were starting to decline. However, food prices often continued to remain fairly high even after the MI had returned to normal. These are probably the reasons why the correlation between the MI and food price movements was found to be relatively weak.[2]

Starvation was not the direct cause of most of the famine mortality, although there *is* evidence of some starvation deaths. Indeed, peak famine mortality was often the result of multiple epidemics associated with the famine. Increased mortality from cholera, dysentery/diarrhoea, and fevers appears to have accounted for most of the excess deaths during these major famines. The mortality from all these causes generally tended to increase simultaneously from the early months of the prime mortality year.

[1] See also Menken and Campbell (1992) and Dyson (1992).

[2] A careful study of short-run variations in food prices, mortality, and fertility over several centuries in medieval England also suggested a much weaker connection between prices and mortality compared with prices and fertility: 64 per cent of annual fluctuations in fertility were associated with yearly variations in prices, compared with 16 per cent in the case of mortality; see Lee (1981), and also Walter and Schofield (1989), especially pp. 37–41.

However, the epidemic of cholera generally occurred a little earlier in the year, particularly during the pre-monsoon months, i.e. during the period of maximum undernutrition (as proxied by the level of food prices) and peak social disruptions (e.g. congregations at relief camps, wandering, scarcity of drinking water, etc.). Peak mortality from dysentery/diarrhoea generally occurred during the monsoon months.

However, epidemic malaria, which usually followed the resumption of rains (with the associated favourable conditions for mosquito breeding) was the single most important factor in accounting for the relatively late occurrence of peak famine mortality. A surge in mortality from fevers during the post-monsoon months, again reflecting the rains–mosquitoes–malaria link, was also a normal feature. The huge scale of epidemic malaria in the course of the famine seems to have been largely explained by the conditions of starvation and consequent debilitation.[3] Thus while

[3] Whitcombe in a recent paper on the late nineteenth-century famines in India views 'famine mortality' as resulting, in greatest part, from a malaria epidemic the outbreak of which, according to her, was largely determined by the 'cruel' whims of climate and consequent quantity of surface water (including irrigation canals) and resultant scale of mosquito breeding; see Whitcombe (1993). However, as we have argued in the context of major historical famines (see section 6 of chapter 2 above), it is indeed difficult to view excess famine mortality as resulting from epidemics (including epidemic malaria) the outbreak of which was not crucially related to large-scale starvation and debilitation. Furthermore, it is worth remembering that attributing a large part of excess mortality primarily to the outbreak of malaria epidemic during these major historical famines entails a certain degree of inference based on *registered* fever mortality, because during this period malaria never appeared as a separate cause of death in the registration data. Indeed, as has been stressed before, owing to the possibility of misclassification of registered deaths among the specified causes one should be cautious while explaining an outbreak of malaria epidemic, especially in the wake of famines. For example, during the Punjab famine of 1899–1900—the famine which Whitcombe has discussed to demonstrate the crucial role of climate in the malaria outbreak in 1900—there is rather strong indication that the registered mortality from fever (and hence assumed malarial mortality) includes a considerable number of cholera deaths. As the Deputy Commissioner of Hissar district (one of the severely affected districts) writes on 1 September 1900: ' . . . in Rawalwas, Hissar *Tahsil* 12 deaths from cholera were reported, whereas 36 actually occurred, and that while 22 cases of fever were reported only 3 actually occurred . . . The total for the *tahsil* [Bhiwani] accordingly shows 187 actual cholera deaths to 82 reported, and 90 fever deaths

a period of acute undernutrition seems to have had somewhat lagged effects on human health and survival, the exact timing of peak mortality from specific epidemics was partly shaped by environmental factors (e.g. the monsoon-caused increase in mosquitoes in the case of malaria, and heat and lack of satisfactory drinking water in the case of cholera), and partly by other influences (e.g. population movements, crowding in the relief camps, and breakdown of sanitary arrangements, encouraging epidemics of cholera and dysentery/diarrhoea).

Although information on socio-economic differentials in famine mortality is extremely limited, there are indications that mortality was higher for the poorer sections of the population. A higher mortality for the poor, it has sometimes been argued, may reflect poorer conditions of living and 'public health factors' rather than food shortage or greater undernutrition *per se*.[4] In fact, a distinction between a 'starvation model' on the one hand and a 'health crisis model' on the other has been proposed to explain different patterns of famine mortality.[5] However, in our view such a sharp distinction is difficult to sustain, especially in the Indian historical context. This is because starvation and nutritional stress during these famines appear usually to have caused large-scale mortality through diseases (i.e. through increased susceptibility) the spread and severity of which were partly aggravated by famine-induced disruptions on both the social and the public health fronts (i.e. through increased exposure). The health crises prompted by crowding, contamination, and migration during these famines seems very often to have been related to famine-induced destitution.[6]

Turning to the relief operations during these famines, we have

---

against 194 reported . . . The explanation seems to be that they [i.e. "lambardars and chaukidars"] often dread the enquiry and trouble necessary on reported outbreak of cholera and do all in their power to minimize the matter or to avoid reporting it at all'; see *Note on the enquiry into the high death-rate in Hissar District by Deputy Commissioner to Commissioner, Delhi (No.1060–GI, dated 1st September, 1900) The Punjab Famine of 1899–1900, Volume II*, Lahore, 1901, p. 170–1.

[4] See Walter and Schofield (1989), especially p. 19, and also de Waal (1989b), p. 116.

[5] See de Waal (1989c).

[6] See also Drèze and Sen (1989), footnote 25, p. 44.

seen that the start of relief provision was often rather late. One of the implications of this was that many people were already debilitated when they joined the relief works, and thus they failed to fulfil the set work standards and often fell prey to disease. On the other hand, we have seen that the decline of relief works sometimes occurred *earlier* than the resumption of the rains. This often resulted from the government's deliberate attempts (e.g. through raising the standards of work or the lowering of wages) to keep down the number of people on relief. In some cases, the provision of relief works does appear to have continued until the resumption of the rains. It seems that the time span of relief provision (especially of relief *works*) was influenced by the trend in overall mortality. When mortality failed to show a considerable rising trend, especially during the early part of the year, relief measures seem to have been run down much earlier than the resumption of the rains. Conversely, when mortality showed a steady increase over time, relief works were continued until the resumption of the monsoon.

On the question of the age composition of famine mortality we have seen that infants, young children, and the elderly—age groups whose mortality rate is very high even in normal times—experienced very large absolute rises in the death rate during the famines. But in terms of proportional rises in mortality, the age pattern of famine vulnerability does not always coincide with the one based on absolute increases in mortality. While a very high normal level of infant mortality reflects both widespread poverty and very poor public health provision in normal times, in terms of proportional increase in mortality, infants appear to have been relatively protected compared to other ages. During normal times infant mortality was almost always higher for males than for females; but female infant mortality usually rose by a larger proportion during famines. However, apropos other age groups, two broad patterns of proportional mortality increases seem to have corresponded with two regions of the subcontinent. First, in south, central, and western India older children and adults experienced relatively large proportional increases in mortality, especially compared to young children. Second, in the north-Indian famines young and older children experienced relatively large proportional increases in mortality, especially when compared to adults. And a relatively greater parental neglect towards children seems to have been largely responsible for the greater famine mortality increase for children in north India (especially in Punjab).[7] Likewise, in connection with the sex differentials in famine mortality (all ages combined) two regional patterns emerged. In the first region (i.e. south, central, and western India) famine mortality of males increased most in proportional terms; but in the north-Indian famines the reverse was true. While the age–sex pattern of famine mortality is probably largely shaped by biological vulnerability and the pattern of afforded 'social protection', the above regional differences seem to have corresponded to India's broad 'north–south' dichotomy in basic cultural and social features. Relatively pronounced anti-female socio-cultural features (e.g. low status of women and related female neglect) in the northern parts (compared with southern, central, and western regions) seem to have outweighed the potential biological and other female advantages in coping with famines.[8]

Our analysis of some historical famines which involved relatively minor mortality has shown that the time patterns of demographic responses were broadly similar to those for the major famines: i.e. relatively early declines in conceptions, comparatively late occurrence of the MI peak, and a generally close correspondence between the movements of the MI and CI. Also, the timing of the outbreak of cholera was generally somewhat earlier than the occurrence of the malaria epidemic, again reflecting seasonal influences. But the main difference with the major famines lay in

[7] Referring to the 'poor condition' of children of some caste groups (e.g. 'Ahirs' and 'Kamins') during the famine of 1899–1900, the Executive Engineer of the Rohtak Division (Punjab) wrote: 'It is to be feared that this deterioration on the part of the children mentioned is to a great extent due to neglect on the part of parents'; see *The Punjab Famine of 1899–1900, Volume III*, Lahore, 1901, p. 20. Observing heavy mortality among children in 1900, the Deputy Commissioner of Hissar district (Punjab) wrote: 'I am strongly convinced that in a severe famine . . . it is the duty of the famine administration to take special care of the children, as parents are apt to neglect them . . . '; ibid., p. 172.

[8] Note that females in the prime reproductive ages appear to have had a relative mortality advantage (compared with males in those ages) in almost all famine locations with the notable exception of Punjab. The female mortality advantage (in proportionate terms) in reproductive years in most cases seems to have resulted (at least partly) from a considerable decline in the number of conceptions and associated decline in pregnancy and childbirth-related deaths during the famine.

the scale of the demographic effects, which were much smaller primarily reflecting, in our view, the lesser associated volume of distress and disruption. The relatively mild distress and disruption levels during these famines were not related to the severity of drought conditions and the scale of crop failure. Better provision of *relief* (e.g. a relatively timely start of relief, and a relatively liberal relief policy)—sometimes helped by the general expansion and diversification of the economy—appears to have played a crucial role in mitigating the scale of adverse demographic consequences in these famines. Also, the relatively high vulnerability of infants, young children and probably elderly people to nutritional stress remains overt during these famines, even though they were prevented from developing into major mortality crises. And the regional dichotomy of sex differentials in famine mortality—particularly the female disadvantage in the childhood years in northern parts of the subcontinent—has again been observed in these 'lesser mortality' famines.

It is worth noting that our analysis of inter-district variation in adverse demographic consequences during major historical famines (i.e. those of 1876–8, 1896–7, 1899–1900, and 1907–8) has put the role of relief into even sharper focus.[9] The correspondence of the regional (i.e. district-level) variation in famine distress (proxied by crop failure) with the variation in the fertility declines has been found to be somewhat stronger than that with the regional variation in the price rises. This reflects the fact that markets were interlinked to some degree.

Regional variation (particularly between the 'famine' and 'non-famine' districts) in mortality increases was found to be much greater during the famine of the 1870s than in the famines of later decades (i.e. those of 1896–7, 1899–1900 and 1907–8). Indeed, there has been a declining trend over time in both the scale and regional disparity of the demographic impact of famines. There has also been a weakening of the strength of the association between the district-level indices of crop failure and the adverse demographic effects. Improved transport and communications (especially railways) over the years seems to have played a significant role in diffusing famine intensity (e.g. through faster and greater movements of both food and population). However,

---

[9] See Maharatna (1994b) for details.

the change in the nature of government relief policy also seems to have played an important role. For example, the much larger increase in mortality and the larger reduction in births during the famine of 1876–8, compared to later famines, seems to relate to the very stringent and harsh relief policy which was adopted.[10]

The occurrence of the Bengal famine in 1943–4 again demonstrated the importance of the government's efforts in the prevention of a subsistence crisis and the occurrence of an associated demographic disaster. Unlike the previous drought-related major famines, the Bengal famine was triggered off by war-induced inflation and the disruption of food supplies. Thus, it was not the food shortage as such, but instead the government's failure in controlling the prices and distribution of food that was at the root of the large-scale distress in Bengal.

Although a substantial literature exists on the demographic impact of the famine, the original registration data for the whole of Bengal have hitherto been unutilized. While Amartya Sen's recent analysis of the famine's demographic impact has been influential, the data he used not only necessitated a separate treatment of post-partition West Bengal and East Bengal, but it appears to have been somewhat unreliable too. The detailed analysis of the demography of the Bengal famine, using the original (and hitherto neglected) registration data for undivided Bengal, has provided us with several new findings. The quantum of excess deaths in the famine has been hotly debated ever since its occurrence. While Sen's recent estimate of 3 million deaths has been widely quoted, applying Sen's own procedure to our new data for undivided Bengal gives figures of 1.8 to 1.9 million excess deaths. But allowing for the pre-famine declining trend in the death rate, an estimate of 2.1 million appears to be more appropriate.

The basic nature of the short-term fertility and mortality responses was broadly similar to that we have found for the earlier major famines. A remarkably early reduction in conceptions in Bengal probably matched the prolonged period of rising prices and other disruptions brought about by the war. In urban Bengal, although conceptions began to decline in as early as 1941, the scale of the overall reduction was much less than in the province as a whole. On the other hand, the time pattern of movements

[10] See Maharatna (1994b).

in the urban MI broadly coincides with that for the whole of Bengal. The urban areas also experienced greater (proportional) excess mortality. All these features may well reflect the influence of rural–urban migration of destitutes.[11]

Deaths from cholera, dysentery/diarrhoea, malaria, and fever shared a rising trend from the middle of 1943. The cholera mortality peak occurred in October 1943, and it was followed by a peak from malaria, dysentery/diarrhoea, and fever occurring about two months later. The smallpox epidemic peaked very much later (in April 1944).

Epidemic malaria constituted the largest component of famine mortality in Bengal. However, in urban areas most of the registered excess deaths were not accounted for by malaria. In fact, the cause composition of urban famine mortality differed from the rural pattern, perhaps partly as a result of differences found even in normal times and partly because large numbers of migrant destitutes died in the urban areas. However, the rural–urban similarity in the time pattern of the MI (despite differences in the cause composition of deaths) reinforces our view that the general course of mortality was largely determined by the somewhat lagged effects of large-scale nutritional stress on human health and survival, while the exact timing of the excess mortality peak was also partly shaped by both the usual seasonal influences and the movement of population.

The newly discovered registration data for Bengal confirms the view that the impact of famine on the number of stillbirths is probably adverse, but is not pronounced. Neo-natal mortality appears to be relatively protected compared to that of infants beyond the neo-natal stage of life. The pattern of the mortality increase by age and sex found for rural Bengal seems to have been similar to that found during the major famines in the south, west, and central regions of India: infants of both sexes experienced a relatively small proportional increase compared to other ages, and female infants suffered larger increases than did male infants.

---

[11] It should also be noted that pre-famine registered death and birth rates were considerably lower in urban areas than those for rural Bengal. Putting registration biases aside, this probably implies both a larger scope for proportionate increase in mortality and a smaller scope for fertility reduction (in proportionate terms) in urban areas.

Young children of both sexes also appear to have experienced a relative mortality advantage (in proportionate terms) compared to older children and adults. Females in the prime reproductive ages appear to have experienced lower mortality increase than males in those ages. And males (all ages combined) experienced a slightly larger proportional increase in mortality than did females.

But in urban Bengal the pattern was quite different. Infants in urban areas appear to have experienced larger mortality increase (proportional) than adults, and female infants seem to have been the most vulnerable group. Young children and elderly people in urban Bengal experienced relatively large increases in mortality, while adult mortality appears to have been least affected. But this urban pattern of age–sex increase in famine mortality probably reflects, in our view, the influence of rural–urban migration, especially by those groups who were largely dependent on adults.

Since a dramatic rise in food prices (in the wake of the war) was the root cause of the Bengal famine of 1943–4,[12] distress prevailed almost everywhere largely because of the existence of fairly integrated markets and speculative activities. Indeed, unlike the drought-related famines, the division between 'famine' and 'non-famine' districts was not made for the Bengal famine. But there was nevertheless considerable regional variation in the demographic impact. Regional variation in price rises showed a weak association with adverse demographic impact. But this probably reflects the relative uniformity of price rises during the Bengal famine.

The regional pattern of mortality increase appears to have been partly shaped by pre-existing environmental, ecological and infrastructural conditions, and the distribution of relief and migration. Malaria endemicity (as measured by the proportionate share of malarial deaths of total fever mortality) appears to have been the most important variable explaining the regional variation in mortality increase— although its overall explanatory power is still rather small. Differences in the cause composition of deaths between the 'heaviest mortality' districts and the 'lowest mortality' districts also suggest the importance of pre-existing levels of malaria endemicity. The greatest increases in malaria deaths during the prime famine period happened in districts which were

12 For a detailed treatment of this issue, see especially Sen (1981), chapter 6.

normally relatively less affected by malaria. This is consistent with our finding that West Bengal—with a lower overall pre-famine malaria incidence—experienced a higher increase in famine mortality. The possible net inflow of people into West Bengal in the wake of pre-partition Hindu–Muslim tensions may have also contributed to West Bengal's relatively prolonged elevation in recorded mortality in the post-famine period. Interestingly, however, the experience of Malda and Dinajpur districts implies that the epidemic phase of famine may well extend beyond the famine period itself. And that the scale of such late outbreaks of epidemics may be extremely severe.

During the Bengal famine the most appropriate form of relief, namely gratuitous food relief,[13] was not only inadequate, but was also very late in coming. In fact, it assumed significance only after the outbreak of the epidemic phase and did not moderate mortality increases. Thus, the regional distribution of relief does not appear to have influenced the pattern of mortality variation. On the contrary, the finding of a positive relationship between district-level relief and mortality increase suggests that the distribution of relief may have been partly influenced by the regional pattern of mortality increase. However, there is also a clear suggestion that food despatch was relatively greater in those districts which were relatively close to the main foci of communication. And lesser malaria endemicity in those favourably located districts (receiving relatively large food despatches) and also migration into those areas may well have contributed to their greater mortality increase (compared to the far-flung districts which received fewer food despatches, and were normally very malarious). On the whole, relief provision, being very late, did not prove successful in moderating mortality increases.

In this connection the experience in Madras during the famine of 1943–4 presents a contrasting episode, where the government's relatively prompt and active intervention in the management and distribution of food combined with a larger provision of relief. Indeed, the lower mortality toll of the Madras famine seems to have been in part a reflection of the government's relatively effective interventions. This again contrasts with the experience of

[13] For a useful general discussion on the pros and cons of food and cash forms of relief, see Sen (1990), pp. 43–5.

adjoining Travancore state, where a much larger mortality increase coincided with a negligible provision of relief. On the other hand, part of the increase in mortality in Orissa—a province adjoining Bengal—seems to have been caused by the death of many migrants from Bengal.

Although the scale of excess mortality was colossal only in Bengal, the broad patterns of demographic responses were somewhat similar in all these locations (i.e. Bengal, Madras, and Orissa). Fertility reduction appears to have been a common feature. Most of the famine mortality can be attributed to the outbreak of epidemics, though some starvation deaths seem to have occurred in all these locations. Epidemics of cholera, malaria, and smallpox happened in succession. The course of famine mortality seems to have been determined largely by the general course of distress and debility—with somewhat lagged effects on health and survival, again being also partly mediated by environmental (e.g. post-monsoon malaria) and other factors (e.g. population movements). Some similarity has also been found in the age and sex patterns of mortality increase in these three locations, and these patterns are broadly consistent with our findings from earlier major famines. The rural–urban contrast in Bengal, which can be viewed as an outcome of famine-induced social crisis (e.g. the cutting-off of dependants from domestic subsistence and their movement towards towns in the hope of finding relief), does not seem to have been prominent in Madras and Orissa. This again probably reflects a lesser severity of distress in these two provinces and a relatively better distribution of relief provisions.

Since the famine of 1943–4 India, unlike Bangladesh, has never experienced a major famine of a comparable scale. This absence of major famines in the contemporary period partly reflects the key political, economic, and demographic changes that had taken place since independence. However, the country still appears to be vulnerable to occasional droughts and food crises. The Bihar famine of 1966–7 and the Maharashtra drought of 1970–3 seem to have been the most important events since 1947. But major disaster has almost always been prevented by relatively timely and effective relief provision.[14] However, the basic patterns of demographic responses

[14] India's democratic system with fairly strong opposition parties, adversarial politics, and independent press seems to have played an important role in

during contemporary crises appear to be similar to those found in the earlier famines. In both the Bihar famine of 1966–7 and the Maharashtra drought of 1970–3, there seems to have been some excess mortality—though it was small compared to the earlier major famines.[15] In the Maharashtra scarcity there were at least 70,000 excess deaths. There was also a pronounced reduction in births—especially in 1973. The cause composition of excess mortality also appears to be similar to that we have found for the past famines: increased importance of cholera, dysentery/diarrhoea, and fevers. The seasonal pattern of mortality, too, shows the influence of normal seasonal and environmental factors (e.g. post-monsoon unfavourable conditions) in shaping the crisis mortality peak. As was found during the past famines with moderate excess mortality, the greater vulnerability of infants, young children, and the elderly has again been observed during the Maharashtra scarcity. This confirms the view that these are the most vulnerable age groups even when a subsistence crisis does not develop into a major mortality crisis (although during a major, famine-induced, mortality crisis they often appear to have experienced a relative mortality advantage—in terms of proportional increases—compared to older children and adults).[16]

Our comparative analysis of the Bihar and Maharashtra episodes has revealed that the distribution of relief provision was comparatively well targeted in Maharashtra, where a negative

instigating a relatively prompt and effective public action in the event of crisis. This contrasts with the experiences in several less democratic countries with less conducive conditions for generation of pressure on government in times of crisis. On this issue, see Sen (1983), Drèze and Sen (1989), Ram (1990), and also Article 19, The International Centre on Censorship, *Starving in Silence*, London, 1990. However, it should also be noted that India's democratic polity appears to have provided less protection against large-scale endemic poverty and hunger, which are less photogenic and harder to politicize. Indeed, an in-built ad hocism in India's relief policy and associated inefficiency in resource allocation—as opposed to a policy for a permanent elimination of weather-related crises—has often been criticized; on these issues, see Morris (1974, 1975) and Jodha (1975)

[15] See Dyson and Maharatna (1992) and also chapter 6 above.

[16] Note that most African famines in the recent period appear to have killed mainly young children (aged one–five years). In fact, a distinction has sometimes been made between famines that kill mainly young children and those that kill both children and adults, the latter reflecting a higher degree of severity; see de Waal (1988), pp. 89–90.

association (based on an inter-district analysis) between mortality and production failure was found. Indeed the relief policy was relatively effective in preventing distress and its associated excess mortality. The core principles of the famine relief strategy during the crisis were broadly the same as those which were laid down in the early 1880s by the first Indian Famine Commission (e.g. generating incomes through the provision of public works, supplemented by gratuitous relief for the weak). But India's present relief system cannot be viewed as a mere legacy of the British administration because significant changes have occurred since independence. While some of these changes relate to practicalities of relief strategy, one fundamental change from the pre-Independence system has been direct government participation in both food supply management and food distribution at controlled prices. Thus, while the pre-independence relief strategy concentrated only on the generation of incomes for vulnerable groups (e.g. through public works programmes supplemented by gratuitous relief), the relief strategy in the post-independence period both generated incomes and ensured that food was available to the needy at commendable prices.[17]

Distress migration from the most severely affected areas also seems to have influenced the regional pattern of mortality. Indeed, the contrasting relationship of mortality and crop failure between Bihar and Maharashtra appears to have been partly related to the differences in communications and integration. The contrast seems to be between Bihar—with relatively limited scope for population mobility, where people died where they lived—and Maharashtra, where a more extensive communications system and much larger urban sector seem to have helped redistribute and limit excess deaths. Thus, while the long-term decline in the frequency and severity of famines since the 1870s appears to have corresponded to the evolution of relief policy towards greater effectiveness and liberality, the (coterminous) expansion in communications and increasing diversification of the economy also

[17] Indeed, from the late 1970s onwards the holding of major national buffer stocks in staple grains—partly as a result of the Green Revolution in several parts—has also helped government tackle food crises and provide the relatively effective relief; see, e.g. Article 19, The International Centre on Censorship, *Starving in Silence*, London, 1990, pp. 6–7, and also Drèze (1990).

seem to have played a role in diffusing, redistributing, and probably limiting the adverse demographic impact of famine. However, characteristic features of demographic responses to famine have been much the same throughout.

Appendix A

Average Monthly Crude Birth and Death Rates During Baseline Pre-Famine Periods in Major Famine Locations

							Month						
	J	F	M	A	M	J	J	A	S	O	N	D
Bombay 1871–4												
CBR	17.2	15.8	17.7	18.0	18.9	19.8	21.1	20.5	19.9	20.2	19.9	18.6
CDR	18.6	16.2	18.1	17.2	17.0	17.3	18.8	20.6	19.0	19.5	20.3	19.0
Madras 1871–5												
CBR	14.2	12.8	15.1	15.8	17.3	18.7	22.9	21.8	22.0	22.1	20.8	18.2
CDR	18.3	14.8	16.7	15.7	15.5	15.3	17.7	18.6	19.4	19.2	21.0	22.2
Central Provinces 1891–4												
CBR	38.0	34.4	38.1	39.8	38.9	34.2	36.5	40.3	42.4	43.9	40.9	38.9
CDR	25.7	23.8	30.8	35.2	35.2	31.6	30.0	35.0	37.9	40.0	37.9	33.1

(cont.)

Table A1 (*cont.*)

						Month						
	J	F	M	A	M	J	J	A	S	O	N	D
Bombay 1891–4												
CBR	32.5	31.0	34.5	34.8	37.0	38.0	37.5	36.5	36.0	36.5	35.3	33.9
CDR	31.2	25.7	27.8	28.0	29.0	26.9	31.9	33.3	30.2	29.8	32.1	32.0
Berar 1891–5												
CBR	34.7	34.6	39.6	34.5	33.1	32.7	37.3	43.6	43.3	44.5	37.2	34.7
CDR	28.1	25.4	36.3	37.8	34.8	26.0	33.1	53.7	58.9	53.2	42.8	36.2
Punjab 1891–5												
CBR	40.4	35.6	36.7	30.3	30.4	28.9	33.4	40.7	47.4	50.0	47.3	46.5
CDR	34.1	27.0	24.5	23.1	29.7	27.2	27.2	26.7	31.2	39.9	39.5	39.2
United Provinces 1901–4												
CBR	44.1	38.2	38.0	36.0	35.6	36.7	43.2	51.1	54.2	56.0	51.9	51.0
CDR	30.1	26.1	30.0	33.4	35.1	34.3	30.6	30.5	36.1	42.5	41.6	40.7

Notes: 1. The above vital rates are based on constant denominators—being the respective populations under registration according to the preceding famines. Thus these monthly schedules above effectively reflect the seasonal variation in the number of registered births and deaths.

2. To facilitate interpretation, all monthly vital rates are annualized by being multiplied by 12.

Sources: See Table 2.1.

Appendix B

Evaluation of the Data Given in the 1951 Census of India Publication, *Vital Statistics, West Bengal, 1941–50*[1]

We evaluate here the demographic data contained in the above publication for West Bengal for the period around 1943–4 in the light of the available registration data for the whole of undivided Bengal.[2] Table B1 compares the numbers of registered deaths in West Bengal obtained from the 1951 Census of India publication and the numbers of registered deaths in undivided Bengal. There is considerable variation in the fraction of deaths indicated to have occurred in West Bengal. In 1942 it is only 28.5 per cent, whereas by 1945 it is almost 8 per cent higher at 36.2 per cent. And although the number of deaths shown for undivided Bengal in 1946 is a provisional figure, the suggestion nevertheless emerges that the fraction in 1946 may have been higher still. Real demographic fluctuations between West Bengal and East Bengal, as well as variation in registration coverage between these areas, may be influencing these comparisons of annual fractions. Nevertheless, the instability in the annual fraction of deaths occurring in West Bengal shown in Table B1 seems somewhat worrying.

The basic question is how this 1951 Indian census report carved out the registered deaths and births for those districts which were split at the time of partition in 1947. In this connection it is important to note that for the following four districts of West Bengal, namely Nadia, West Dinajpur, Malda, and Jalpaiguri (which were split, and were thus parts of former larger undivided

---

[1] Census of India 1951, Volume VI, Part 1B, *Vital Statistics, West Bengal 1941–50*, New Delhi, 1952.

[2] Government of Bengal, Health Directorate, *Bengal Public Health Report: Alipore.*

districts) the ratios of both births and deaths as given in the 1951 census publication[3] to the respective totals for the undivided districts as given in the *Bengal Public Health Reports*[4] for each year between 1941 and 1945 were respectively 0.5, 0.3, 0.7, and 0.7. This clearly suggests that the data for these districts were derived by applying a *fixed* proportional norm for all the relevant years. This way of deriving the numbers of births and deaths for the split districts may well bias conclusions drawn about the demographic impact of the famine (see the relevant sections of the text in chapter 4).

TABLE B1

Recorded Vital Events for West Bengal Compared with Registered Vital Events in Undivided Bengal 1941–6

Year	West Bengal	Undivided Bengal	Per cent in West Bengal
Deaths			
1941	384,220	1,184,850	32.4
1942	347,886	1,222,164	28.5
1943	624,266	1,908,622	32.7
1944	577,375	1,726,870	33.4
1945	448,600	1,238,133	36.2
1946	414,687	1,068,996	38.8
Births			
1941	541,280	1,594,291	34.0
1942	506,578	1,448,299	35.0
1943	440,014	1,151,556	38.2
1944	377,376	957,210	39.4
1945	457,356	1,301,314	35.1
1946	524,365	1,478,857	35.5

Notes: 1. See notes to Table 4.2.

Sources: See Table 4.2.

[3] Census of India 1951, Volume VI, Part 1B, Table 1.1–1.5, pp. 20–3.
[4] Government of Bengal, Health Directorate, *Bengal Public Health Report:* Alipore, relevant years.

It is notable that in an appendix to the 1951 Indian census publication the number of births and deaths for all the districts in West Bengal are given for years since 1870.[5] Interestingly, these numbers of deaths and births for the above split districts do not match exactly with those we have just referred to above (as given in the text of the census volume). The number of deaths for these split districts as given in the text of the census volume are somewhat higher (except for Jalpaiguri) throughout the period 1941–5 than are those given in its Appendix. For 1946 the *Bengal Public Health Report* produced data for only West Bengal. And for 1946 the numbers of births and deaths in these four split districts of West Bengal were all exactly the same in both the text and appendix of the census publication as in the *Bengal Public Health Report.*[6] For each of the four split districts, we calculated the ratios of deaths and births, as given in the appendix to the census publication, to the respective totals for the corresponding undivided former district as given in the *Bengal Public Health Reports* during the period 1938–45 (see Table B2). It is interesting that these ratios for both deaths and births show year-to-year fluctuations of considerable magnitude, except for Jalpaiguri for which all these ratios are 0.70. This implies that in the case of Jalpaiguri the numbers of births and deaths as given in the appendix to the 1951 census of India publication were derived by applying a constant fraction (i.e. 0.70) to the total numbers of registered deaths and births as given for the undivided district in the *Bengal Public Health Reports.*

But now the question arises as to why the ratios for the other three districts vary so markedly from one year to another. One possibility is that real demographic fluctuations between the boundaries of East Bengal and West Bengal as well as variations in the registration coverage between these areas produced such variations in the ratios found in Table B2. This in turn implies that for these three districts which were split in 1947, both deaths and births for the whole period as reported in the appendix to the 1951 census publication were meticulously derived from the registration data at the necessary disaggregated level, strictly in accordance with the divided geographical boundaries. If this is the case then

[5] See Census of India 1951, Volume VI, Part 1B, Appendix IV, pp. 67–8.
[6] *Bengal Public Health Report for 1946* provides data only for West Bengal.

TABLE B2

Ratios of Births and Deaths in the Four Split Districts in West Bengal (as Given in the Appendix to the Census Publication) to the Respective Totals in those Undivided Districts (as Given in the Bengal Public Health Reports)

	Nadia	West Dinajpur	Malda	Jalpaiguri
1938				
Births	0.485	0.297	0.733	0.700
Deaths	0.486	0.311	0.727	0.700
1939				
Births	0.465	0.247	0.729	0.700
Deaths	0.499	0.246	0.741	0.700
1940				
Births	0.488	0.300	0.718	0.700
Deaths	0.436	0.276	0.751	0.700
1941				
Births	0.489	0.273	0.753	0.700
Deaths	0.444	0.285	0.773	0.700
1942				
Births	0.506	0.271	0.740	0.700
Deaths	0.437	0.263	0.749	0.700
1943				
Births	0.483	0.285	0.792	0.700
Deaths	0.478	0.293	0.720	0.700
1944				
Births	0.524	0.301	0.673	0.700
Deaths	0.458	0.321	0.740	0.700
1945				
Births	0.582	0.297	0.651	0.700
Deaths	0.483	0.283	0.737	0.700

Sources: Census of India 1951, Volume VI, Part IB, *Vital Statistics, West Bengal 1941–50*, Appendix IV, pp. 67–8; Government of Bengal, Health Directorate, *Bengal Public Health Report.* Alipore, relevant years.

the question remains: Why was it necessary to apply a fixed-proportions formula to derive the numbers of deaths and births as given in the text of the census publication (which in fact were the data used by Sen and others)? Actually we cannot be sure whether these data in the appendix are real or not. If they are real (i.e. not calculated on a fixed-proportions formula) the question of why it was also necessary to apply a fixed age-distribution formula to the total number of deaths for West Bengal remains unanswered.

Appendix C

Growth Balance Estimation of Death Registration Completeness in Undivided Bengal, 1940–1942

A useful, though sometimes limited, technique for assessing the death registration coverage is the 'Growth Balance' method advanced by Brass.[1] We briefly describe its application to the data for Bengal around the 1941 census. The method involves the following assumptions: (1) that the population is both stable and closed; (2) that the completeness of death registration is the same at every age; (3) that age-reporting is accurate. Table C1 presents the age distribution of average registered deaths in 1940–2 and also of the 1941 census population. Cumulating these data gives the values of d_x and p_x respectively, i.e. the numbers of deaths and population above age x. Approximate estimates of n_x (the numbers of people aged exactly x) can be obtained from adjacent census population age groups; thus the numbers aged 10 can be estimated as $\frac{1}{10}$ the numbers aged 5–14 [i.e. $31,179 = \frac{1}{10} (175,163 + 136,624)$]. Then we compute the partial birth rates (n_x/p_x) and death rates (d_x/p_x) by age. Under the above assumptions the relationship between these partial rates should be linear, and the slope of this line should provide a correction factor for the level of death registration coverage. The relationship for Bengal is shown in Figure C1. The slope of the regression line based upon all eight age points is 1.34, implying a 75 per cent coverage level of registered deaths in 1940–2.

However, by themselves, we cannot treat these estimates as particularly robust because conditions in Bengal probably departed from some of the method's requisite assumptions. For example, recording of age (in both the Census and at the time of death registration) was certainly subject to systematic biases (e.g.

[1] Brass (1975); also United Nations (1983), pp. 139–45.

TABLE C1

Growth Balance Method Applied to Death Registration Data for Bengal, Both Sexes, 1940–2

Age group	Average registered deaths 1940–2	Mid-1941 population	Age: x	Registered deaths above age x: d_x	Population above age x: p_x	Population at exact age x: n_x	Partial birth rate: n_x/p_x	Partial death rate: d_x/p_x
<1	246,540	29,868						
1–4	180,266	138,880	5	745,893	1,048,055	34,391	.0328	.0143
5–9	86,799	175,163	10	659,094	872,892	31,179	.0357	.0152
10–14	42,625	136,624	15	616,469	736,268	24,874	.0338	.0169
15–19	51,243	112,118	20	565,226	624,150	23,858	.0382	.0182
20–29	121,146	228,422	30	444,080	395,728	20,264	.0512	.0226
30–39	105,643	176,864	40	338,437	218,864	14,385	.0657	.0312
40–49	95,912	110,837	50	242,525	108,027	8,724	.0808	.0452
50–59	89,265	63,644	60	153,260	44,383	4,647	.1047	.0696
60+	153,260	44,383						
Total	1,172,699	1,216,803						

Notes: 1. In calculating the partial death rates, the values of p_x were scaled-up by a factor of 49.6367 in order to allow for the fact that the 1941 Bengal census age data are only available on a sample basis. This factor gives a corresponding Bengal population in mid-1941 of 60,398,085.

2. The least-squares regression line to all eight age points is $y = 0.0164 + 1.3381x$. Hence the implied CF for death registration completeness is 1.34 and the estimated level of death registration is 75 per cent.

Sources: For the 1941 census age data, see Census of India 1941, Volume IV, *Bengal, Tables*, Delhi, 1942, p. 110. For the death data, see the sources listed in Table 4.4.

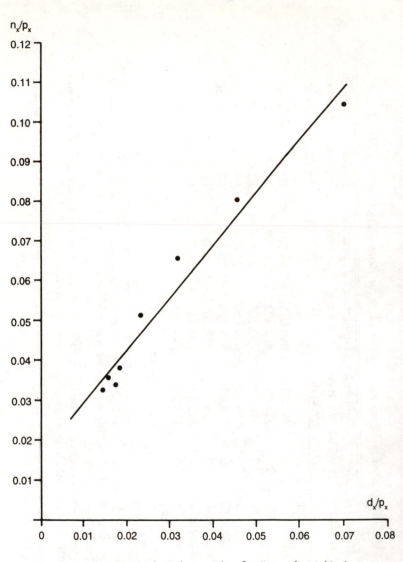

FIG. C1   Growth Balance Plot for Bengal, 1940–2

exaggeration at older ages). In addition, we know that Bengal experienced significant net in-migration in the 1920s and 1930s. It is difficult to evaluate how such considerations might affect the estimates. Figure C1 also shows that different values of correction factor might result if we were to omit certain age points when calculating the slope of the line. Nevertheless, the estimates may be broadly consistent with some of the other assessments of death registration coverage given in Table 4.3.

Appendix D

Comparison of Monthly Average Prices of Rice in the Calcutta Market with the Provincial Average Rice Prices Given in the Pinnell Papers

Month & year	The wholesale price of rice (Rs per maund)		'Provincial price of coarse rice' (Rs per maund)	Wholesale price of rice in Calcutta (Kalma mill cleaned No. 1) (Rs per maund)
	Bengal	Calcutta		
	(1)	(2)	(3)	(4)
1943				
January	9.00	11.25		n.a.
February	11.46	13.75		n.a.
March	13.75	19.30		23.00–24.00
April	20.73	19.30		23.00–24.00
May	26.85	30.60		31.00–32.00
June	27.19	31.65		31.00–32.00
July	29.56	30.69	29.56	33.00
August	31.39	32.34	30.25	35.00
September			23.50	32.00
October			22.31	20.00*
November			19.63	20.00*
December			15.13	17.00*
1944				
January			14.69	
February			14.50	

(cont.)

Table D1 (*cont.*)

Month & year	The wholesale price of rice (Rs per maund)		'Provincial price of coarse rice' (Rs per maund)	Wholesale price of rice in Calcutta (Kalma mill cleaned No. 1) (Rs per maund)
	Bengal	Calcutta		
	(1)	(2)	(3)	(4)
March			14.50	
April			14.81	
May			15.75	
June			15.56	
July			15.19	
August			14.13	
September			12.94	
October			11.81	

Notes: 1. The prices marked * are the maximum controlled rates.
2. The prices in column (4) are those quoted at the end of each month.
3. The figures for Bengal in column 1 are averages for about 70 markets.
4. L.G. Pinnell, ICS, Bengal's first civil supplies director (a former district officer and secretary to two Governors), was largely responsible for the Government's food policies, in the crucial period from August 1942 – April 1943; he then resigned. L.G. Pinnell was indeed closely linked to the course of events especially in 1943. He took charge of the Bengal Development Department in late 1945.

Sources: Columns (1) and (2): the Pinnell Papers, Confidential, Department of Civil Supplies, Bengal, 'Further information desired by the Commission', Appendix E(2), p. 30; column (3): the Pinnell Papers, Confidential, 'Reference – The last sentence of paragraph 2 of annexure 1 to Famine Inquiry Commission's letter No. FC(E)/10, dated 8th September 1944'; column (4): Government of India, Department of Commercial Intelligence and Statistics, *Monthly Statement of Wholesale Prices of Certain Selected Articles at Various Centres in India, December 1943*, Delhi, Government of India Press, 1945.

Appendix E

*Average Monthly Crude Birth and Death Rates
During Pre-famine Baseline Period 1936–40,
All-Bengal and Urban Bengal*

	All-Bengal		Urban Bengal	
Month	*CBR*	*CDR*	*CBR*	*CDR*
January	30.92	21.73	18.35	15.48
February	29.17	17.71	16.40	13.63
March	32.21	20.13	16.37	14.98
April	26.77	21.01	14.65	14.78
May	22.35	17.47	13.65	13.21
June	19.43	15.21	12.15	11.36
July	18.58	17.78	13.15	12.52
August	19.57	16.92	14.33	12.99
September	23.85	17.86	14.51	12.52
October	30.79	20.35	17.28	12.76
November	36.03	24.88	19.41	15.14
December	35.43	28.31	16.95	15.75

Notes: 1. All rates above are calculated by using a constant denominator—being the respective populations according to the 1941 census. So, all these rates effectively reflect monthly variations in the numbers of registered births and deaths. And these average monthly births and deaths schedules are used in the calculation of the conception and mortality indices.

2. Due to non-availability of data on urban births by month prior to 1940 the urban CBRs are the averages of 1940 and 1941. All monthly rates are annualized by being multiplied by 12.

Sources: *Bengal Public Health Report* cited in Table 4.5.

Bibliography

Agarwal, B. (1990), 'Social Security and the Family: Coping with Seasonality in Rural India', *Journal of Peasant Studies*, vol. 17, no. 3: 341–412.

Ahmad, Nafis (1958), *An Economic Geography of East Pakistan*, London: Oxford University Press.

Akhtar, R. and A.T.A. Learmonth (1986), 'Resurgence of Malaria in India 1965–76', in R. Akhtar and A.T.A. Learmonth (eds.), *Geographical Aspects of Health and Disease in India*, New Delhi: Concept Publishing.

Alamgir, M. (1980), *Famine in South Asia: Political Economy of Mass Starvation*, Cambridge, Mass.: Oelgeschlager, Gunn & Hain.

Ambirajan, S. (1978), *Classical Political Economy and British Policy in India*, Cambridge: Cambridge University Press.

—— (1989), 'Food, Famine and Hunger in Tamil Nadu: 1850–1900', in Singh et al., vol. 2.

Appadurai, A. (1984), 'How Moral is South Asia's Economy?—A Review Article', *Journal of Asian Studies*, vol. 43, no. 3.

Arnold, D. (1988), *Famine*, Oxford: Basil Blackwell.

—— (1991), 'Social Crisis and Epidemic Disease in the Famines of Nineteenth-Century India', paper presented at the Society for the Social History of Medicine Conference on Famine and Disease, Cambridge: Christ's College.

Ashton, B., K. Hill, A. Piazza and R. Zeitz (1984), 'Famines in China 1958–61', *Population and Development Review*, vol. 10, no. 4: 613–46.

Aykroyd, W.R. (1974), *The Conquest of Famine*, London: Chatto & Windus.

Bairagi, R. (1986a), 'Seasonal Food Shortage and Female Children in Rural Bangladesh', *American Journal of Clinical Nutrition*, 43: 330–2.

—— (1986b), 'Food Crisis, Nutrition and Female Children in Rural

Bangladesh', *Population and Development Review*, vol. 12, no. 2: 307–15.

Baishya, P. (1975), 'Man-made Famine', *Economic and Political Weekly*, vol. 10, no. 21: 821–2.

Baker, C.J. (1984), *An Indian Rural Economy 1880–1955: The Tamil Countryside*, Oxford: Clarendon Press.

Bang, F.G. (1978), 'The Role of Disease in the Ecology of Famine', *Ecology of Food and Nutrition*, vol. 7, no. 1: 1–15.

Barclay, G.W. (1958), *Techniques of Population Analysis*, New York: John Wiley & Sons.

Bardhan, P. (1974), 'On the Life and Death Questions', *Economic and Political Weekly*, Special Number, vol. 9, nos 32–4: 1293–304.

—— (1982), 'Little Girls and Death in India', *Economic and Political Weekly*, vol. 17, no. 36: 1448–50.

—— (1987), 'On the Economic Geography of Sex Disparity in Child Survival in India: A Note', paper presented at the workshop on Differential Female Health Care and Mortality, Dhaka, January.

Basu, A. (1989a), 'Is Discrimination in Food Really Necessary for Explaining Sex Differentials in Childhood Mortality?', *Population Studies*, vol. 43, no. 2: 193–210.

—— (1989b), 'Culture and the Status of Women in North and South India', in Singh et al., vol. 2.

Behar, M., W. Ascoli and N.S. Scrimshaw (1958), 'An Investigation into the Causes of Deaths in Children in Four Rural Communities in Guatemela', *Bulletin of the World Health Organization*, vol. 19, no. 6: 1093–103.

Bentley, C.A. (1925), *Malaria and Agriculture in Bengal*, Calcutta: Bengal Secretariat.

Berg, Alan (1971), 'Famine Contained: Notes and Lessons from the Bihar Experience', in Blix et al.

Bhatia, B.M. (1963), *Famines in India: A Study in Some Aspects of the Economic History of India (1860–1945)*, London: Asia Publishing House.

—— (1967), *Famines in India: A Study in Some Aspects of the Economic History of India (1860–1965)*, London: Asia Publishing House, second edition.

—— (1975), 'Famine and Agricultural Labour: A Historical Survey', *Indian Journal of Industrial Relations*, vol. 10, no. 4: 575–94.

—— (1991), *Famines in India: A Study in Some Aspects of the Economic History of India with Special Reference to Food Problem (1860–1990)*, third revised edition, Delhi: Konark Publishers.

Blix, G., Y. Hofvander and B. Vahiquist (eds.) (1971), *Famine: A Symposium Dealing with Nutrition and Relief Operations in Times of Disasters,* Uppasala: Almquist and Wiksell/Swedish Nutrition Foundation.

Bongaarts, J. (1980), 'Does Malnutrition Affect Fecundity? A Summary of Evidence', *Science,* 208: 564–9.

Bongaarts, J. and M. Cain (1982), 'Demographic Responses to Famine', in Cahill (1982).

Brass, W. (1975), *Methods for Estimating Fertility and Mortality from Limited and Defective Data,* North Carolina: Carolina Population Centre.

Brennan, L. (1984), 'The Development of the Indian Famine Codes: Personalities, Politics and Policies', in Currey and Hugo (1984).

—— (1988), 'Government Famine Relief in Bengal, 1943', *The Journal of Asian Studies,* vol. 47, no. 3: 541–66.

Cahill, K. (1982) (ed.), *Famine,* New York: Orbis Book.

Caldwell, J.C., P.H. Reddy and Pat Caldwell (1986), 'Periodic High Risks as a Cause of Fertility Decline in a Changing Rural Environment: Survival Strategies in the 1980–83 South Indian Drought', *Economic Development and Cultural Change,* vol. 34, no. 4: 677–702.

Caldwell, J.C., P.H. Reddy, Pat Caldwell, I. Gajanayake, W.K. Gaminiratne, I. Pieris and B. Caldwell (1992), 'A Note on Conscious Planning', mimeo, forthcoming in *Health Transition Review.*

Chambers, J.D. (1972), *Population, Economy and Society in Pre-Industrial England,* London: Oxford University Press.

Chambers, R., R. Longhurst and A. Pacey (eds.) (1981), *Seasonal Dimensions to Rural Poverty,* London: Frances Pinter.

Chand, G. (1939), *India's Teeming Millions, A Contribution to the Study of the Indian Population Problem,* London: George Allen & Unwin.

Chatfield, C. (1984), *The Analysis of Time Series: An Introduction,* London: Chapman and Hall, third edition.

Chattopadhyay, B. (1991), *Food Insecurity and the Social Environment,* Calcutta: K.P. Bagchi.

Chattopadhyaya, K.P. and R. Mukherjea (1946), 'A Plan for Rehabilitation', in P.C. Mahalanobis, R. Mukherjea and A. Ghosh (eds.) (1946), *Famine and Rehabilitation in Bengal,* Calcutta: Statistical Publishing Society.

Chen, L.C. and A.K.M.A. Chowdhury (1977), 'The Dynamics of Contemporary Famine', *International Population Conference,* Mexico, vol. 1: 409–26.

Chen, L.C., A.K.M.A. Chowdhury and S.L. Hoffman (1980), 'Anthropometric Measurement of Protein-Energy Malnutrition and Subsequent Risk of Mortality Among Pre-School Aged Children', *American Journal of Clinical Nutrition*, vol. 33: 1836–45.

Chen, L.C., E. Huq and D'Souza (1981), 'Sex-Bias in the Family Allocation of Food and Health Care in Rural Bangladesh', *Population and Development Review*, vol. 7, no. 1: 55–70.

Chowdhury, S.R. (1989), 'The Unprecedented Growth of Population in Bengal in the 1930s: An Effort to Find Out the Real Mechanism', M.Sc. Demography Thesis, London School of Economics, September.

Christophers, S.R. (1910), 'On Malaria in the Punjab', in *Proceedings of the Imperial Conference held at Simla in October 1909*, Simla: Government of India Press.

Cornish, W.R. (1878), *Annual Report of the Sanitary Commissioner for Madras for 1877*, Madras: Government Press.

—— (1879), *Annual Report of the Sanitary Commissioner for Madras for 1878*, Madras: Government Press.

Crawford, J.A. (1901), *Report on the Famine in the Hyderabad Assigned Districts in the Year 1899–1900*, Hyderabad, 2 vols.

Currey, B. (1978), 'The Famine Syndrome: Its Definition for Preparedness and Prevention in Bangladesh', *Ecology of Food and Nutrition*, vol. 7, no. 2: 87–98.

Currey, B. and G. Hugo (eds.) (1984), *Famine as a Geographical Phenomenon*, Riedel: Dordrecht.

Currie, K. (1991), 'British Colonial Policy and Famines: Some Effects and Implications of "Free Trade" in the Bombay, Bengal and Madras Presidencies, 1860–1900', *South Asia*, vol. XIV, no. 2: 23–56.

Dando, W.A. (1980), *The Geography of Famine*, London: Edward Arnold.

Das, T. (1949), *Bengal Famine (1943)*, Calcutta: Calcutta University.

Das Gupta, M. (1987), 'Selective Discrimination Against Female Children in India', *Population and Development Review*, vol. 13, no. 1: 77–100.

Davis, K. (1951), *The Population of India and Pakistan*, Princeton: Princeton University Press.

De Waal, A. (1988), 'Famine Early Warning System and the Use of Socio-Economic Data', *Disasters*, vol. 12, no. 1: 80–91.

—— (1989a), *Famine that Kills*, Oxford: Oxford University Press.

—— (1989b), 'Population and Health of Eritreans in Waad Sherifei: Implications for the Causes of Excess Mortality in Famines', mimeo, Oxford: Nuffield College.

De Waal, A. (1989c), 'Famine Mortality: A Case Study of Darfur, Sudan, 1984–5', *Population Studies*, vol. 43, no. 1: 5–24.

Dhillon, H., J. Dhamoa and B. Cowan (1979), 'Reaching the Child in Need', *Health and Population*, vol. 2, no. 1: 5–25.

Drèze, J. (1988), *Famine Prevention in India*, Development Economics Research Programme, Discussion Paper No. 3, STICERD, London School of Economics.

—— (1990), 'Famine Prevention in India', in Drèze and Sen (1990), vol. 2.

Drèze, J. and A. Sen (1989), *Hunger and Public Action*, Oxford: Clarendon Press.

Drèze, J. and A. Sen (eds.) (1990), *Political Economy of Hunger*, vols 1 and 2, Oxford: Clarendon Press.

—— (1991), *Political Economy of Hunger*, vol. 3: Endemic Hunger, Oxford: Clarendon Press.

D'Souza, S. and L.C. Chen (1980), 'Sex Differentials in Mortality in Rural Bangladesh', *Population and Development Review*, vol. 6, no. 2: 257–70.

Dutta, H.K. and A.K. Dutta (1978), 'Malaria Ecology: A Global Perspective', *Social Science and Medicine*, vol. 12, no. 2D: 69–84.

Dyson, T. (1988), 'Excess Female Mortality in India: Uncertain Evidence on a Narrowing Differential', in Srinivasan and Mukherji (1988).

—— (1989a), 'The Historical Demography of Berar, 1881–1980', *Indian Economic and Social History Review*, vol. 26, no. 2: 168–201.

—— (1991a), 'On the Demography of South Asian Famines, Part I', *Population Studies*, vol. 45, no. 1: 5–25.

—— (1991b), 'On the Demography of South Asian Famines, Part II', *Population Studies*, vol. 45, no. 2: 279–97.

—— (1992), 'Famine Reactions', *Health Transition Review*, vol. 2, no. 1: 107–13.

Dyson, T. (ed.) (1989b), *India's Historical Demography: Studies in Famine, Disease and Society*, London: Curzon Press.

Dyson, T. and M. Moore (1983), 'On Kinship Structure, Female Autonomy and Demographic Behaviour in India', *Population and Development Review*, vol. 9, no. 1: 35–60.

Dyson, T. and A. Maharatna (1991a), 'Excess Mortality During the Bengal Famine: A Re-evaluation', *Indian Economic and Social History Review*, vol. 28, no. 3: 281–97.

Dyson, T. and A. Maharatna (1991b), 'On the Demographic Consequences of the Bihar Famine of 1966–67 and the Maharashtra Drought of 1970–73', paper presented at the Society for the Social History of Medicine Conference on Famine and Disease , Christ's College, Cambridge; forthcoming in *Economic and Political Weekly*.

Elliott, A.C. (1881), 'Famine Histories', *Parliamentary Papers 1881, Volume 71, Part 1*, pp. 1–45.

Famine Inquiry Commission (1945a), *Report on Bengal*, New Delhi: Government of India Press.

—— (1945b), *Final Report*, Madras: Government Press.

Foege, W.H. (1971), 'Famine, Infections and Epidemics', in Blix et al. (1971).

Fornum, N.R. and L.W. Stanton (1989), *Quantitative Forecasting Methods*, Boston: PWS-KENT Publishing Company.

Fry, A.B. (1912), *First Report on Malaria in Bengal*, Calcutta.

Ghosh, A.K. (1982), 'Food Supply and Starvation: A Study of Famines with Reference to the Indian Subcontinent', *Oxford Economic Papers*, vol. 34, no. 2: 368–89.

Glass, D.V. and D.E.C. Eversley (1965), *Population in History: Essays in Historical Demography*, London: Edward Arnold.

Gottfried, R.S. (1983), *The Black Death: Natural and Human Disaster in Medieval Europe*, London: The Free Press.

Government of Bengal (1944a), *A Scheme for Relief and Rehabilitation in Bengal*, Revenue Department, Calcutta.

Government of Bengal (1944b), *A Plea for the Rehabilitation of Bengal's Rural and Industrial Economy*, Department of Industries, Calcutta.

Government of Bombay (1878), *Annual Report of the Sanitary Commissioner for the Government of Bombay for 1877*, Bombay: Government Press.

Government of Bombay (1878), *Government of Bombay Gazettes for 1877*, Bombay.

Government of Bombay (1879), *Government of Bombay Gazettes for 1878*, Bombay.

Government of Bombay (1895), *Thirty-First Annual Report of the Sanitary Commissioner for the Government of Bombay, 1894*, Bombay: Government Press.

Government of Bombay (1903), *Report on the Famine in the Bombay Presidency, 1899–1900*, 2 vols, Bombay.

Government of Bombay (1907), *Report on the Famine in the Bombay Presidency, 1905–1906*, Bombay: Government Press.

Government of Bombay (1913), *Report on the Famine in the Bombay Presidency, 1911–12*, Bombay.

Government of the Central Provinces (1901), *Report on the Famine in the Central Provinces in 1899–1900*, 2 vols, Nagpur: Secretariat Press.

Government of the Hyderabad Assigned Districts (1898), *Report on the Sanitary Administration of the Hyderabad Assigned Districts for the Year 1897*, Hyderabad: Government Press.

Government of the Hyderabad Assigned Districts (1901), *Report on the Sanitary Administration of the Hyderabad Assigned Districts for the Year 1900*, Hyderabad: Government Press.

Government of India (1946), *Annual Report of the Health Commissioner with the Government of India for 1943 and 1944*, Delhi: Government Press.

Government of India (1947), *Appendices to Annual Reports of the Public Health Commissioner with the Government of India for the Period 1940–1944*, Delhi: Government Press.

Government of India (1972), *Civil Registration System in India: A Perspective*, New Delhi: Office of the Registrar General.

Government of India (1990), *The Drought of 1987; Response and Management*, Ministry of Agriculture, New Delhi, 2 vols.

Government of Madras (1878), *Fourteenth Annual Report of the Sanitary Commissioner for Madras for 1877*, Madras.

Government of Madras (1879), *Fifteenth Annual Report of the Sanitary Commissioner for Madras for 1878*, Madras.

Government of Madras (1944), *Madras in 1943 (Outline of the Administration)*, Madras: Government Press.

Government of the North-Western Provinces and Oudh (1898), *Resolution on the Administration of Famine Relief in the North-Western Provinces and Oudh During 1896 and 1897*, Allahabad: Government Press.

Government of Punjab (1898), *The Punjab Famine of 1896–1897*, Lahore: Government Press, 2 vols.

Government of Punjab (1901), *The Punjab Famine of 1899–1900*, Lahore, 3 vols.

Government of Punjab (1903), *Annual Report of the Sanitary Commissioner for the Government of Punjab for the Year 1902*, Lahore: Government Press.

Government of the United Provinces of Agra and Oudh (1909a), *Resolution on the Administration of Famine Relief in the United Provinces of Agra and Oudh During the Years 1907 and 1908*, Allahabad: Government Press.

Government of the United Provinces of Agra and Oudh (1909b), *Annual Report of the Sanitary Commissioner of the United Provinces of Agra and Oudh for 1908*, Allahabad.

Government of the United Provinces of Agra and Oudh (1910a), *Report on the Administration of the United Provinces of Agra and Oudh 1908–1909*, Allahabad.

Government of the United Provinces of Agra and Oudh (1910b), *Annual Report of the Sanitary Commissioner of the United Provinces of Agra and Oudh for 1909*, Allahabad.

Greenough, P.R. (1982), *Prosperity and Misery in Modern Bengal: The Famine of 1943–44*, New York: Oxford University Press.

—— (1992), 'Inhibited Conception and Women's Agency: A Comment on One Aspect of Dyson's "On the Demography of South Asian Famines"', *Health Transition Review*, vol. 2, no. 1.

Guha, S. (1991), 'Mortality Decline in Early Twentieth Century India: A Preliminary Enquiry', *Indian Economic and Social History Review*, vol. 28, no. 4: 371–92.

Guilmoto, C.Z. (1991), 'Towards a New Demographic Equilibrium: The Inception of Demographic Transition in South Asia', mimeo, Centre d'Etudes de l'Inde et de l'Asie du Sud, Paris.

Guz, D. (1989), 'Population Dynamics of Famine in Nineteenth Century Punjab, 1896–7 and 1899–1900', in Dyson (1989b).

Harrison, G. (1978), *Mosquitoes, Malaria and Man: A History of the Hostilities Since 1880*, London: John Murray.

Harrison, G.A. (ed.) (1988), *Famines*, Oxford: Oxford University Press.

Harriss, B. (1989), 'Differential Female Mortality and Health Care in South Asia', *Journal of Social Studies*, no. 44: 3–123.

—— (1990), 'The Intrafamily Distribution of Hunger in South Asia', in Drèze and Sen (1990), vol. 1.

Hay, R.W. (1986), 'The Political Economy of Famine', *Nutrition and Health*, 4: 71–82.

Hebert, J.R. (1987), 'Social Ecology of Famine in British India: Lessons for Africa in the 1980's?', *Ecology of Food and Nutrition*, vol. 20, no. 2: 97–108.

Higham, T. (1897), *Report on the Management of Famine Relief Works*, Simla: Government of India, Revenue and Agriculture, Government Press.

Hill, A. (1987), 'Demographic Responses to Food Shortages in the Sahel', paper presented at the Expert Consultation on Population and Agriculture and Rural Development, FAO, Rome, June–July.

Hobsbawm, E.J., A. Mitra, K.N. Raj, I. Sachs and A. Thorner (eds.) (1980), *Peasants in History: Essays in Memory of Daniel Thorner*, Calcutta: Oxford University Press.

Holderness, T.W. (1897), *Narrative of the Famine in India in 1896–97*, Simla: Government of India, Department of Revenue and Agriculture (Famine), Government Press.

Hugo, G. (1984), 'The Demographic Impact of Famine: A Review', in Curry and Hugo.

Jain, S.P. (1955), 'Computed Birth and Death Rates in India During 1941–1950', Annexure III of Appendix II of 1951 Census of India, *Volume 1, India, Part I-B-Appendices to the Census Report, 1951*, New Delhi.

Jodha, N.S. (1975), 'Famine and Famine Policies: Some Empirical Evidence', *Economic and Political Weekly*, vol. 10, no. 41: 1609–23.

Johnson, D.G. (1973), 'Famine', in *Encyclopaedia Britannica*, fourteenth edition.

Kane, P. (1988), *Famine in China, 1959–61, Demographic and Social Implications*, London: Macmillan Press.

Kavalseth, T. (1985), 'Cautionary Note About R^2', *The American Statistician*, vol. 39, no. 4 (pt. 1): 279–85.

Keys, A., A. Henschel, O. Michelson and H.L. Taylor (1950), *The Biology of Human Starvation*, vol. II, Minneapolis: University of Minnesota Press.

Kidane, A. (1989), 'Demographic Consequences of the 1984–85 Ethiopian Famine', *Demography*, vol. 26, no. 3: 515–22.

Klein, I. (1972), 'Malaria and Mortality in Bengal, 1840–1921', *Indian Economic and Social History Review*, vol. 9, no. 2: 132–60.

—— (1979), 'Death and Population in India: The Demographic Revolution', paper presented at the Association of Asian Studies Convention, Los Angeles, March.

Klein, I. (1984), 'When the Rains Failed: Famine, Relief and Mortality in British India', *Indian Economic and Social History Review*, vol. 21, no. 2: 185–214.

—— (1990), 'Population Growth and Mortality in British India, Part II: The Demographic Revolution', *Indian Economic and Social History Review*, vol. 27, no. 1: 33–64.

Knight, Sir Henry (1954), *Food Administration in India 1939–47*, Stanford: Stanford University Press.

Krishnamachari, K.A.V.R., N.P. Rao and K.V. Rao (1974), 'Food and Nutritional Situation in the Drought Affected Areas of Maharashtra: A Survey and Recommendations', *The Indian Journal of Nutrition and Dietetics*, 11.

Kulkarni, S.N. (1974), *Survey of Famine Affected Sinnar Taluka*, Pune: Gokhale Institute of Politics and Economics.

Kumar, D. (ed.) (1983), *The Cambridge Economic History of India*, vol. 2: *c*.1757 – *c*.1970, Cambridge: Cambridge University Press.

Kumar, G. (1989), 'Gender, Differential Mortality and Development: The Experience of Kerala', *Cambridge Journal of Economics*, vol. 13, no. 4: 517–39.

Kynch, J. and A.K. Sen (1983), 'Indian Women: Well-being and Survival', *Cambridge Journal of Economics*, vol. 7, 3/4: 163–80.

Langford, C.M. (1984), 'Sex Differentials in Mortality in Sri Lanka: Changes Since the 1920s', *Journal of Biosocial Science*, vol. 16, no. 3: 399–410.

Langford, C.M. and P. Storey (1991), 'Sex Differentials in Sri Lanka in the Early Twentieth Century and Some Comparisons with the Situation in India', mimeo, London School of Economics and Political Science.

Lardinois, R. (1985), 'Famine, Epidemics and Mortality in South Asia: A Reappraisal of the Demographic Crisis of 1876–78', *Economic and Political Weekly*, vol. 20, no. 11: 454–65.

Learmonth, A.T.A. (1980), 'Reflections on the Regional Geography of Disease in Late Colonial South Asia', *Social Science and Medicine*, vol. 14, no. 14D: 271–6.

Lee, R. (1981), 'Short-Term Variation: Vital Rates, Prices and Weather', in Wrigley and Schofield.

Mahalanobis, P.C., R. Mukherjea and A. Ghosh (1946), 'A Sample Survey of After-Effects of the Bengal Famine of 1943', *Sankhya*, vol. 7, part 4: 337–400.

Maharatna, A. (1993), 'Malaria Ecology, Relief Provision and Regional Variation in Mortality During the Bengal Famine of 1943–44', *South Asia Research*, vol. 13, no. 1: 1–26.

—— (1994a), 'The Demography of the Bengal Famine of 1943–44: A Detailed Study', *Indian Economic and Social History Review*, vol. 31, no. 2: 169–216.

—— (1994b), 'The Regional Variation in the Demographic Consequences of Famines in the Late Nineteenth Century and Early Twentieth Century India', *Economic and Political Weekly*, vol. 29, no. 23: 1399–1410.

Mari Bhat, P.N., S. Preston and T. Dyson (1984), *Vital Rates in India, 1961–1981*, Washington, D.C.: National Academy Press.

Martorell, M. and T.J. Ho (1984), 'Malnutrition, Morbidity and Mortality', *Population and Development Review*, vol. 10 (Supplement): 49–68.

Masefield, G.B. (1963), *Famine: Its Prevention and Relief*, Oxford: Oxford University Press.

Mayer, Jean (1975), 'Management of Famine Relief', *Science*, vol. 188.

McAlpin, M.B. (1974), 'Railroads, Prices and Peasant Rationality: India 1860–1900', *Journal of Economic History*, vol. 34.

—— (1979), 'Death, Famine and Risk: The Changing Impact of Crop Failures in Western India, 1870–1920', *Journal of Economic History*, vol. 39, no. 1: 143–58.

—— (1983), *Subject to Famine: Food Crises and Economic Change in Western India, 1860–1920*, Princeton: Princeton University Press.

—— (1985), 'Famines, Epidemics, and Population Growth: The Case of India', in Rotberg and Rabb (1985).

McGregor, I.A. (1982), 'Malaria: Nutritional Implications', *Review of Infectious Diseases*, vol. 4, no. 4: 798–804.

Menken, J. and C. Campbell (1992), 'Age Patterns of Famine-Related Mortality Increase: Implications for Long-Term Population Growth', *Health Transition Review*, vol. 2, no. 1.

Miller, B.D. (1981), *The Endangered Sex: Neglect of Female Children in Rural North India*, Cornell: Cornell University Press.

—— (1989), 'Changing Patterns of Juvenile Sex Ratios in Rural India', *Economic and Political Weekly*, vol. 24, no. 22: 1229–36.

Mills, I.D. (1986), 'The 1918–19 Influenza Pandemic—The Indian Experience', *Indian Economic and Social History Review*, vol. 23, no. 1: 1–40.

Mohanty, B. (1989), 'Case Study of the Indian Famines of 1896–97 and 1899–1900', in Singh et al., vol. 2.

Mokyr, J. (1980), 'The Deadly Fungus: An Econometric Investigation into the Short-Run Demographic Impact of the Irish Famine, 1846–51', *Research in Population Economics*, vol. 2: 237–77.

—— (1983), *Why Ireland Starved: A Quantitative and Analytical History of the Irish Economy, 1800–1850*, London: George Allen & Unwin.

Morris, D.M. (1974), 'What is a Famine', *Economic and Political Weekly*, vol. 9, no. 44: 1855–64.

—— (1975), 'Needed: A New Famine Policy', *Economic and Political Weekly*, Annual Number, vol. 10, no. 5–7: 283–94.

Mosely, W.H. (ed.) (1978), *Nutrition and Human Reproduction*, New York: Plenum Press.

Mukherjee, K. (1947), 'Famine Epidemics and Measures of Health Rehabilitation', *Modern Review*, February.

—— (1965), *Agriculture, Famine and Rehabilitation in South Asia: A Regional Approach*, Santiniketan: Visva Bharati University.

Murray, M.J., A.B. Murray, C.J. Murray and M.B. Murray (1975), 'Refeeding-Malaria and Hyperferramia', *Lancet*, 122: 653–4.

—— (1976), 'Somali Food Shelters in the Orgden and their Impact on Health', *Lancet*, 123, 12: 1283–5.

Murray, J. and A. Murray (1977), 'Suppression of Infection by Famine and its Activation by Refeeding—A Paradox?', *Perspectives in Biology and Medicine*, vol. 20, no. 4.

Murray, J., A.B. Murray, N.J. Murray and M.B. Murray (1990), 'Susceptibility to Infection During Severe Primary Undernutrition and Subsequent Refeeding: Paradoxical Findings', mimeo, Department of Medicine, University of Minnesota.

Murton, B. (1984), 'Spatial and Temporal Patterns of Famine in Southern India', in Currey and Hugo.

Newman, L.F. (ed.) (1990), *Hunger in History: Food Shortage, Poverty and Deprivation*, Oxford: Basil Blackwell.

O'Grada, C. (1988), *Ireland Before and After the Famine: Explorations in Economic History 1800–1925*, Manchester: Manchester University Press.

Oughton, E. (1982), 'The Maharashtra Droughts of 1970–73: An Analysis of Scarcity', *Oxford Bulletin of Economics and Statistics*, vol. 44, no. 3: 169–97.

Peng, Xizhe (1987), 'Demographic Consequences of the Great Leap Forward in China's Provinces', *Population and Development Review*, vol. 13, no. 4: 639–70.

Porter, A. (1889), *The Diseases of the Madras Famine 1877–78*, Madras: Government Press.

Post, J.D. (1976), 'Famine, Mortality and Epidemic Diseases', *Economic History Review*, vol. 29, no. 1: 14–37.

—— (1990), 'Nutritional Status and Mortality in Eighteenth-Century Europe', in Newman (1990).

Prabhakar, M.S. (1975), 'Death in Barpeta', *Economic and Political Weekly*, vol. 10, no. 10: 423–5.

Qureshi, S. (1988), *The British Annexation of Sind*, Bromsgrove: Council of British Pakistanis, Monograph No. 1.

Ram, N. (1990), 'An Independent Press and Anti-hunger Strategies: The Indian Experience', in Drèze and Sen (1990), vol. 2.

Ramakrishnan, S.P. (1954), 'Studies on *Plasmodium berghei Vincke* and *Lips*', *Indian Journal of Malariology*, vol. 8, no. 2: 89–96.

Ravallion, M. (1987), *Markets and Famines*, Oxford: Clarendon Press.

Razzaque, A. (1989), 'Sociodemographic Differentials In Mortality During the 1974–75 Famine in a Rural Area of Bangladesh', *Journal of Biosocial Science*, vol. 21, no. 1: 13–22.

Razzaque, A., N. Alam, L. Wai and A. Foster (1990), 'Sustained Effects of the 1974–75 Famine on Infants and Child Mortality in Rural Area of Bangladesh', *Population Studies*, vol. 44, no. 1: 145–54.

Rivers, J.P.W. (1982), 'Women and Children Last: An Essay on Sex Discrimination in Disasters', *Disasters*, vol. 6, no. 4: 256–67.

—— (1988), 'Nutritional Biology of Famines', in Harrison.

Robson, J.R.K. (1981), *Famine: Its Causes, Effects and Management*, New York: Gordon and Breach.

Rogers, L. (1897), *Report of an Investigation of the Epidemic of Malarial Fever or Kala-Azar in Assam*, Shillong: Assam Secretariat Printing Office.

Rotberg, R.I. and T.K. Rabb (eds.) (1985), *Hunger and History: The Impact of Changing Food Production and Consumption Patterns on Society*, Cambridge: Cambridge University Press.

Sarkar, Sumit (1972), 'Hindu–Muslim Relations in Swadeshi Bengal, 1903–1908', *Indian Economic and Social History Review*, vol. 9, no. 2: 161–216.

Scott and Wild (1991), 'Transformations and R^2', *The American Statistician*, vol. 45, no. 2: 127–9.

Scrimshaw, N.S., C.E. Taylor and J.E. Gordon (1968), *Interactions of Nutrition and Infection*, Geneva: World Health Organization.

Seaman, J. and J. Hatt (1980), 'Markets and Famines in the Third World', *Disasters*, vol. 4, no. 3: 283–97.

Seavoy, R.E. (1986), *Famine in Peasant Societies*, New York: Greenwood Press.

Sen, A.K. (1980), 'Famine Mortality: A Study of Bengal Famine of 1943', in Hobsbawm et al.

—— (1981), *Poverty and Famines: An Essay on Entitlement and Deprivation*, Oxford: Clarendon Press.

—— (1983), 'Development: Which Way Now?', *Economic Journal*, vol. 93, no. 372: 745–62.

—— (1990), 'Food, Economics and Entitlements', in Drèze and Sen, vol. 1.

Sen, A.K. and S. Sengupta (1983), 'Malnutrition of Children and the Rural Sex Bias', *Economic and Political Weekly*, vol. 19, nos 19–21, Annual Number: 855–64.

Sen, Shila (1976), *Muslim Politics in Bengal 1937–1947*, New Delhi: Impex India.

Sengupta, S.C. (1986), 'Sex Preferences and Protein-Calorie Malnutrition', *Journal of Family Welfare*, 32: 59–64.

Singh, S.N., M.K. Premi, P.S. Bhatia and A. Bose (eds.) (1989), *Population Transition in India*, vols 1 and 2, Delhi: B.R. Publishing Corporation.

Sivaswamy, K.G. and Associates (1945), *Food Famine and Nutritional Diseases in Travancore (1943–44)*, Coimbatore: Servindia Kerala Relief Centre.

Sopher, D. (1980), 'The Geographical Patterning of Culture in India', in D. Sopher (ed.), *An Exploration of India: Perspectives on Society and Culture*, London: Longman.

Srinivasan, K. and S. Mukherji (eds.) (1988), *Dynamics of Population and Family Welfare 1987*, Bombay: Himalaya.

Srivastava, H.S. (1968), *The History of Indian Famines and Development of Famine Policy, 1858–1918*, Agra: Sri Ram Mehta.

Stein, Z. and M. Susser (1978), 'Famine and Fertility', in Mosely.

Stein, Z., M. Susser and F. Marolla (1975), *Famine and Human Development: The Dutch Hunger Winter of 1944/45*, New York: Oxford University Press.

Subramanian, V. (1975), *Parched Earth, the Maharashtra Drought 1970–73*, Bombay: Orient Longman.

Taylor, C.E. (1985), 'Synergy among Mass Infections, Famines and Poverty', in Rotberg and Rabb.

The International Centre on Censorship (1990), *Starving in Silence*, Article 19, London.

Tomkins, A.M. (1986), 'Protein-Energy Malnutrition and Risk of Infection', *Proceedings of the Nutrition Society*, 45: 289–304.

Tomkins, A. and F. Watson (1989), *Malnutrition and Infection: A Review*, London: Clinical Nutrition Unit, London School of Hygiene and Tropical Medicine.

United Nations (1983), *Manual X: Indirect Techniques for Demographic Estimation*, New York.

Uppal, J.N. (1984), *Bengal Famine of 1943: A Man-Made Tragedy*, Delhi: Atma Ram & Sons.

Valaoras, V.G. (1946), 'Some Effects of the Famine on the Population of Greece', *Milbank Memorial Fund Quarterly Bulletin*, vol. 24, no. 3: 215–23.

Visaria, L. and P. Visaria (1983), 'Population (1757–1947)', in Kumar.

Waldron, I. (1976), 'Why do Women Live Longer than Men?', *Social Science and Medicine*, vol. 10, nos 7–8.

Walter, J. and R. Schofield (1989), *Famine, Disease and Social Order in Early Modern Society*, Cambridge: Cambridge University Press.

Watkins, S.C. and J. Menken (1985), 'Famines in Historical Perspective', *Population and Development Review*, vol. 11, no. 4: 647–75.

Whitcombe, E. (1990), 'Famine Mortality', paper presented at the BASAS Annual Conference, Edinburgh, April.

—— (1993), 'Famine Mortality', *Economic and Political Weekly*, 5 June: 1169–79.

Wrigley, E.A. and R. Schofield (1981), *Population History of England 1541–1871: A Reconstruction*, London: Edward Arnold.

Zurbrigg, S.H. (1988), 'Hunger and Epidemic Malaria in Punjab', mimeo.

Zurbrigg, S.H. (undated), 'The Meaning of "Intense Malaria"', mimeo.

Index